RIVER ART

SUSQUEHANNA INTERNATIONAL FINE ART COMPETITION - 2010

BY

BARON WERTHEIMER

Cover image: *The Lower Fork* by Ed Letven

RIVER ART: SUSQUEHANNA INTERNATIONAL FINE ART COMPETITION - 2010
Copyright © 2010, by Sunbury Press, Inc.
Cover Copyright ©, 2010 by Sunbury Press, Inc. and Ed Letven.

All rights reserved, including the right to reproduce this book, or portions thereof, in any form or by any means, electronic or mechanical, including photocopying, recording, or by any information storage and retrieval system, without permission in writing from the publisher.

FIRST SUNBURY PRESS EDITION
Printed in the United States of America
January 2011

ISBN 978-1-934597-21-7

Published by:
Sunbury Press, Inc.
100 South Front Street
Lemoyne, PA   17043

www.sunburypress.com

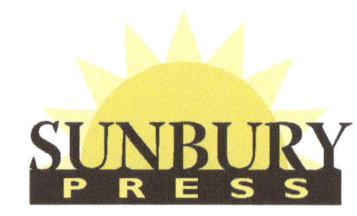

Lemoyne, Pennsylvania   USA

Here, on the river's verge, I could be busy for months without changing my place, simply leaning a little more to right or left."

Paul Cezanne (1839-1906)

DEDICATION

Thank you to all who have participated in the contest: 438 entries from 171 artists in no less than 7 countries!

A special thank you to the jurors, Monica Smith-Talbott, MFA - Professor of Art at Harrisburg Area Community College and Erin Sparler, MFA - Professor of Digital Arts at Central Penn College.

Lawrence von Knorr
& Tammi Knorr

West Shore Gallery, Inc.
Sunbury Press, Inc.

INTRODUCTION

With the opening of West Shore Gallery in Wormleysburg, PA in the summer of 2010, the owners, Lawrence and Tammi Knorr, wanted to make a 'splash'. Given the gallery's location along the Susquehanna River, flowing water was a daily encounter and an easy choice for the theme of the gallery's first contest.

The first Susquehanna International Fine Art Competition was held from September through December, 2010. There was no entry fee – in keeping with the desire of the sponsors to provide an opportunity to all artists to participate, regardless of their financial situation.

Many others felt there must be a catch! Perhaps it is this book that is the hook? For the record, all finalists were invited to participate in the book for no additional cost. Any artist desiring copies of this book have been offered them at the same wholesale price the bookstores will pay.

Finally, this book serves as the program for the River Art Exhibition, to be held at West Shore Gallery from February 11th to March 10th, 2011. Hopefully, you are browsing this book while enjoying a glass of wine and the many works included in the exhibition!

PROSPECTUS

The theme of this year's contest was "River Art". All entries were to include *a river, real or imagined, in their composition.* While most utilized the theme literally, many used the theme metaphorically.

Entries were divided into seven categories: Oil/Acrylic, Watercolor, Drawings/Sketches, Mixed Media/Collage, Photography, Digital and Other. Ten finalists were selected in each category, except for Oil/Acrylic, which had an overwhelming number of entries. Category winners were selected, along with an overall winner, whose work was determined to be most attractive for the book cover.

Regarding the jurors, Monica Smith-Talbott and Erin Sparlor: Monica is a Professor of Art at Harrisburg Area Community College and Erin is a Professor of Digital Arts at Central Penn College. Both hold Master of Fine Arts degrees. Erin judged the Photography and Digital categories. Monica judged all of the other categories.

This catalog presents the work of the finalists who wished to be in the book. The work is arranged by category, in no particular order, except the lead image is the winning entry for the category (if the artist participated in the book).

Unless otherwise noted, all of the work is for sale. Prices have not been included in the catalog, but can be found on the information card accompanying each piece in the exhibition. At the time of publication, it was not yet determined which artists would be able to participate in the exhibition, though all finalists were invited.

DIGITAL

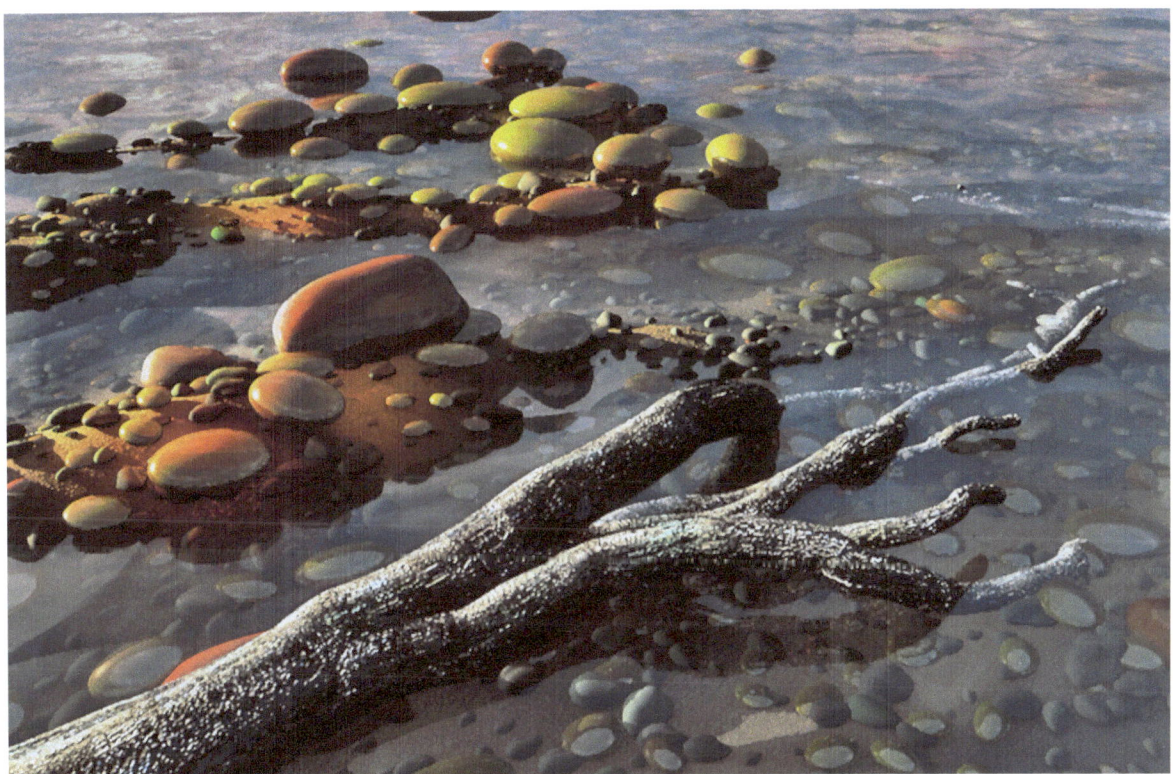

"Red Rocks" (2010) by Mark DeMent, USA, from Fresno, California - 1st place in Digital category. "This is a digital illustration in which I am exploring techniques to generate a feel of traditional media. I enjoy creating landscapes, places that could be real but are not."

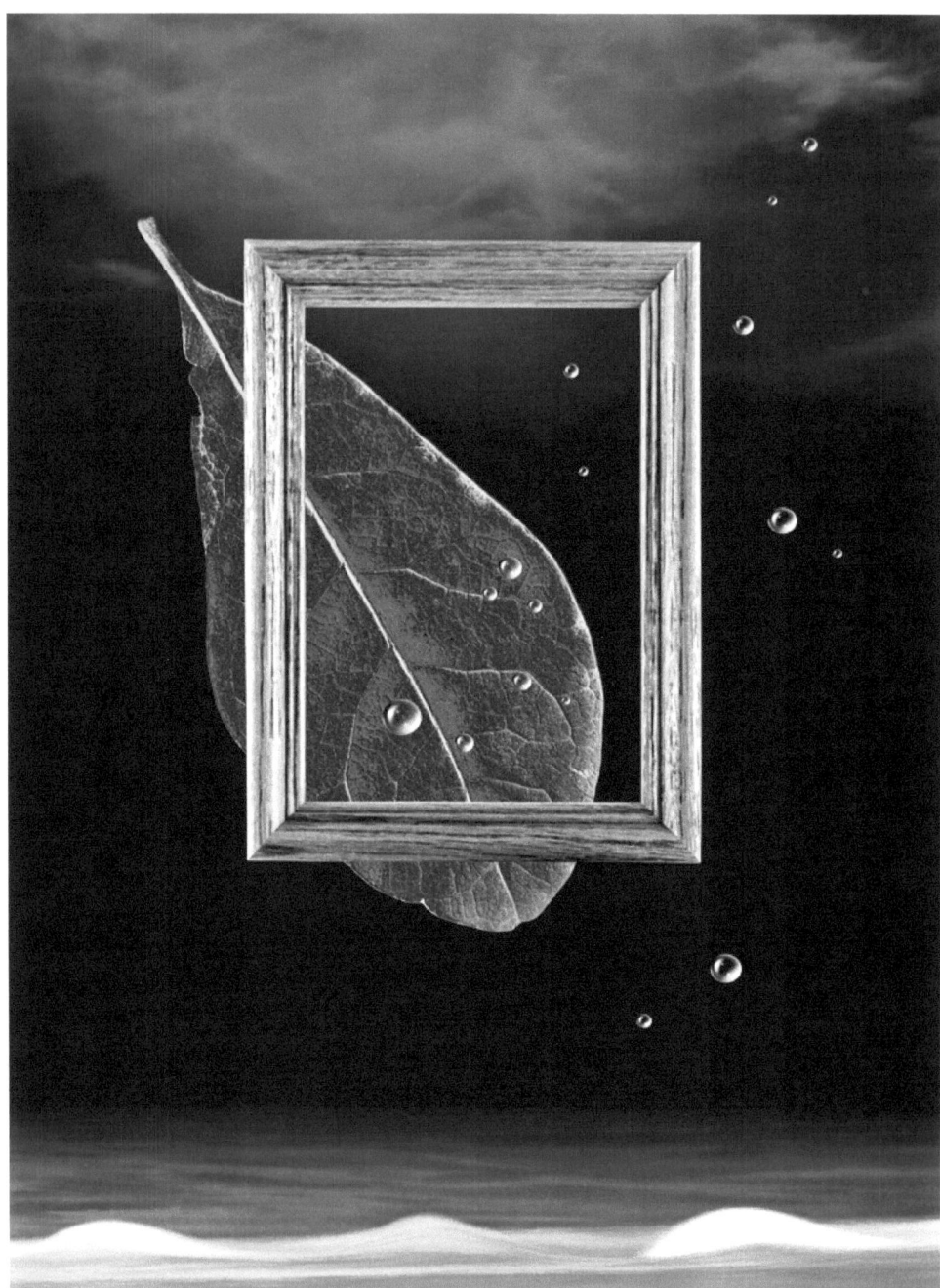

"Artless Art" (2003) by Jing Zhou, Chinese living in USA - digital photography on archival paper. "The motif behind this image was generated from my experience with both art and Ch'an, called Zen in Japanese. Master Suzuki-roshi said, 'If one really wishes to be master of an art... one has to transcend technique so that the art becomes an 'artless art' growing out of the Unconscious.' In my opinion, when one reaches an enlightened stage of spiritual development, s/he is not only an artist in terms of art but also an 'artist of life'."

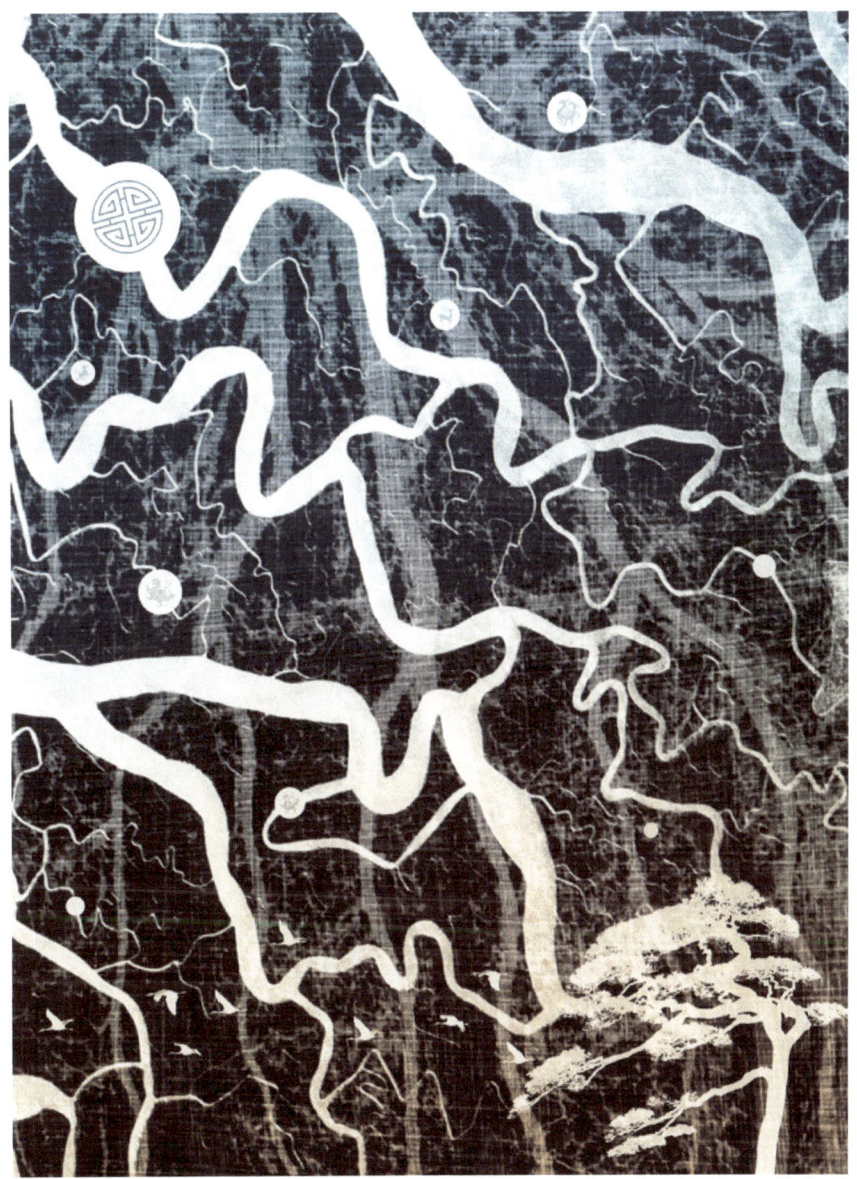

"Totality" (2010) by Jing Zhou, Chinese living in USA - digital mixed media on archival paper. "The concept of life, death, and reincarnation has followed humanity through the ages. In the history of human experience we continuously seek the understanding of the interconnectedness of life. Flowing high in the sky, the nerve-like white lines are part of the Ganges river delta formed over thousands of years. The river channels at the lower right extend from an ancient pine tree on Mt. HuangShan in China. Surrounded by cranes, this aged pine symbolizes longevity, perseverance, and origin of life. Visually deluding, the root-like patterns in the background are indeed blood veins of a human hand. The white circles carrying primal icons become symbolic indicators of dreams, thoughts, transcendence, and human consciousness."

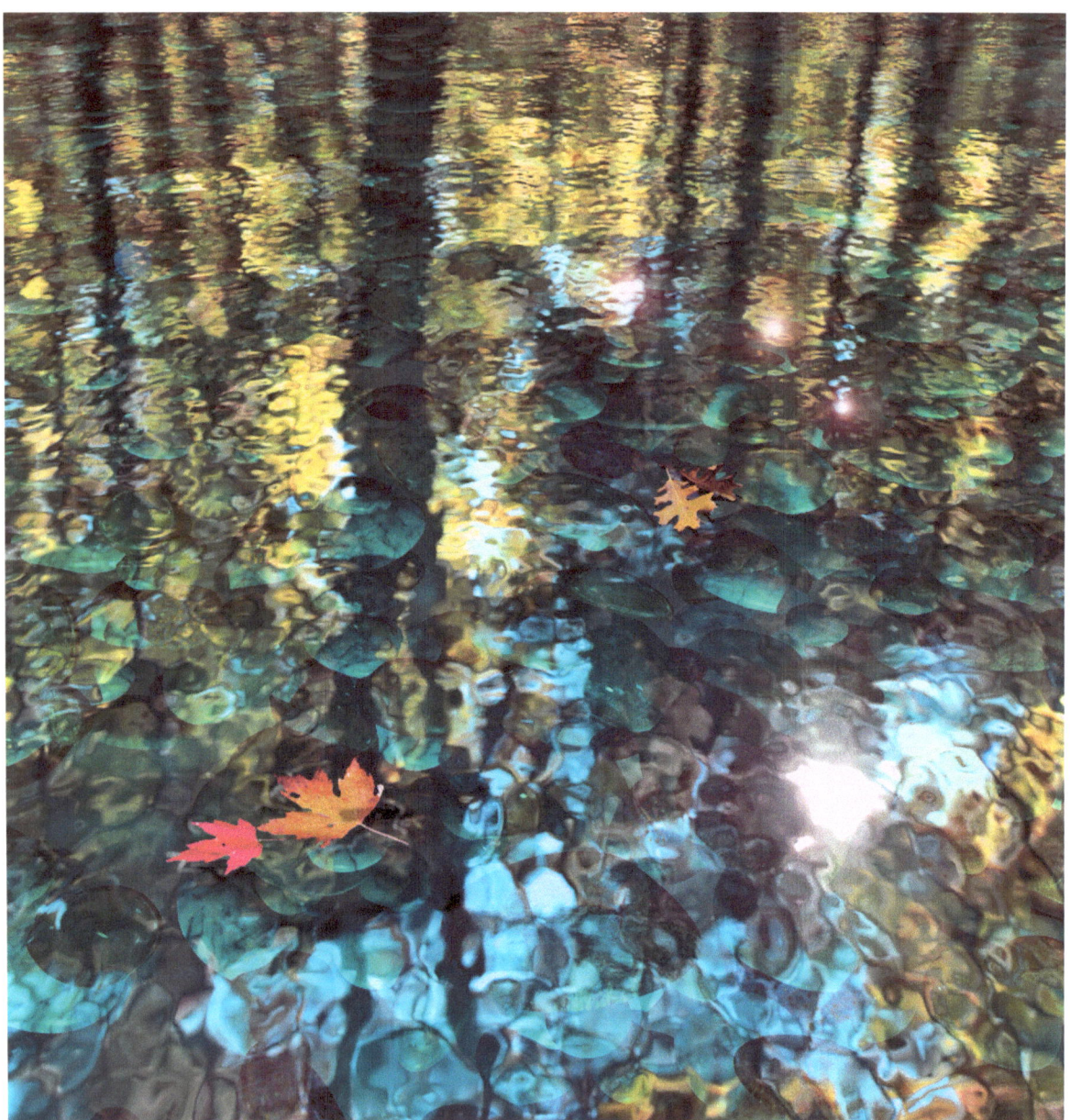

"Floating Leaves" (2010) by Mark DeMent, USA, from Fresno, California - digital image. "This is a digital painting of a more abstract view of the river I enjoy. I am continually creating new points of view for my landscapes imagining places that could be real but are not."

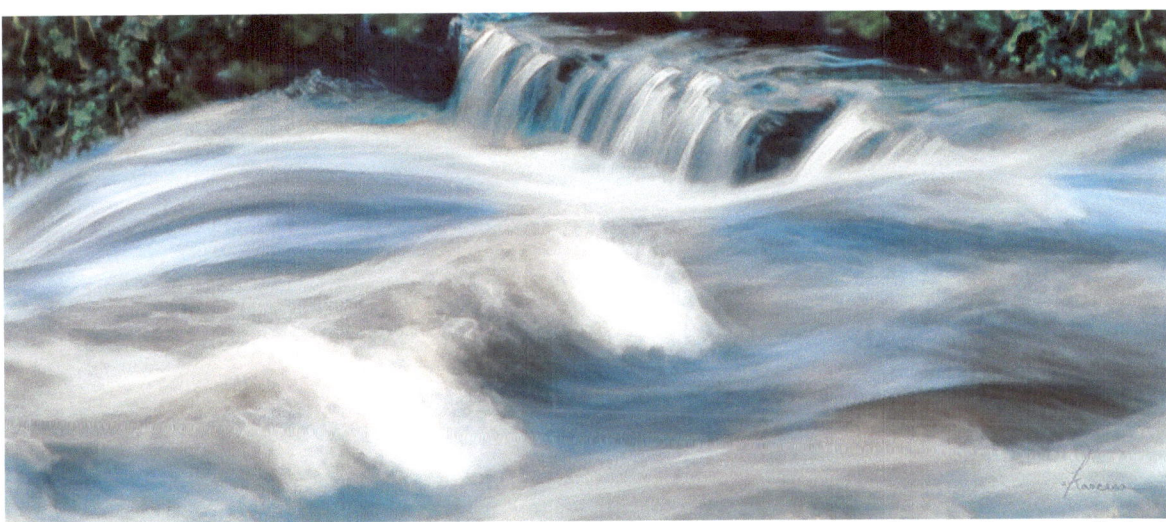
"River Rapids" (2008) by Frances A. Miller, USA, from Florida's Space Coast - digital image. "I was at Child's Park in Pennsylvania to photograph the beautiful waterfalls there when I saw these rapids in the stream above a fall. Water is a most fascinating subject, endlessly enchanting as it flows, sparkles, slides and tumbles over the earth."

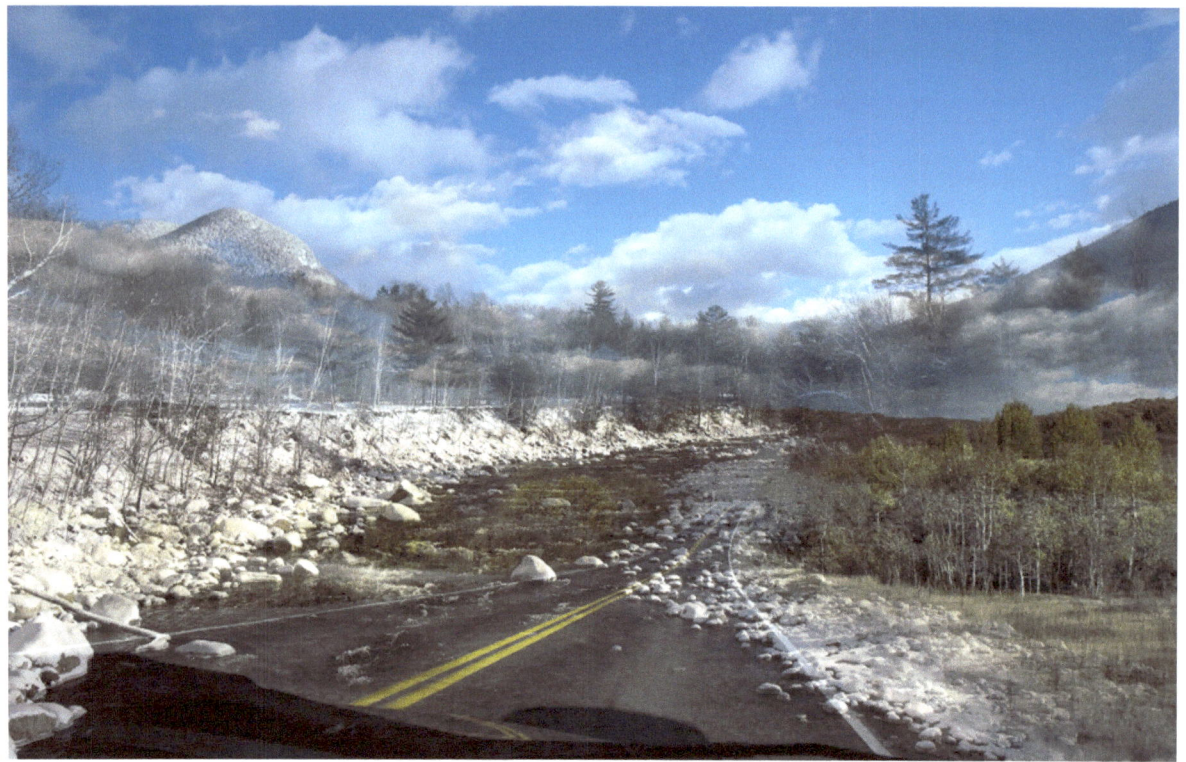

"Holzwege 30" (2009) by Deborah Orloff, USA, from Sylvania, Ohio - digital photomontage. "*Holzwege*, the German word for wood-path, refers to paths in the forest that lead nowhere. These paths meander through the woods and end abruptly; you never know where they will take you. Thus, the concept of a wood-path can be seen as a metaphor for life's uncertainty. There are points in our lives when we are focused; it is as if we are on a clear path toward our goals. Other times, we feel unsure of where we are heading, or a chosen course ends unexpectedly and we must suddenly reevaluate our direction. I am exploring these ideas in a new body of work in which I create ambiguous landscapes through the layering of multiple photographs. I combine the images digitally to create surreal, new spaces where one photograph disappears into the next. These invented landscapes function as metaphors for the universal experience we all have inevitably, when our lives suddenly change; Just when you think you know where you're going, unexpected circumstances dictate a change of plans. Ultimately the images are meant to be ethereal and optimistic, conveying the sense of wonder that exists when we open ourselves up to new possibilities and realize that change is often fortuitous. While the word *holzwege* suggests a dead-end, the connotation is not necessarily negative. Rather, the inability to move forward presents opportunities for exploration, transformation, and previously unimagined destinies."

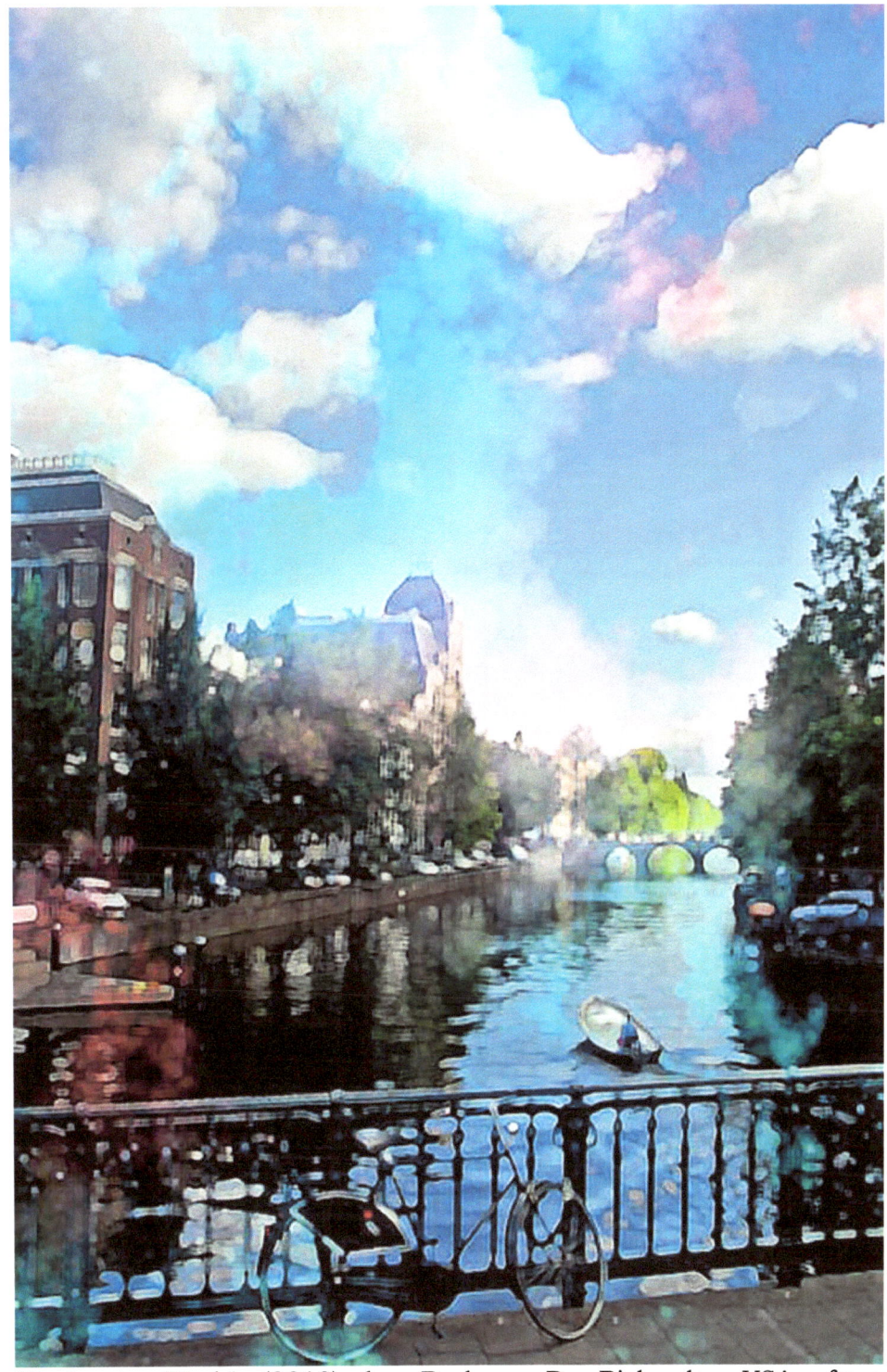

"Early to Work" (2010) by Barbara D. Richards, USA, from Wickenburg, Arizona and Heber, Utah - digital image. "My work starts with pictures that I have taken. I then create my work of art using Photoshop. This photo was taken early morning in Amsterdam."

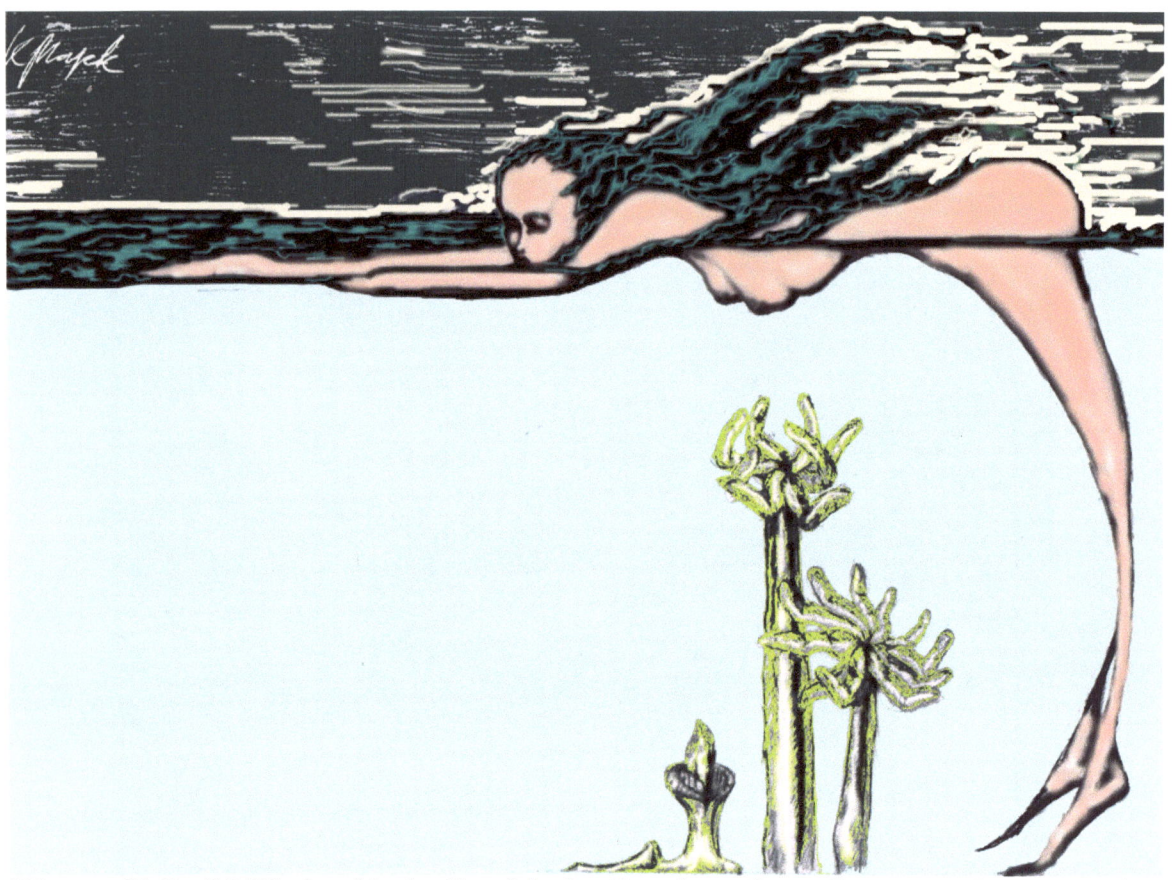

"Water Girl" (2007) by Mark Kovalchuk, Russian, from Rostov-on-Don, Russian Federation - digital painting. "Fantasy art: Most of my art works you can see at my website: www.paintingsilove.com/artist/markkovalchuk."

DRAWINGS & SKETCHES

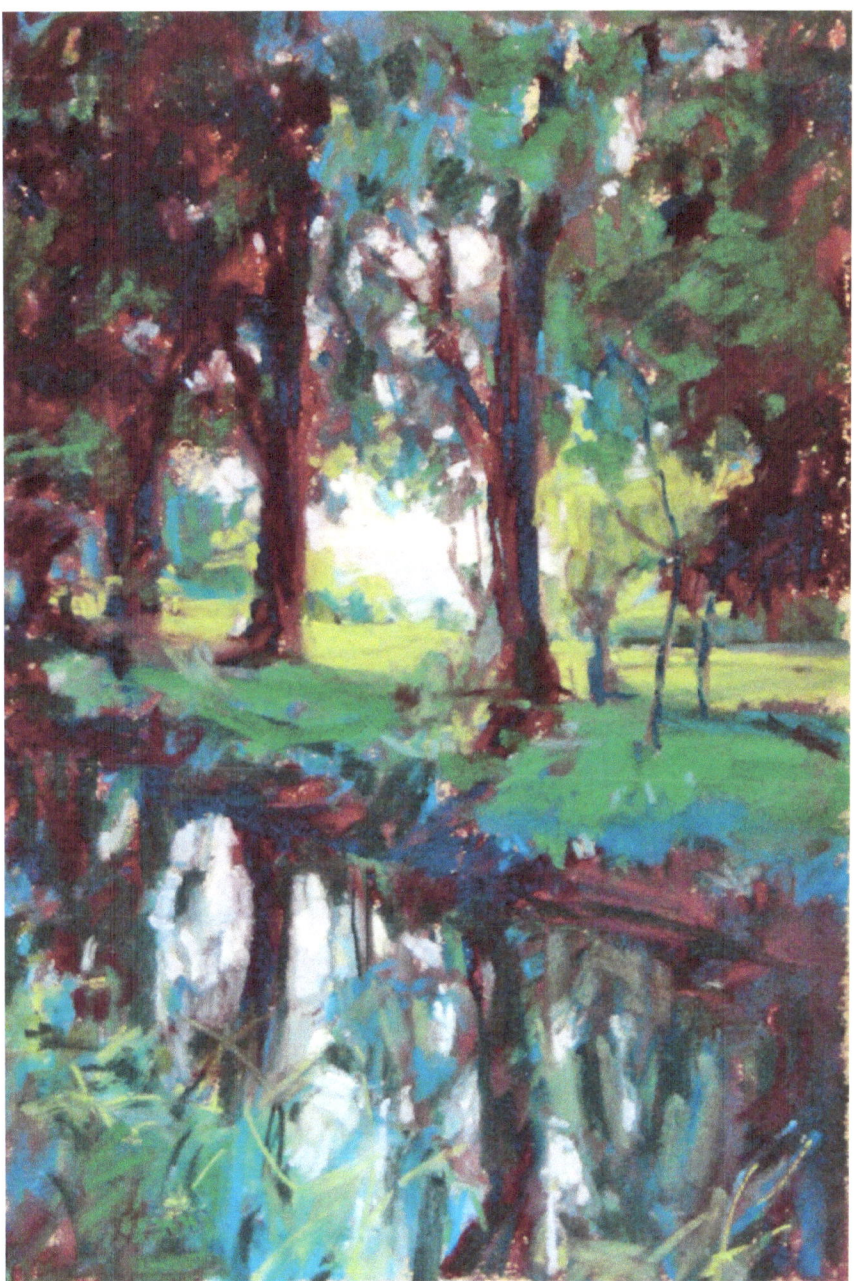

"By the River" (2010) by Nancy Ness, USA, from Adirondack Park, New York - soft pastel - 1st place in Drawing/Sketches category. "After a wonderful trip to France, I chose one of my photos to use as reference for this piece. I wanted to capture the rich color and tranquil beauty of the day."

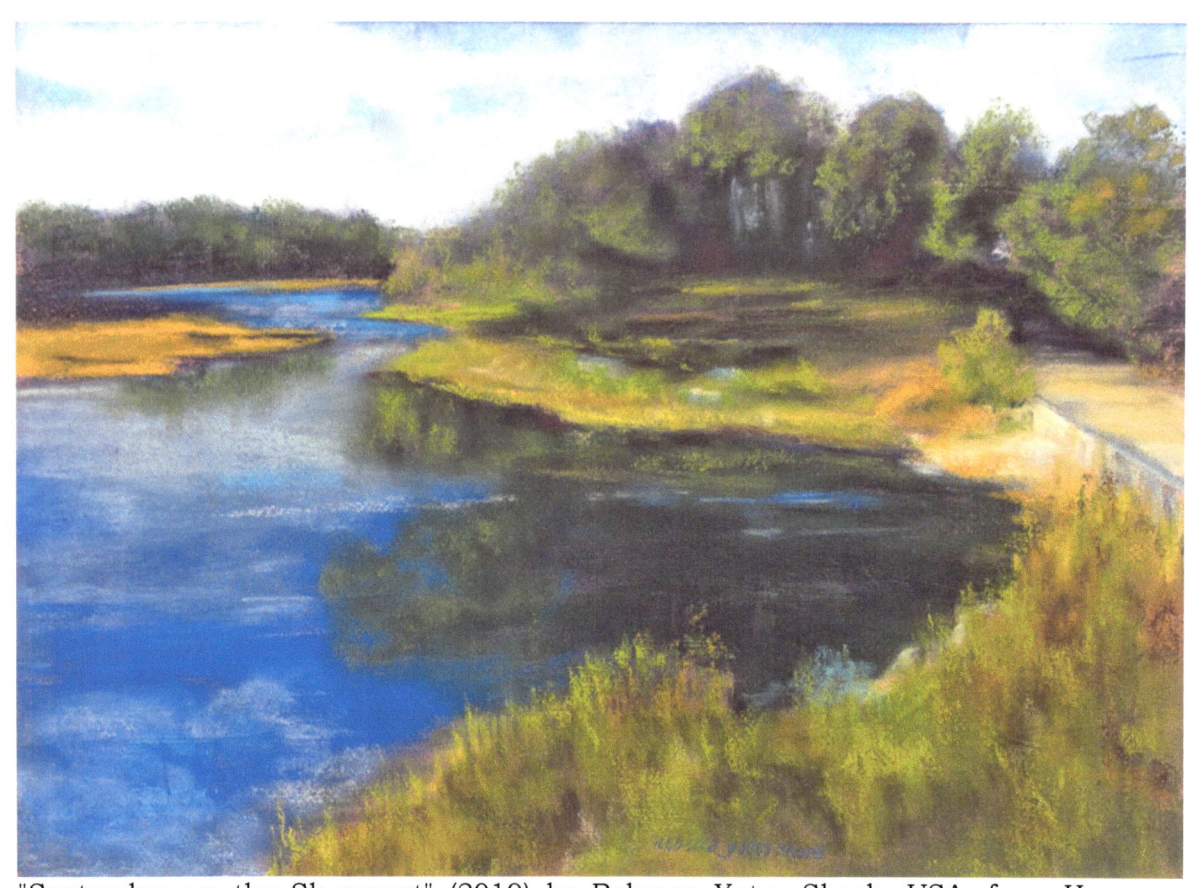

"September on the Sheepscot" (2010) by Rebecca Yates Shorb, USA, from Hanover, Pennsylvania - pastel. "My passion is Plein Air Painting. It is my joy to share these experiences with some 25 other artists each summer in Maine. As we paint together and I critique the group, we grow in skill and friendship. Both of these images were created in Mid-Coast Maine."

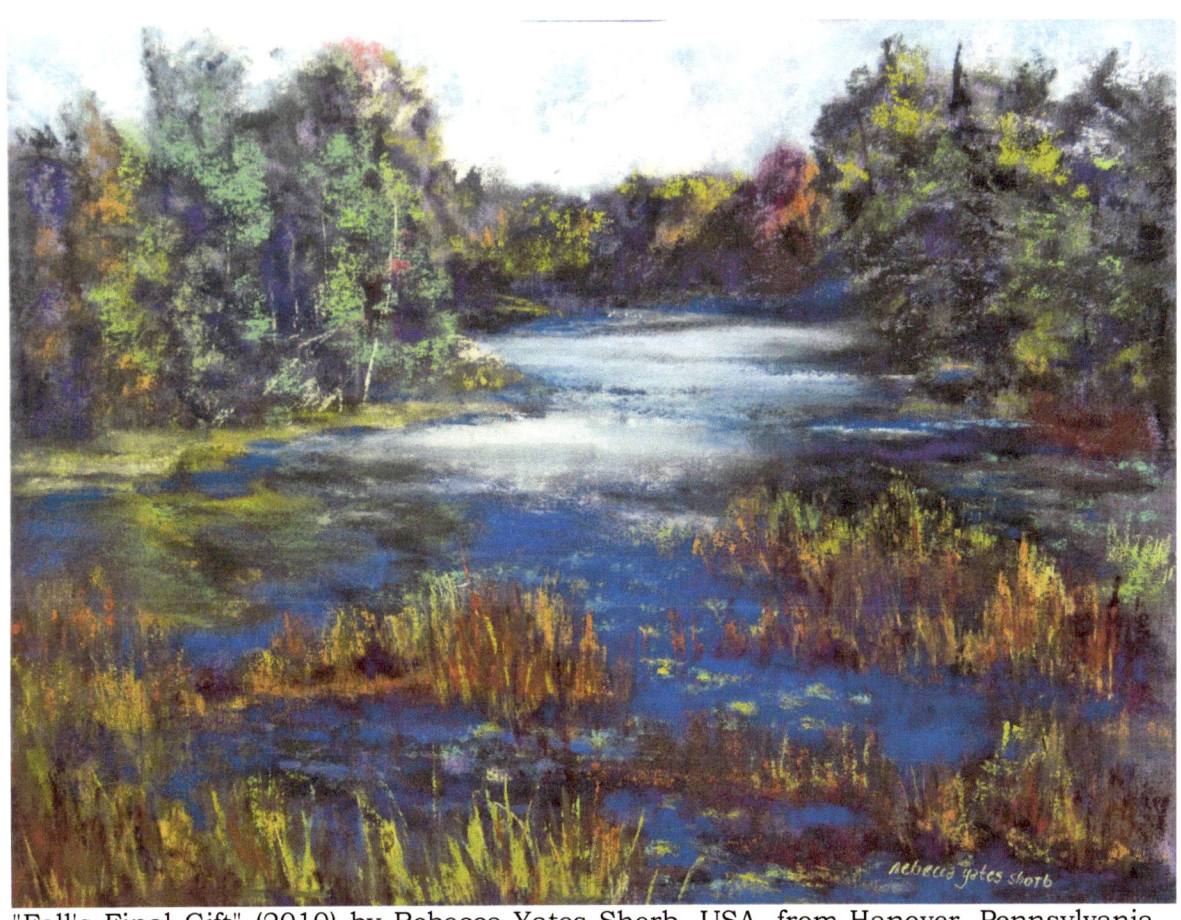
"Fall's Final Gift" (2010) by Rebecca Yates Shorb, USA, from Hanover, Pennsylvania - pastel.

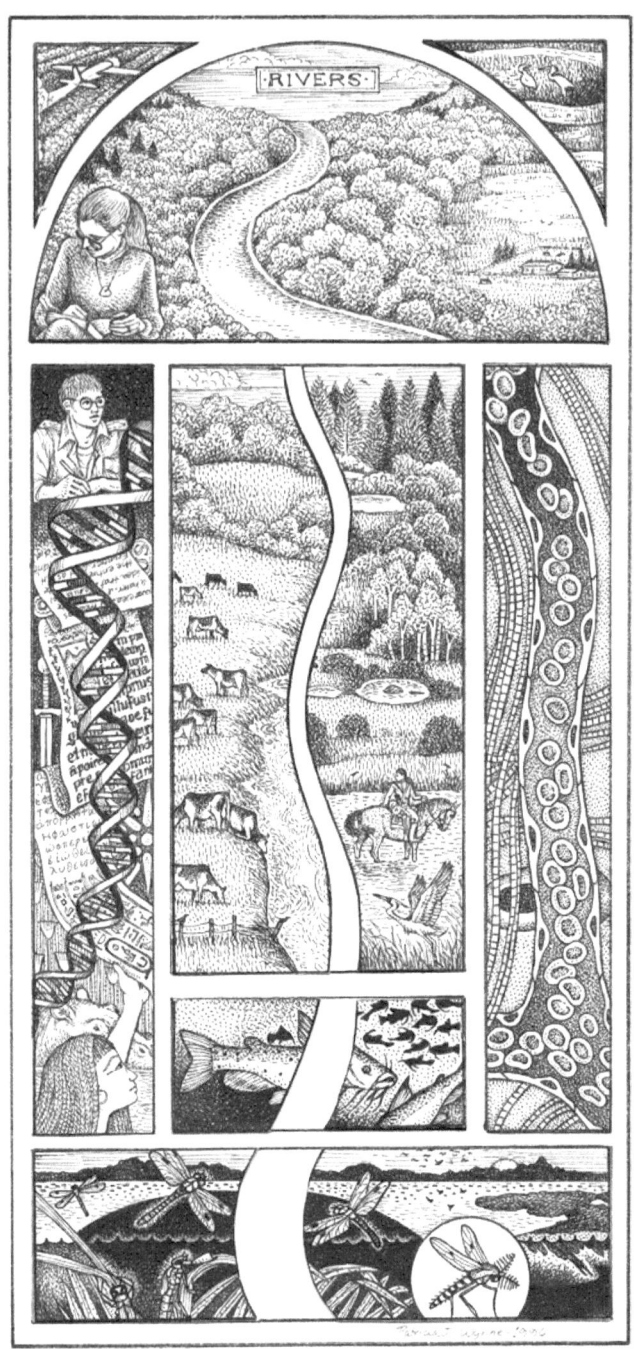

"Rivers" (1996) by Patricia J. Wynne, USA, from New York, New York - pen and ink. "I did Rivers while working on a series of drawings for the *New York Times*. It occurred to me that rivers flowed not only through pristine and polluted land but also through our bodies, our cells, our thoughts and our cultural history. The result was this little drawing."

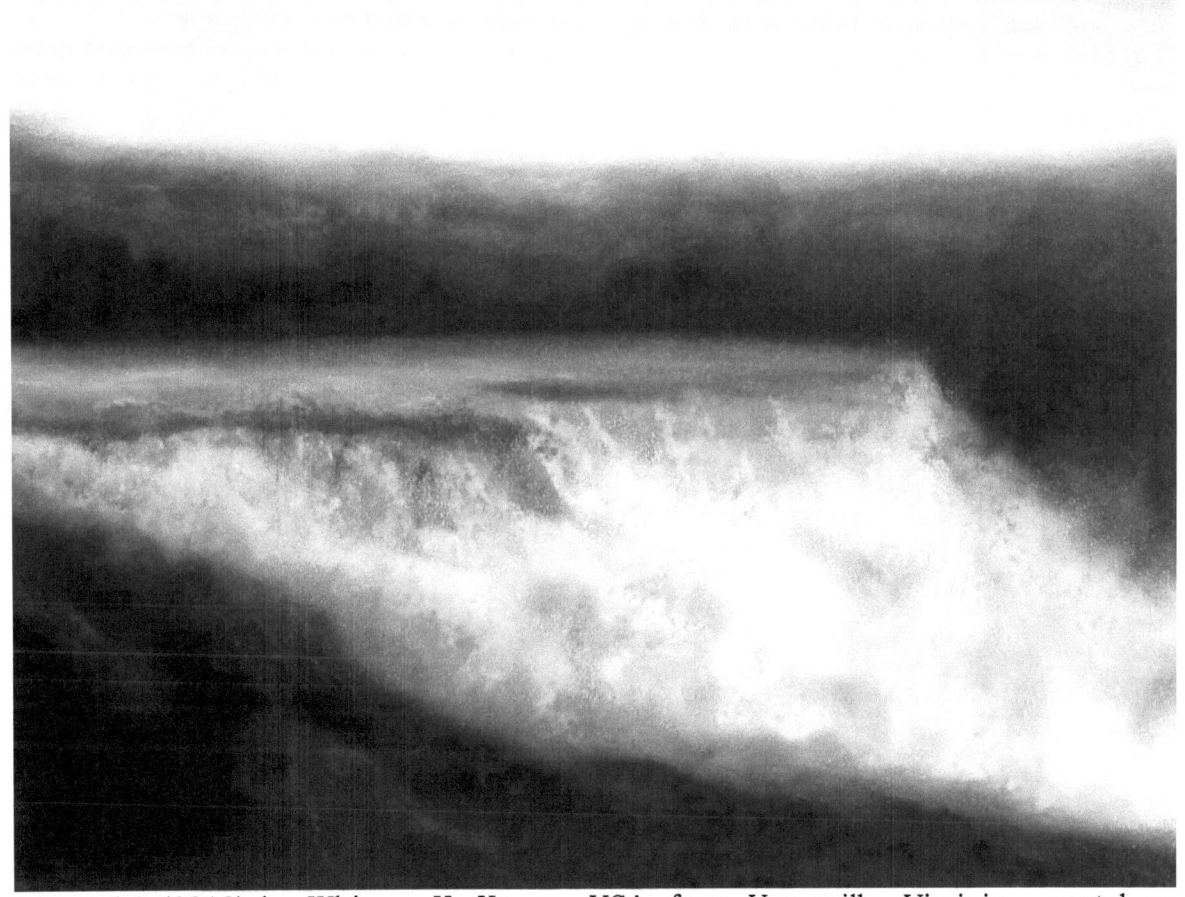
"Cascade" (2010) by Whitney K. Knapp, USA, from Upperville, Virginia - pastel on paper. "There is an ineffable quality about the sky that I find fascinating. It's intangible yet governing presence over the palpable landscape is crucial to my work. I'm interested in the atmospheric relationships between sky and surface, and ultimately, their reconciliation. This exploration is both perceptual and metaphorical. Through sky, I seek to allude to the Divine, while I reference my own environment by the depiction of land or subject."

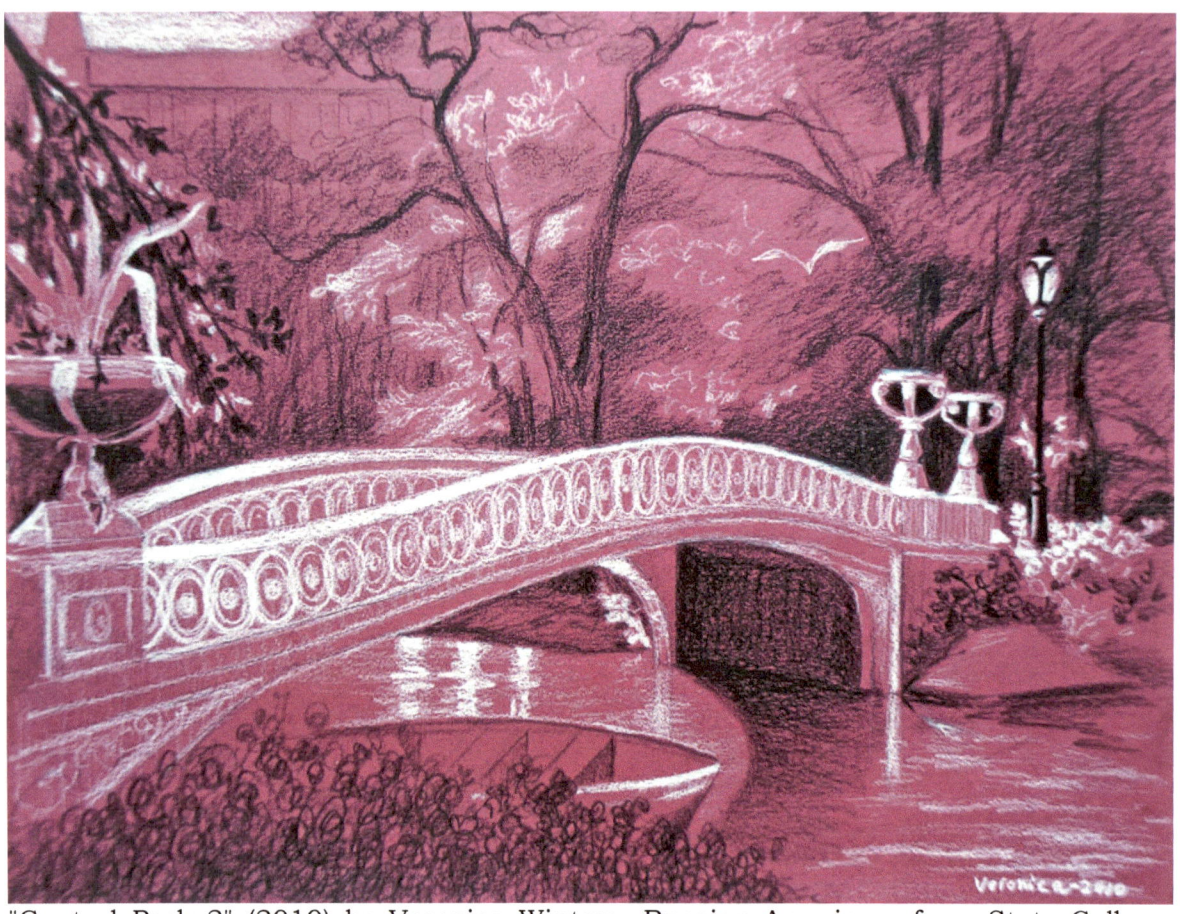

"Central Park 2" (2010) by Veronica Winters, Russian-American, from State College, Pennsylvania - drawing. "Veronica Winters creates realist mystical environments based on her travels and field notes. She works in two mediums: oils and colored pencil. Her work can be found on-line at www.veronicasart.com. Veronica has published several art books and her artwork is in private collections in the U.S. and Europe."

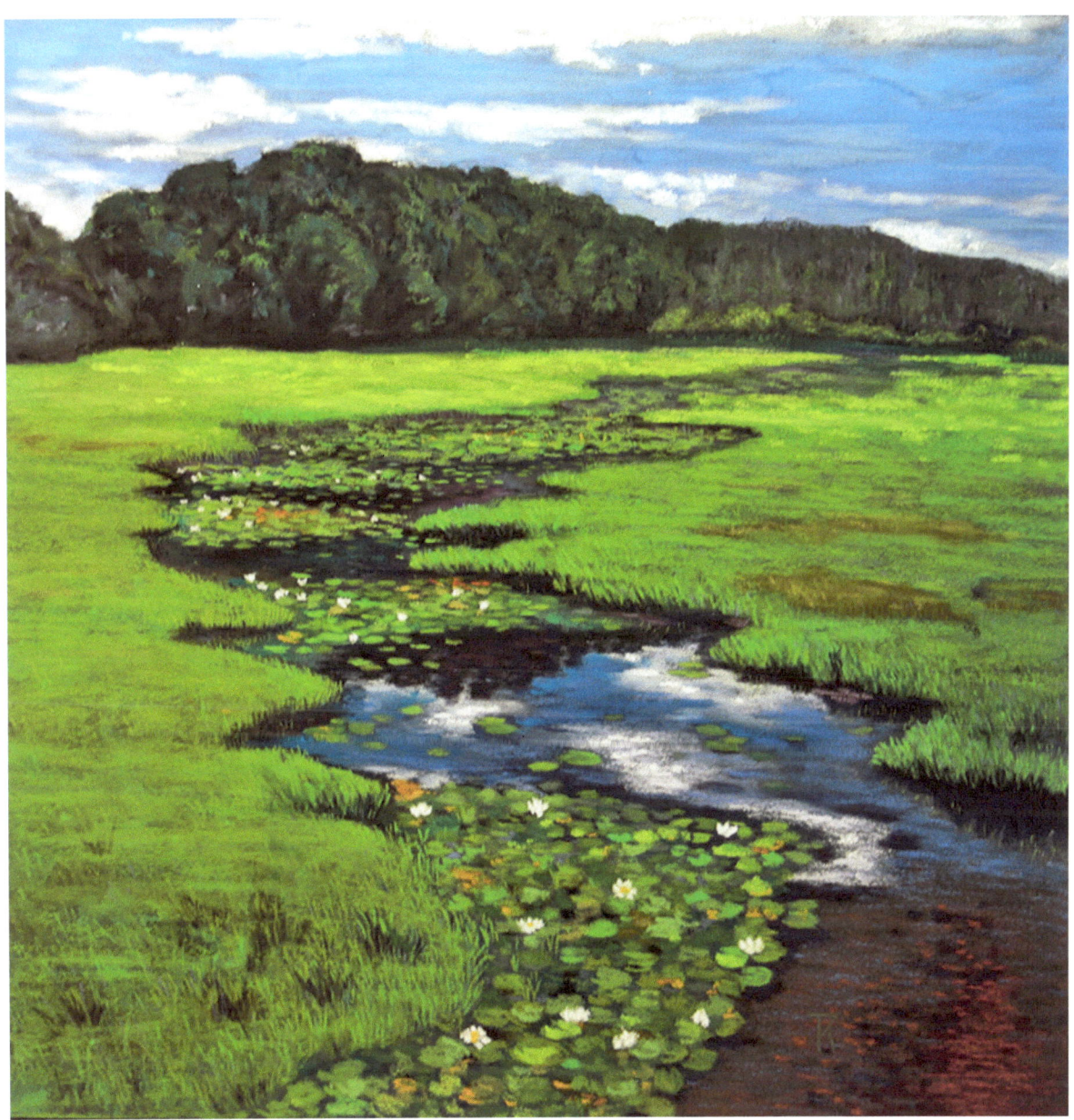

"Waterway with Lilies" (2010) by Tatiana Myers, Russian-American, from Duncannon, Pennsylvania - drawing. "This painting was inspired by the beauty of Susquehanna River lowlands. This is one of pastel paintings I have done in my series of works dedicated to Creeks, Lakes and waterways of Central PA."

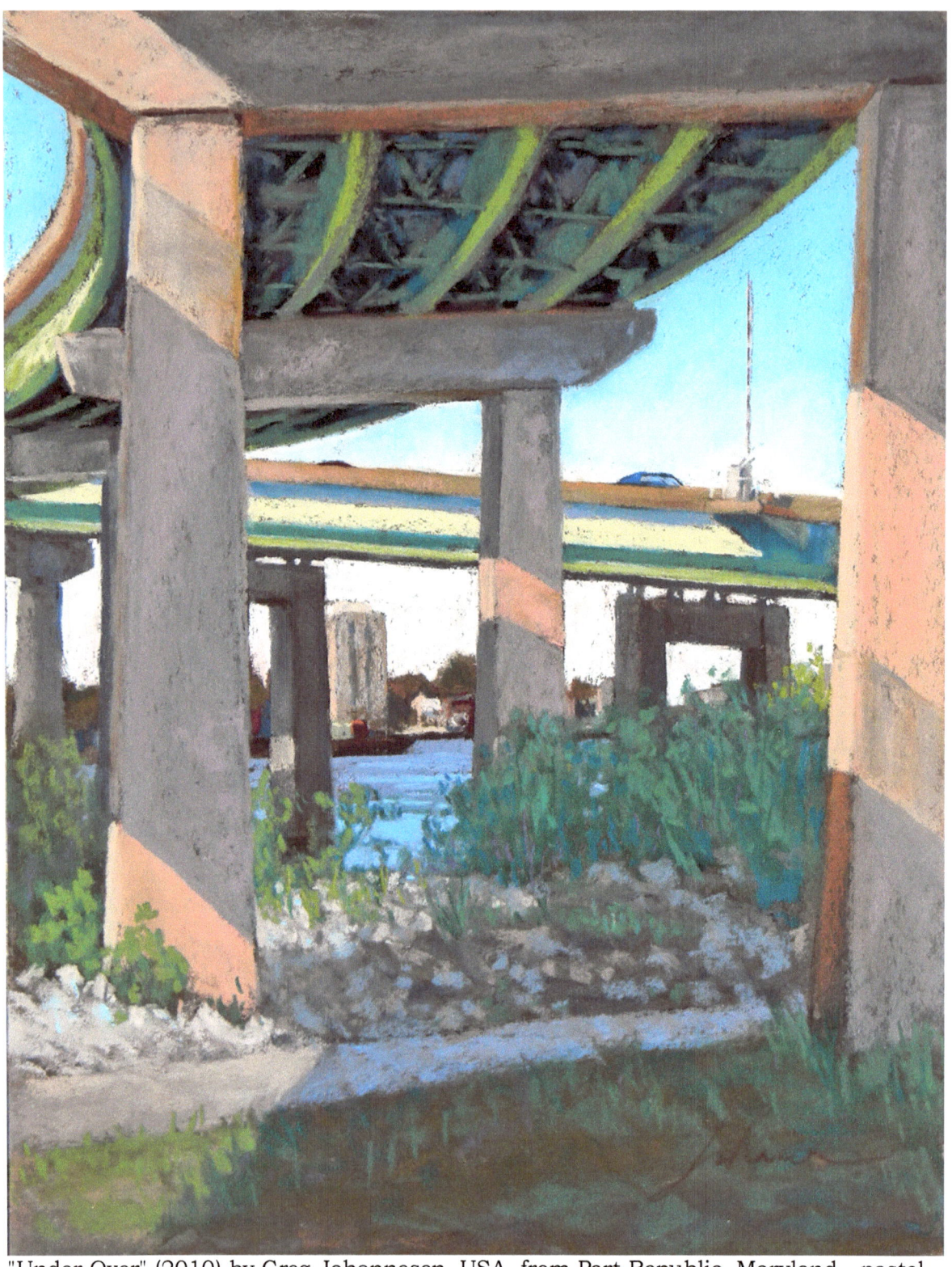

"Under Over" (2010) by Greg Johannesen, USA, from Port Republic, Maryland - pastel.

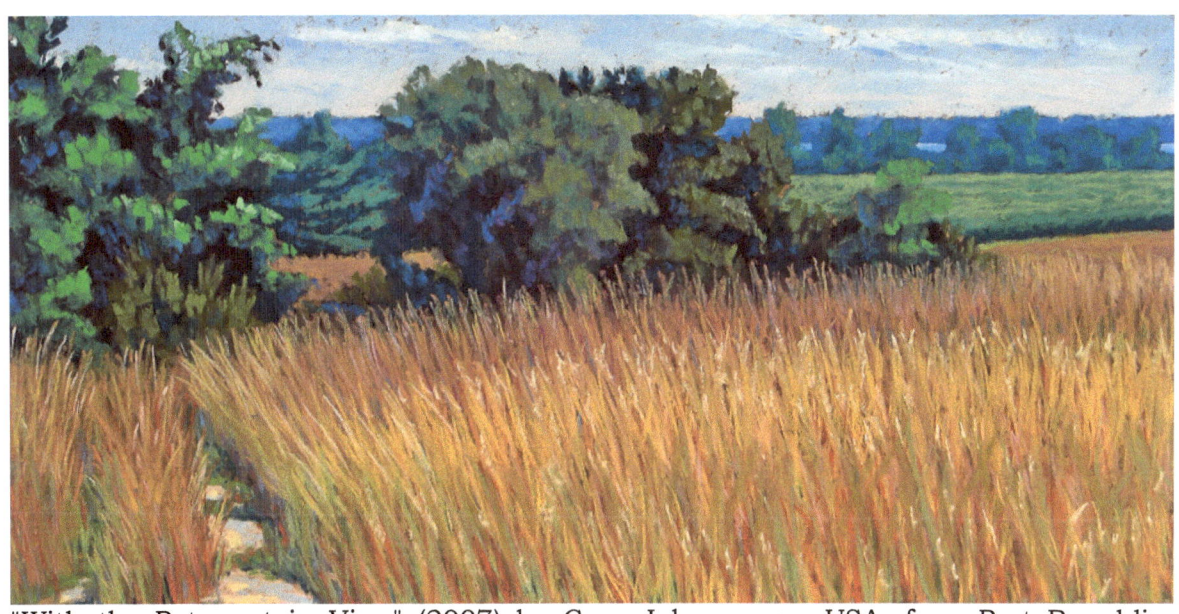
"With the Patuxent in View" (2007) by Greg Johannesen, USA, from Port Republic, Maryland - pastel. "My process begins by taking my 'studio' outdoors, painting en plein air, so that I can experience that which I am humbly trying to recreate on paper. I find that immersing myself in the outdoors somehow liberates my creativity. I paint exclusively with pastels which enable me to produce quick, vibrant, and expressive pieces."

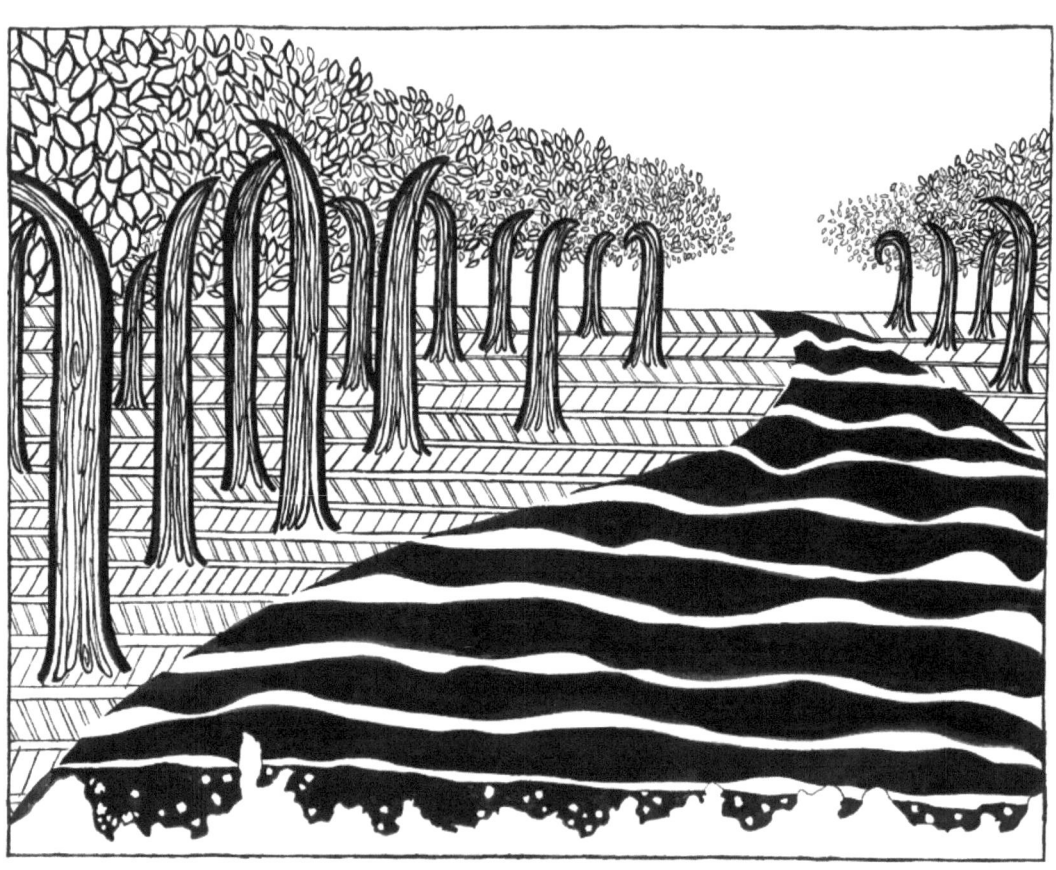

"Embelle" (2010) by Shannon Chong, USA, from Miramar, Florida- pen and ink. "What makes life beautiful is our perception and how we interpret what we see before us. When I observe a subject, I see beyond the actual object and start to transform what I see into repeating shapes and patterns on my piece of paper or canvas. This love for embellishment and exaggeration can be seen in my work, 'Embelle'."

MIXED MEDIA & COLLAGE

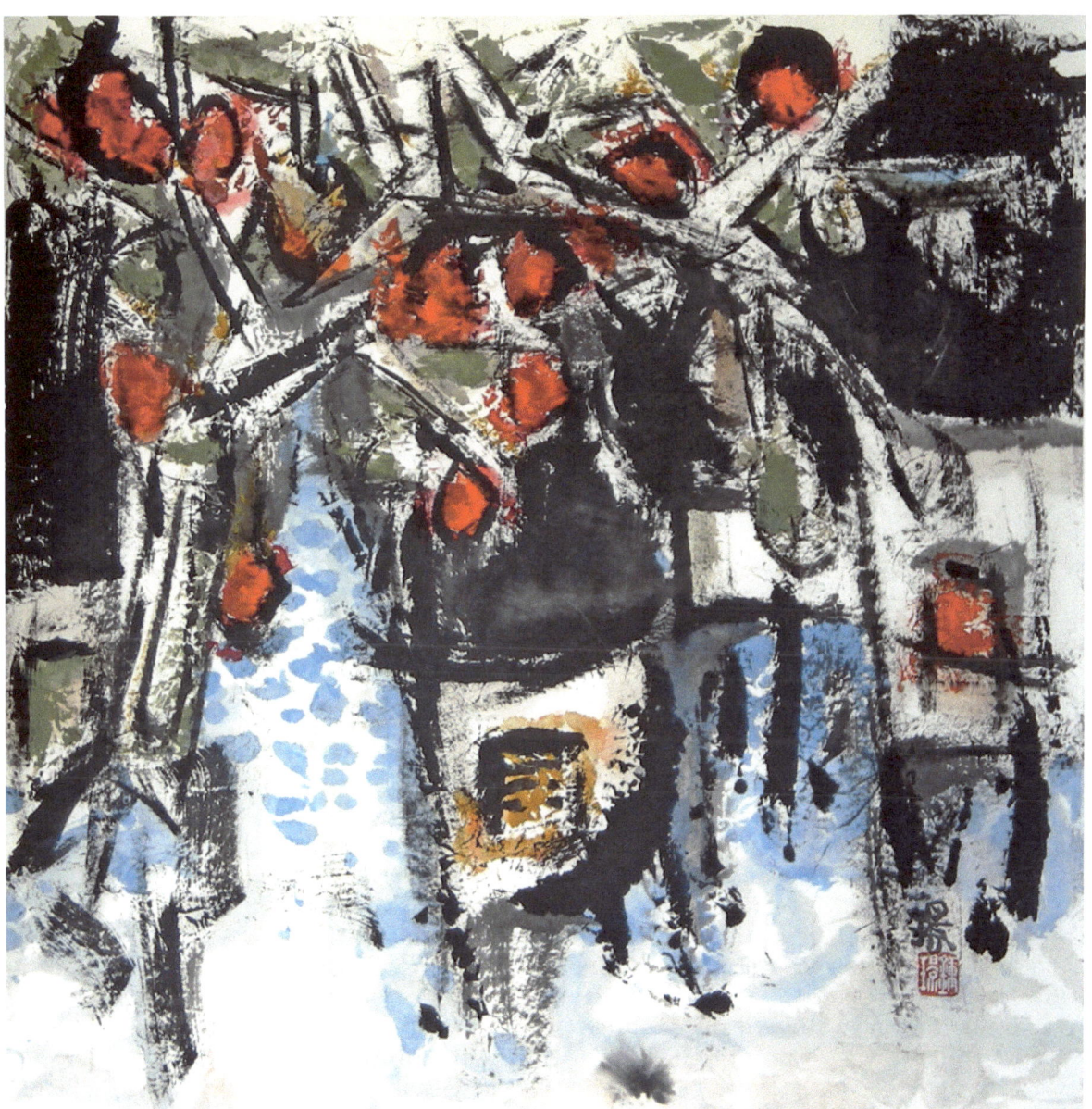

"Fishing Village" (2008) by Jing Chung, Malaysia - ink and acrylic on paper. "You find these sorts of villages along the river of Malaysia. The houses are built on stilts away from the high-tide line, just in case the river runs over high-tide line during flood."

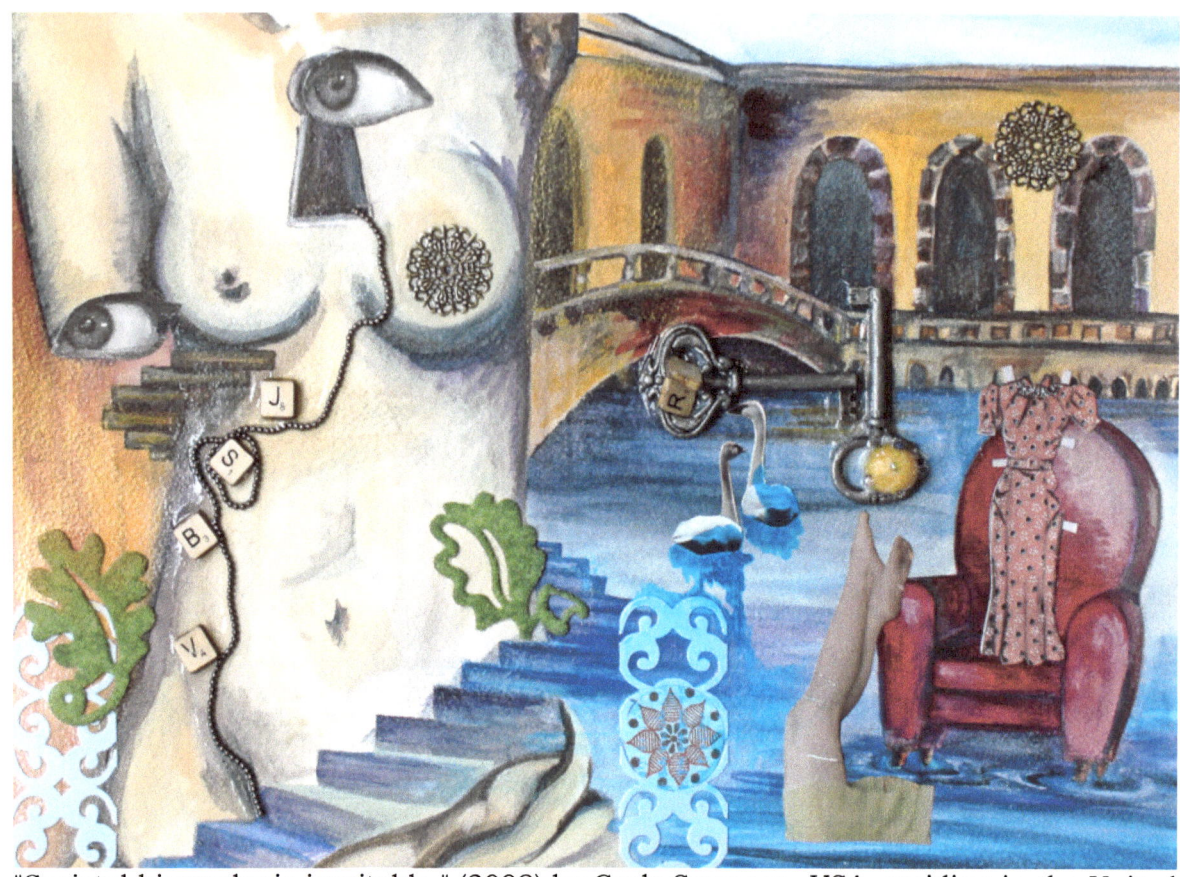

"Societal hierarchy is inevitable " (2008) by Carly Swenson, USA, residing in the United Kingdom - watercolor collage, found objects, paper, felt, matte medium. "My art is a juxtaposition of classic, conceptual and ordinary images to create aesthetically intriguing and thought provoking pieces. I find historical changes in art, culture, religious interpretations and social conventions infinitely fascinating and I incorporate those concepts into my art. In the majority of my work, I combine identifiable images and ideas to create a surreal appearance and dreamlike effect. I prefer my pieces to allow viewers to make their own interpretations on the comparisons, commentary or observations depicted in my work. I enjoy the use of common animals, objects and other easily recognizable forms because people will create their own associations with such things allowing their minds and feelings to find a meaning in a piece. I choose to work in mixed media because it gives me the freedom to utilize different supplies, while adding textures and tangible materials creates an affect that I find alluring. Ultimately, I want my work to express what I can't verbally articulate."

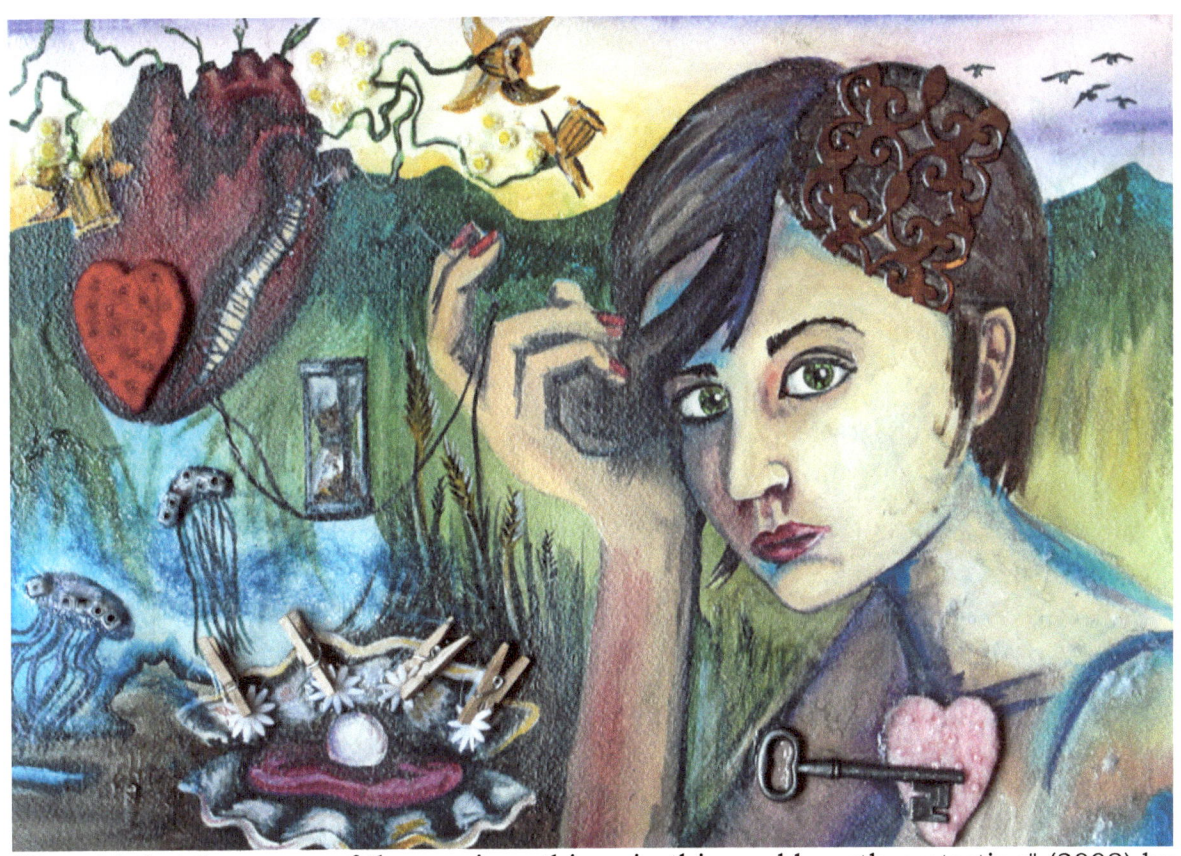

"He said that I was one of the precious things in this world worth protecting" (2008) by Carly Swenson, USA, residing in the United Kingdom - watercolor collage, found objects, paper, felt, matte medium.

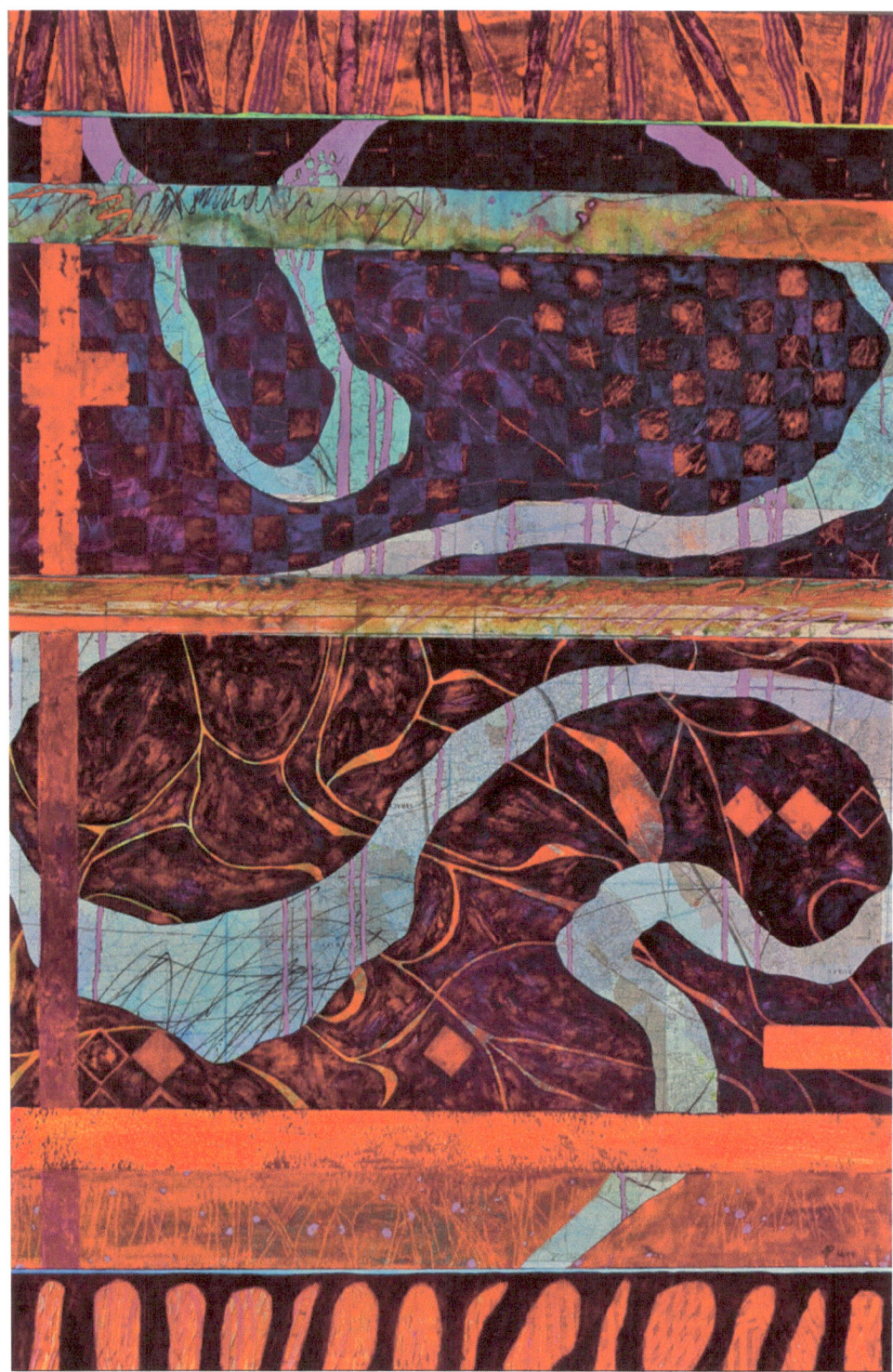
"Night River Meditation Shawl " (2004) by John Lyon Paul, USA, from Ithaca, New York - acrylic and mixed media on collaged elements. "One of a series of 'Shawls' meant to be entered in meditation, and imaginatively wrapped around our bodies as we do so. It is night. The river speaks. This is a listening meditation." Photo by Gary Hodges.

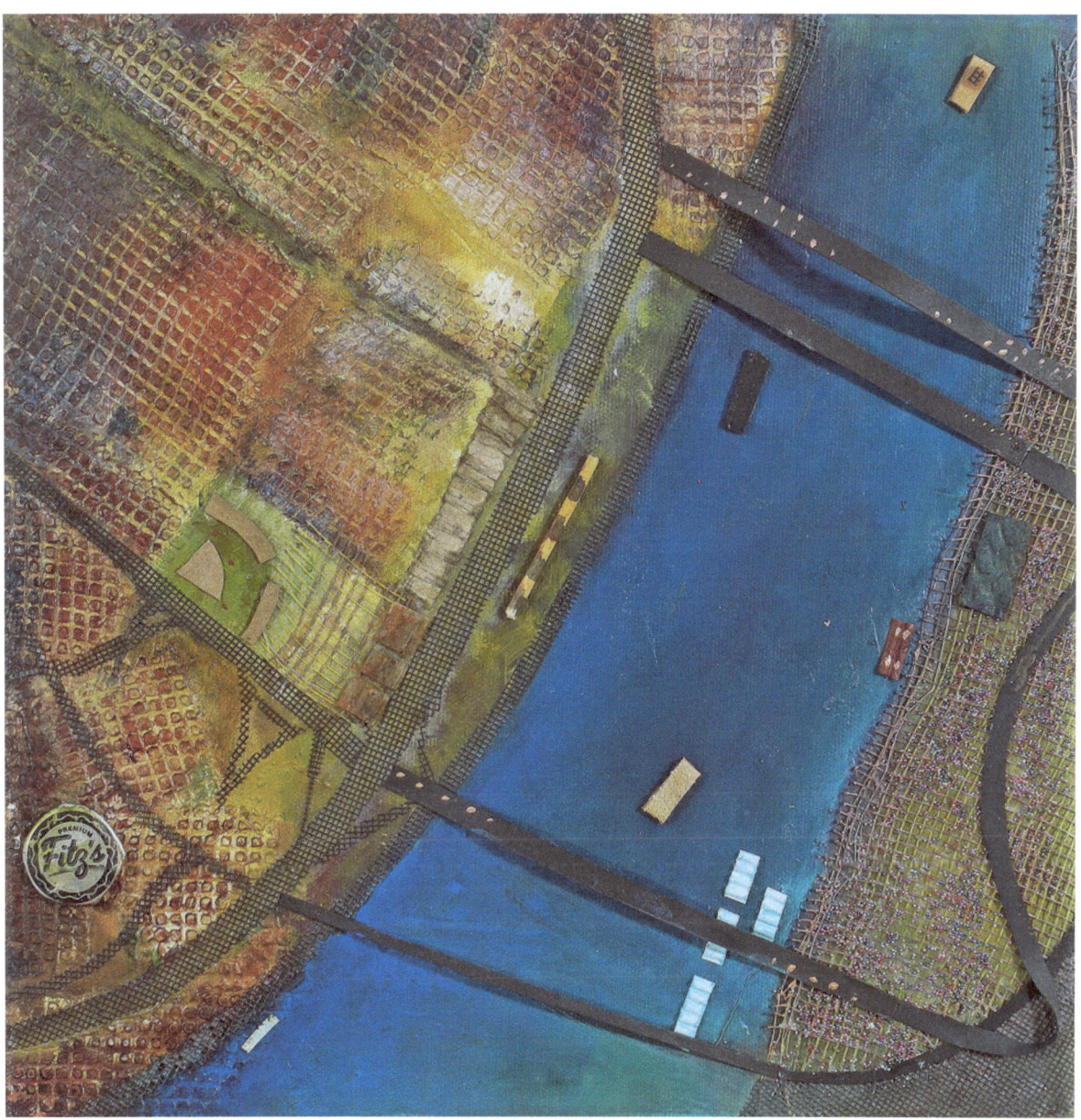

"Riverfront" (2010) by Janice Schoultz Mudd, USA, from St. Louis, Missouri - acrylic on canvas, paper, corrugated cardboard, fiberglass screen, wood, metal bottle cap, woven wire, glass beads, acrylic medium. "'Riverfront' is based on an aerial view of the Mississippi levee area in St Louis, Missouri. The city of St Louis lies to the west of the river. Highway interchanges, bridges, the new ballpark, the arch, and of course, river barges, are part of today's landscape. In late 2009, a two year highway construction project came to an end and the closed highway was reopened. In 2006, the St Louis Cardinals moved to a new stadium. The landscape had changed and you had to be a bird or a pilot to fully appreciate it. "Riverfront" is a loose aerial interpretation of these changes; a snapshot capturing the essence of the impact river and city make on each other.

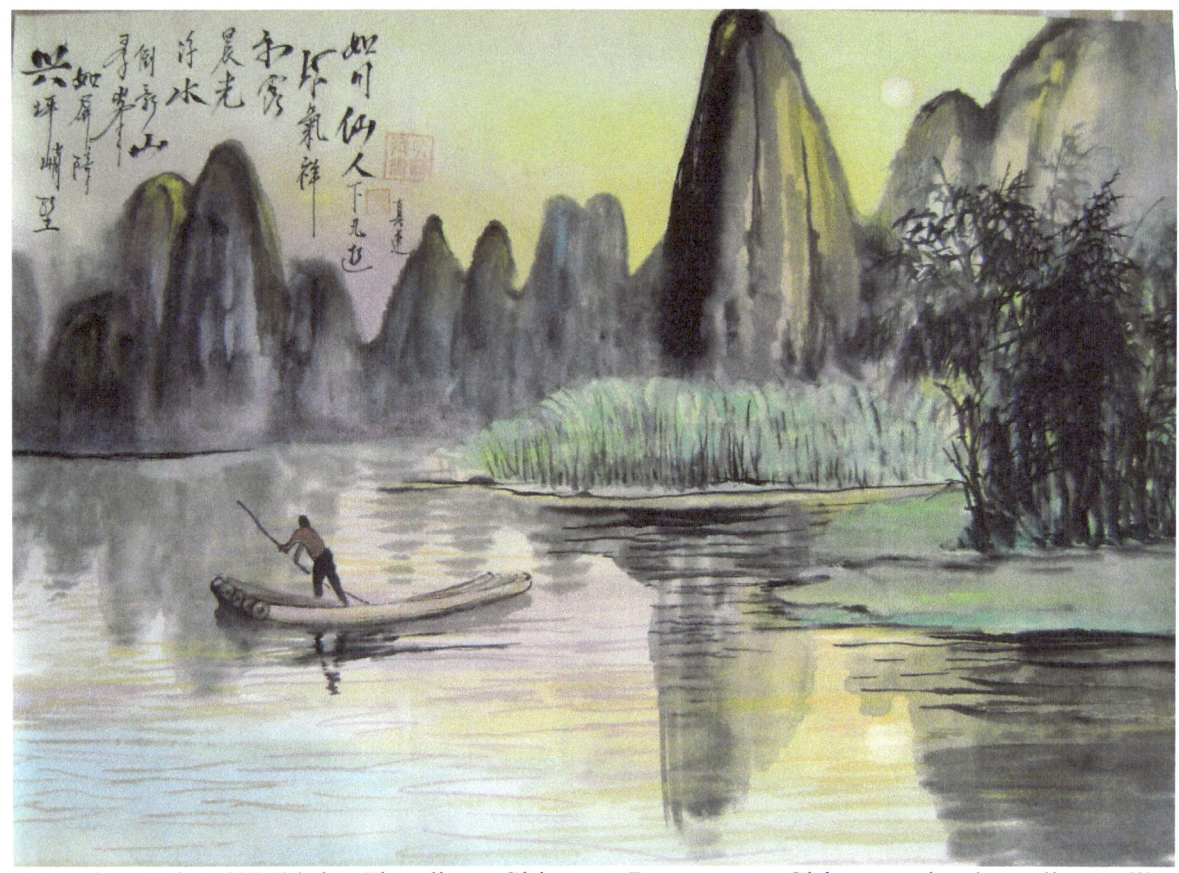

"Morning Trip" (2007) by Zhenlian, Chinese, Dongguan, China - mixed media. "I like both oil paintings and Chinese paintings. In oil painting I like the richness of its colors. I love to cover my canvas with a profusion of colors in their dream-like imageries. I am often inspired by nature, flowers, waters, trees, fruits, etc, I don't paint what I see but express what I feel, I often see the theme of a subject before me, and I choose to express it in colors and forms, like Renoir I believe that a painting should be beautiful. My paintings are meditative and poetic. They make you feel easy and relaxed, because I usually add a humorous touch to my themes. Most of my paintings are conceptual realistic in style, that is to say my paintings appear very realistic but there are always some imaginative elements in the composition of my works. I think I would rather call this Conceptual Romanticism. My paintings are integrations of the real and the imaginative."

OIL & ACRYLIC

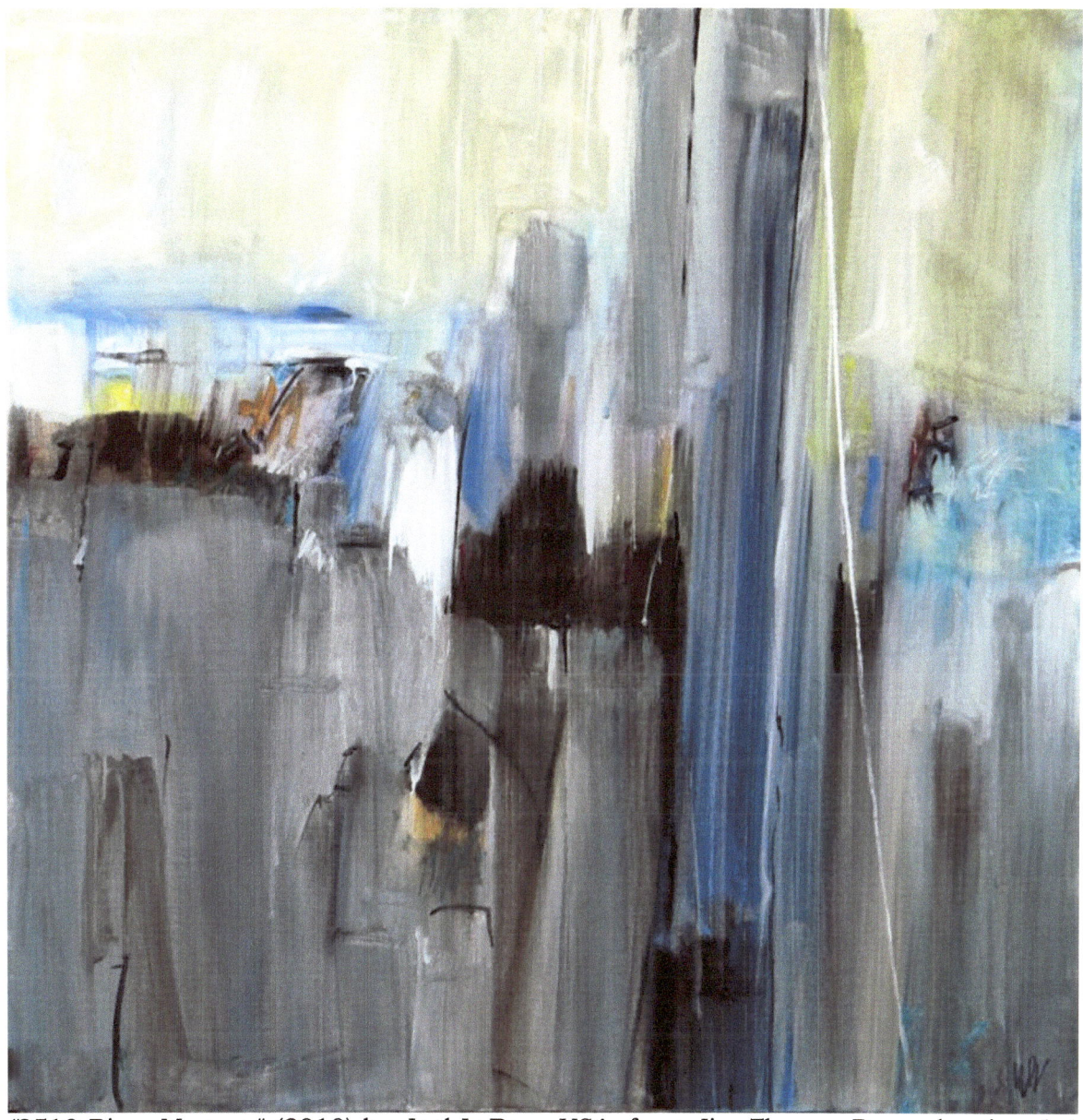

"9510 River Memory" (2010) by Joel LeBow, USA, from Jim Thorpe, Pennsylvania - 1st place in the Oil/Acrylic category. "My works examine the human condition, both physical and metaphysical. We live in a multi-layered universe containing memories of places, people and emotions. My mission over the past 60 years has been to make the viewer remember and to *feel*."

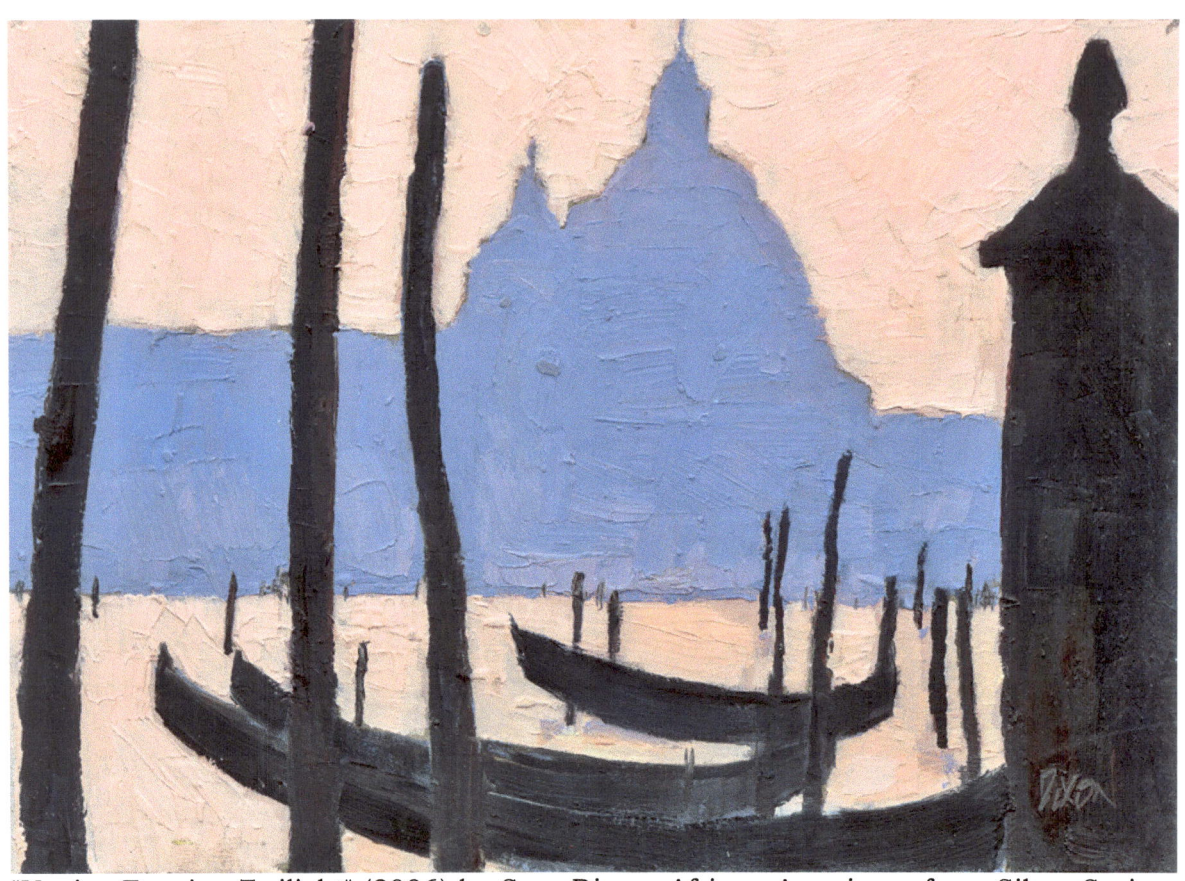

"Venice Evening Twilight" (2006) by Sam Dixon, African-American, from Silver Spring, Maryland - oil. "I never made a conscious decision to be an artist, art just seemed to come to me."

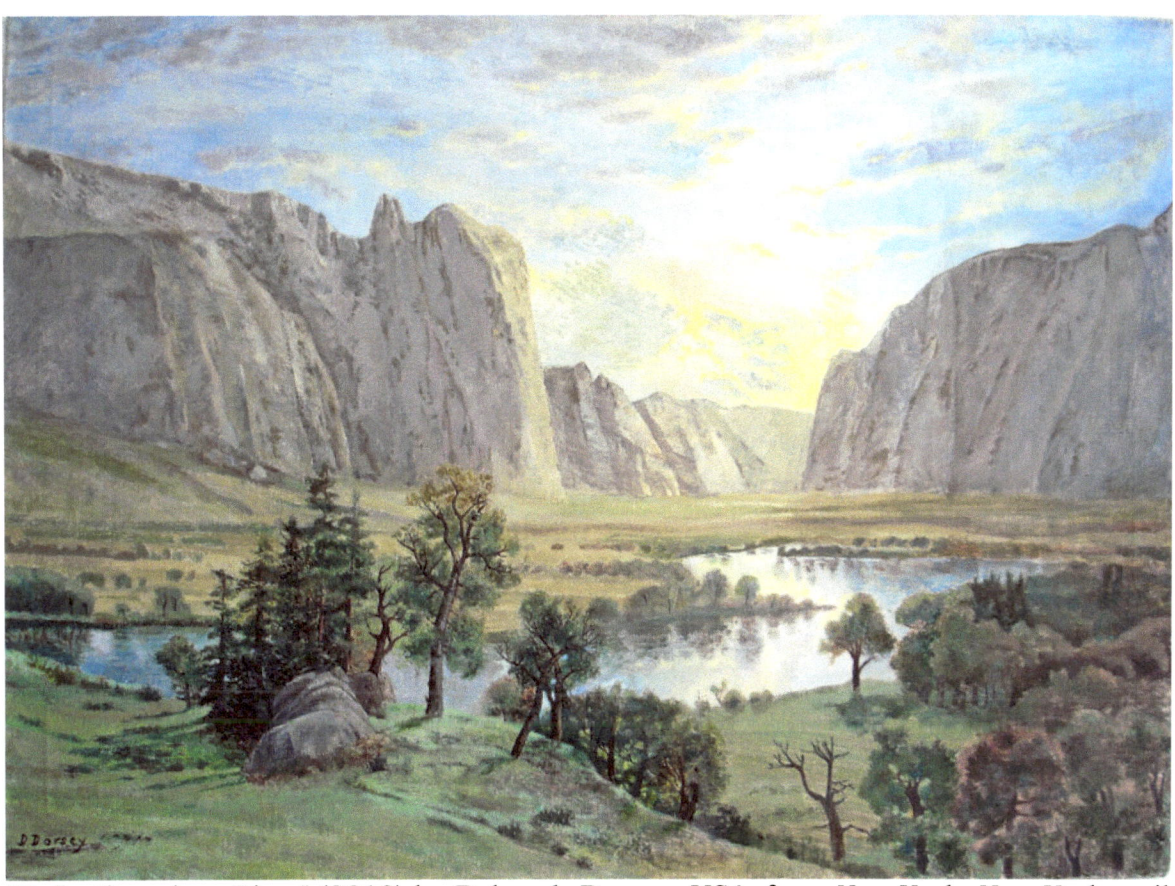

"Reflections in a River" (2010) by Deborah Dorsey, USA, from New York, New York – oil on linen. "Landscape painting is a mood as well as an evocation of place. It describes weather and brings the seasons of the year to life. Technique is the means used to describe the landscape; for me, it is color, drawing and design. Whenever possible I paint on the spot in oils. Working en plein air is an exercise in perception. Painting outdoors the artist observes the changes in mood and the play of light and shade. The artist is constantly comparing one color in nature to the other. If the artist is aware of the constant movement around her - sky, water, even wild animals, her work will never be rigid but full of life."

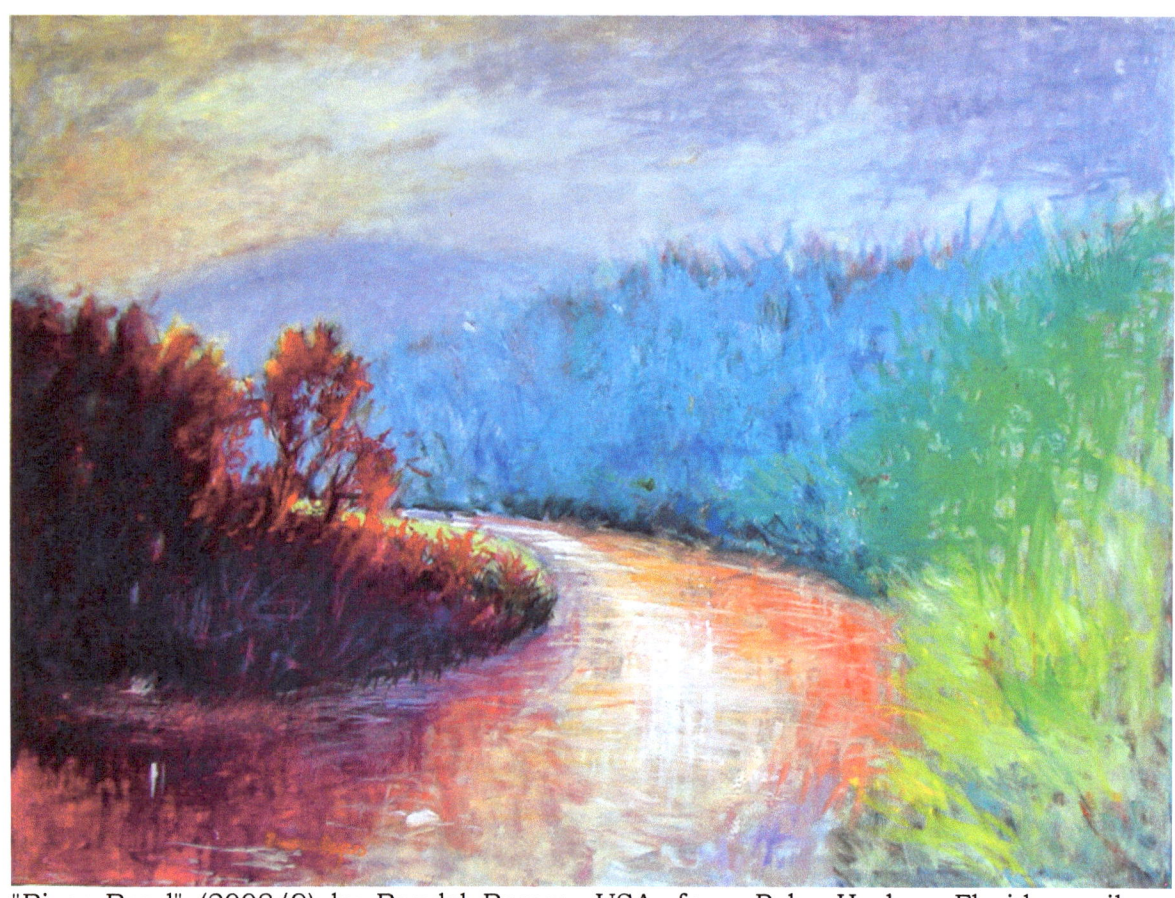

"River Bend" (2008/9) by Randel Rogers, USA, from Palm Harbor, Florida – oil on canvas. "River Bend is a painting that I did from sketches en plein air while on a month-long fellowship in the mountains of Vermont. The time there had been quite productive as well as magical. I wanted to transpose that feeling into this painting."

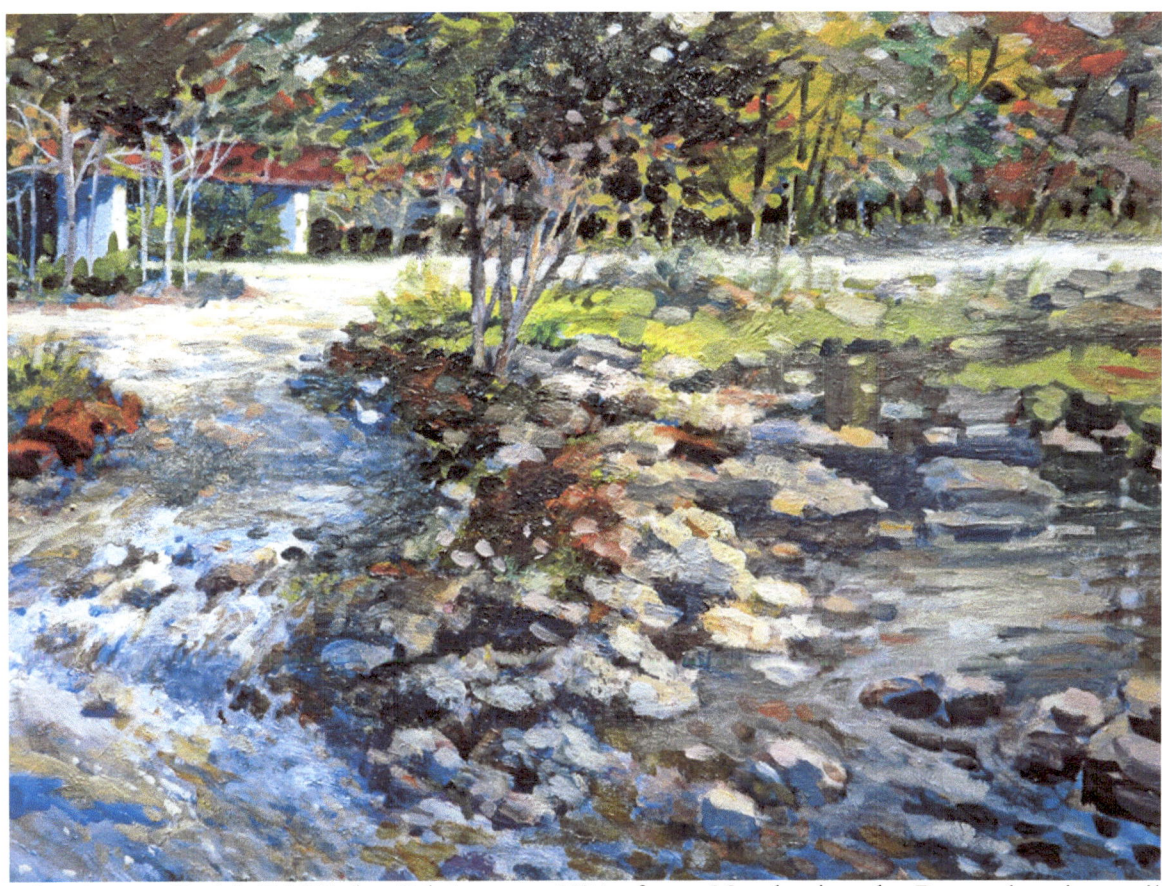
"The Lower Fork" (2009) by Ed Letven, USA, from Meadowbrook, Pennsylvania – oil (selected as the Grand Prize cover image). "Plein Air study of Montgomery County's Pennypack as rapids swirl around a small island form a pool of still water. There had been a heavy rain and beyond is the main stream. I imagined its gathering strength as it joins the mighty Delaware waterway only a few miles away."

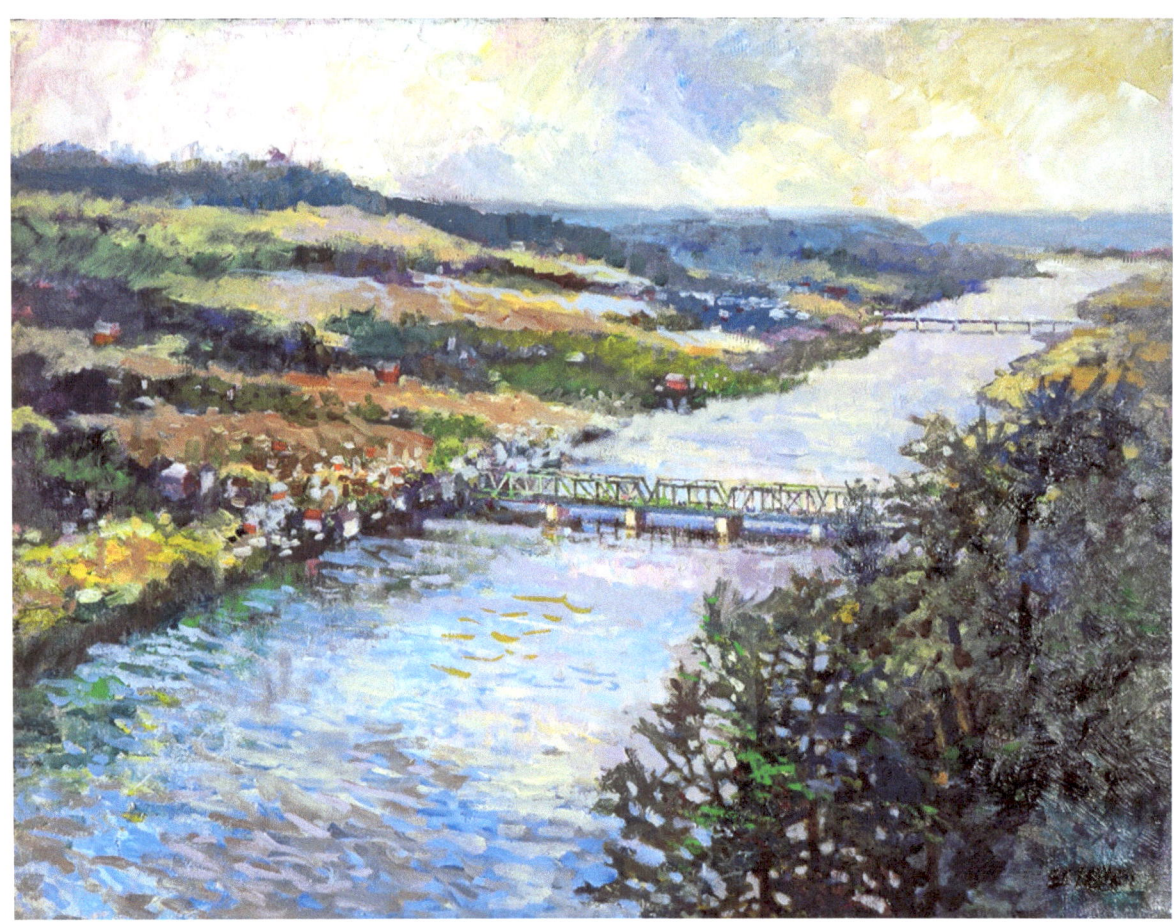

"Delaware View from Goat Hill" (2009) by Ed Letven, USA, from Meadowbrook, Pennsylvania – oil. "This view was painted 'plein air' looking down from Goat Hill (George Washington's lookout point) toward Trenton. The Delaware river flows south under the famed New Hope Bridge. It was delightful to paint on location with this bird's eye view of a long powerful mirror that reflected all the colors of the sky in late afternoon."

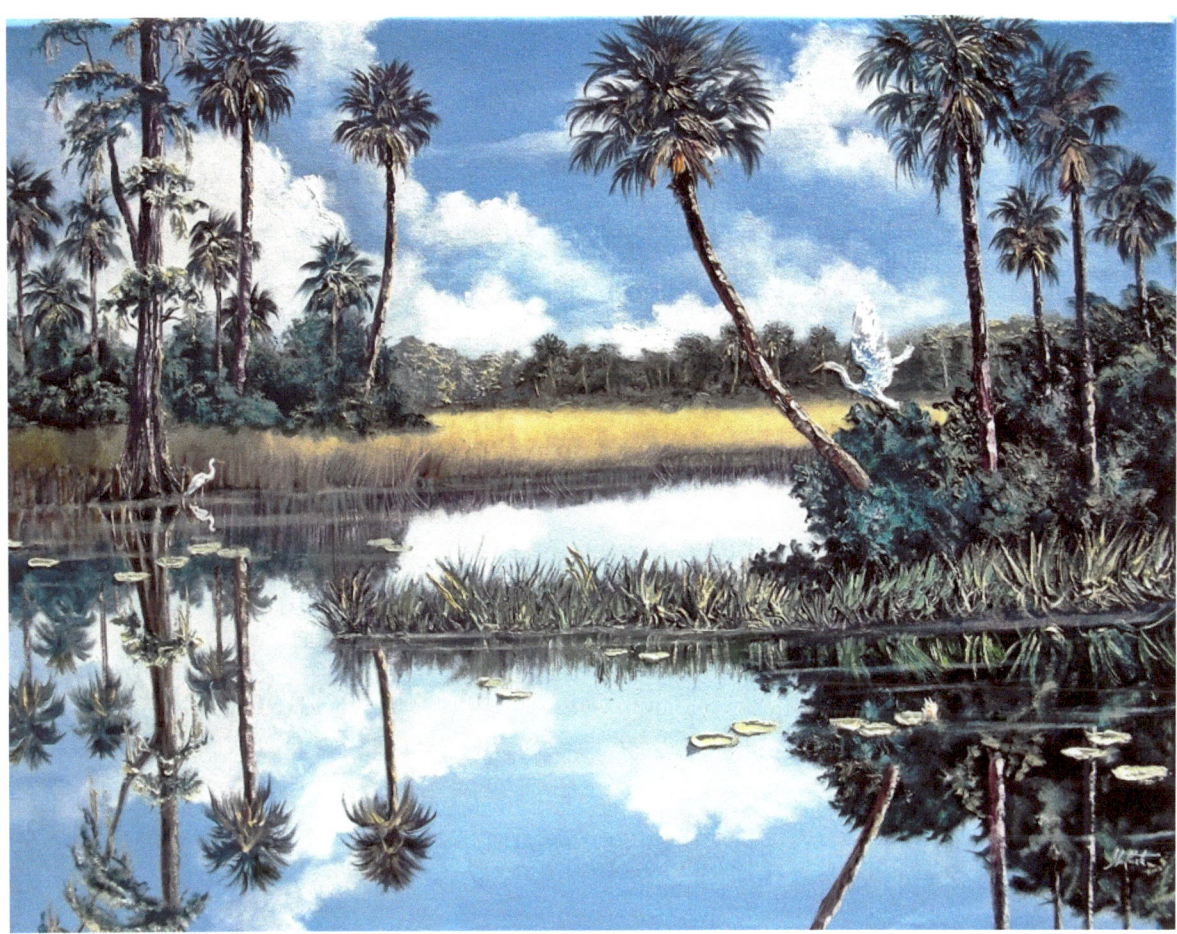

"Summer Reflections" (2010) by Dennis Shattuck, USA, from Palm Bay, Florida – oil. "The painting is a view of many places in nature viewed on the Sebastian River where I lived for three years before my father, my best friend, passed away. The girl I fell in love with, for the first time in many years, worked the river running her river boat tours every day with me as the first mate. We were going to get married, but her old boyfriend came back into the picture and my heart was broken. Inspired by AE Backus of the High Way Men, where they had their beginning also."

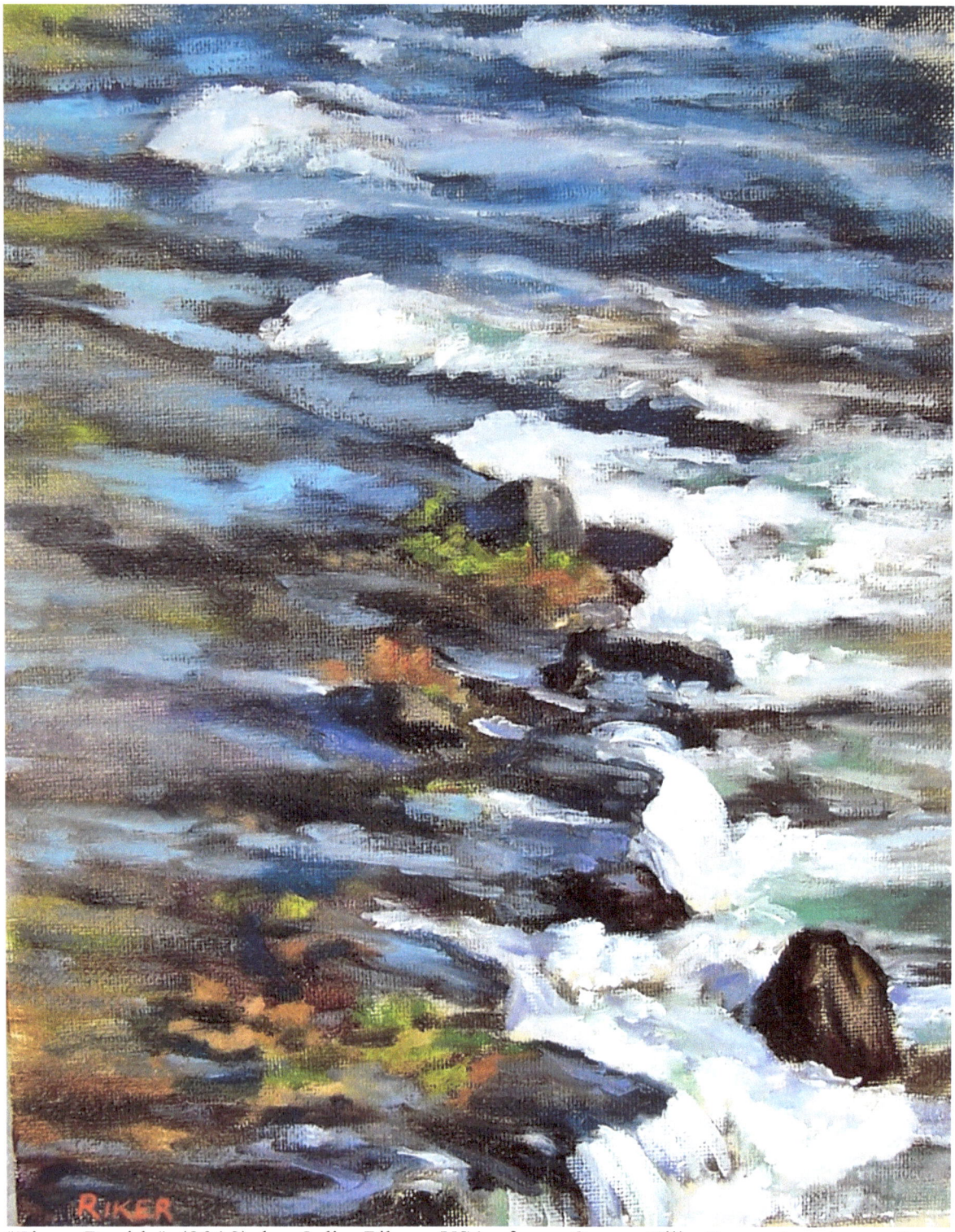
"River Rapids" (2010) by Julie Riker, USA, from Camp Hill, Pennsylvania – oil on canvas. "While painting this on location I was mesmerized by the sound of the running water and become lost in following the movement of the water with my brush markings."

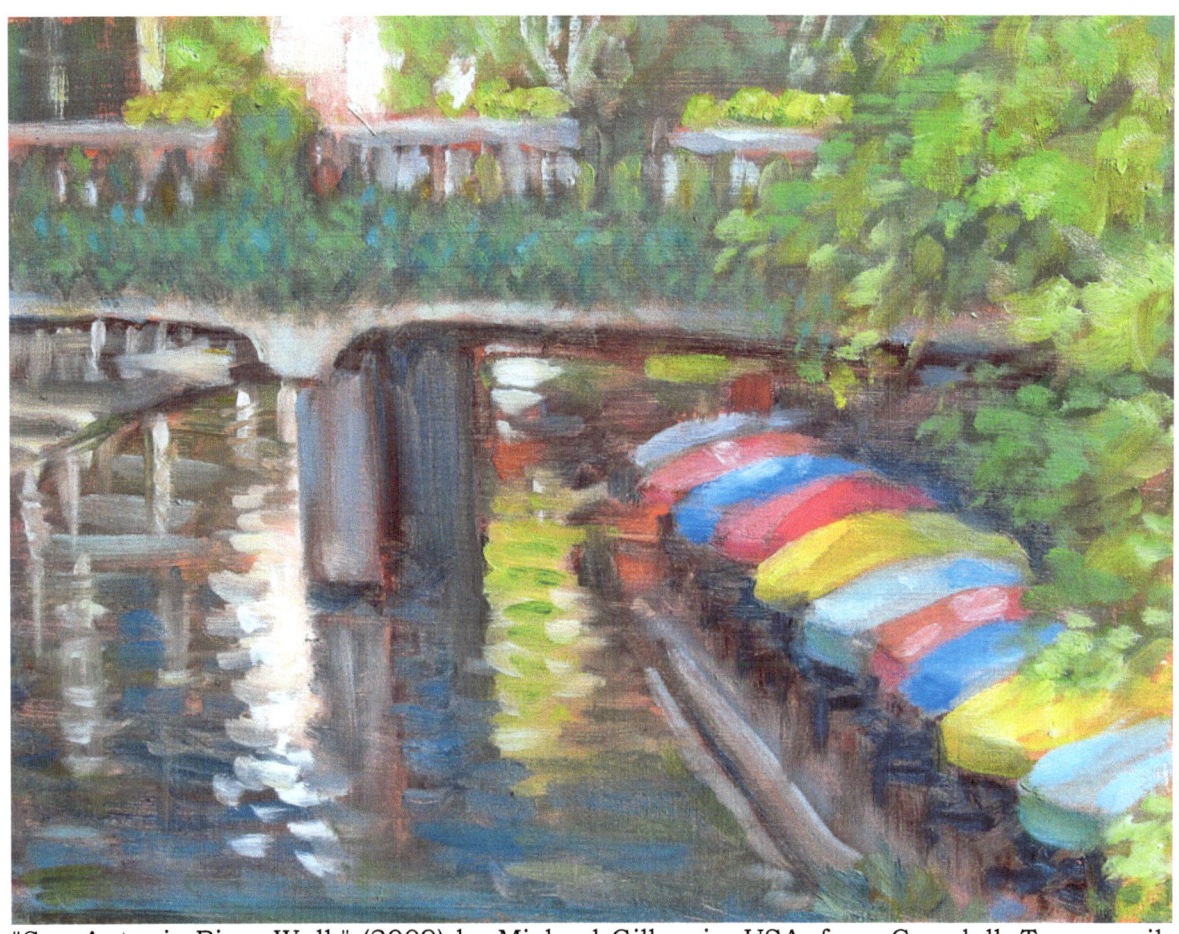

"San Antonio River Walk" (2009) by Michael Gillespie, USA, from Crandall, Texas – oil. "A small painting based on a photo I took from a bridge. I wanted it to be impressionistic, emphasizing the colorful umbrellas, the foliage, and the reflections in the water."

PHOTOGRAPHY

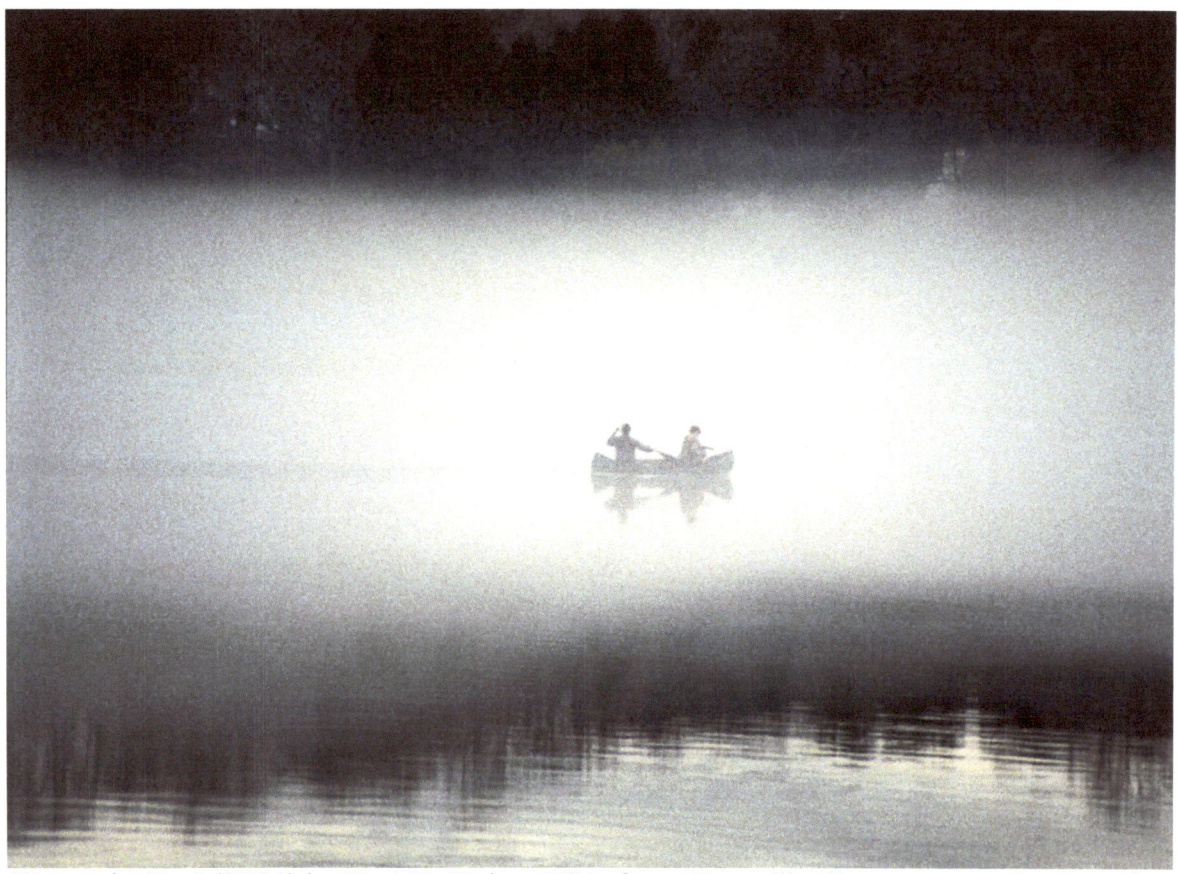

"Canoe in Fog" (2001) by Kurt K. Weiss, USA, from Knoxville, Tennessee – photography. "This photo was taken in January 2001 on the Tennessee River in Knoxville, Tennessee at the National Guard Armory. There was a layer of fog on the river. I was taking pictures of the river with the fog, when these two men in the canoe came rowing out of nowhere. What good luck!!! Even though this photo appears to be black and white, it was shot on Color Fuji REALA 100 film, with a Nikon F5 camera and a Nikon 70-300mm lens. My website is www.weissphotography.com."

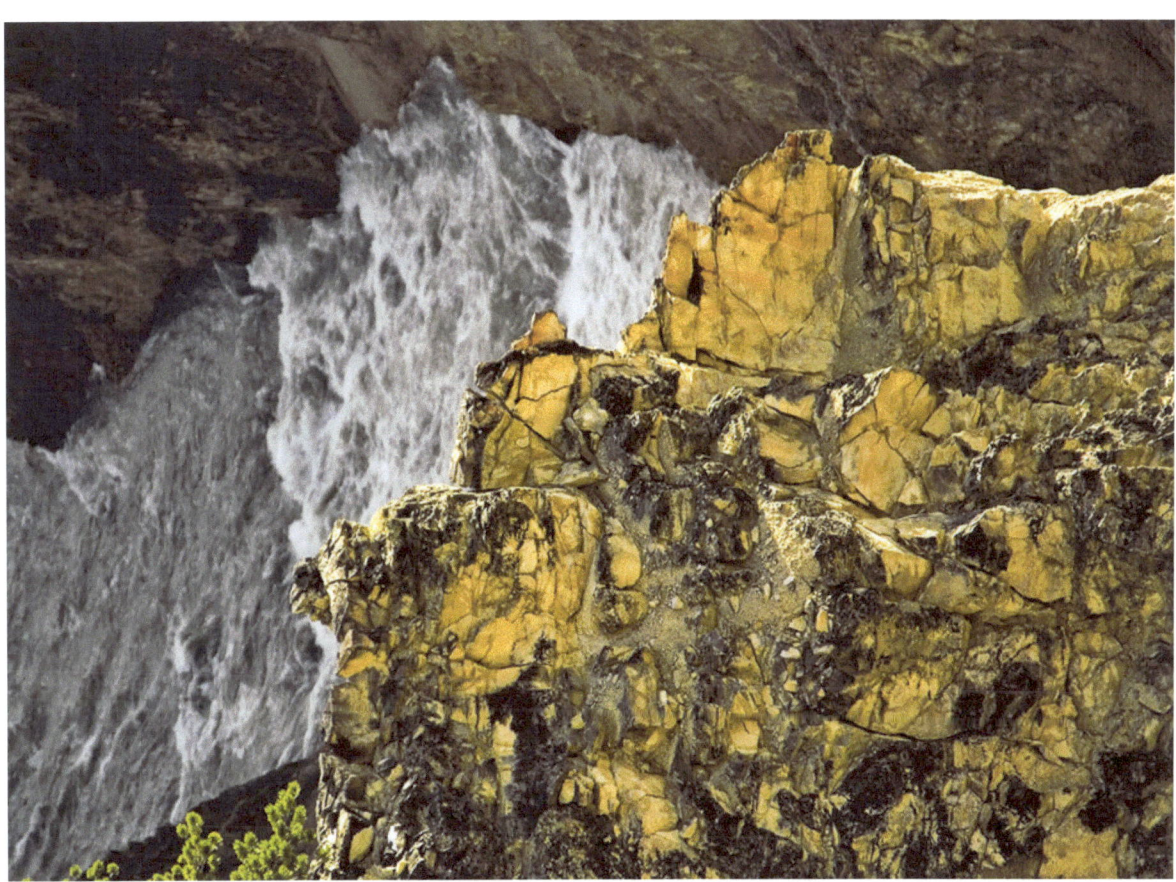
"Water Force 1" (2009) by Judith Nylen, USA, from Brooklyn, New York – photograph. "The force of water has literally sliced the yellow rock formations in the Grand Canyon, Yellowstone, Wyoming. As a photographer, I have explored the basic abstract elegance of water, organic and fluid, the balance of texture, the tension of form and edge. 'Water Force 1' explores the edge between land and water where two of earth's primordial elements dance continuously. To quote Lao Tzu, 'In the world there is nothing so submissive and weak as water. Yet for attacking that which is hard and strong, nothing can surpass it.' The attack of this explosive river creates a most expressive, resistant edge providing an endless expedition into textural and contextual forms."

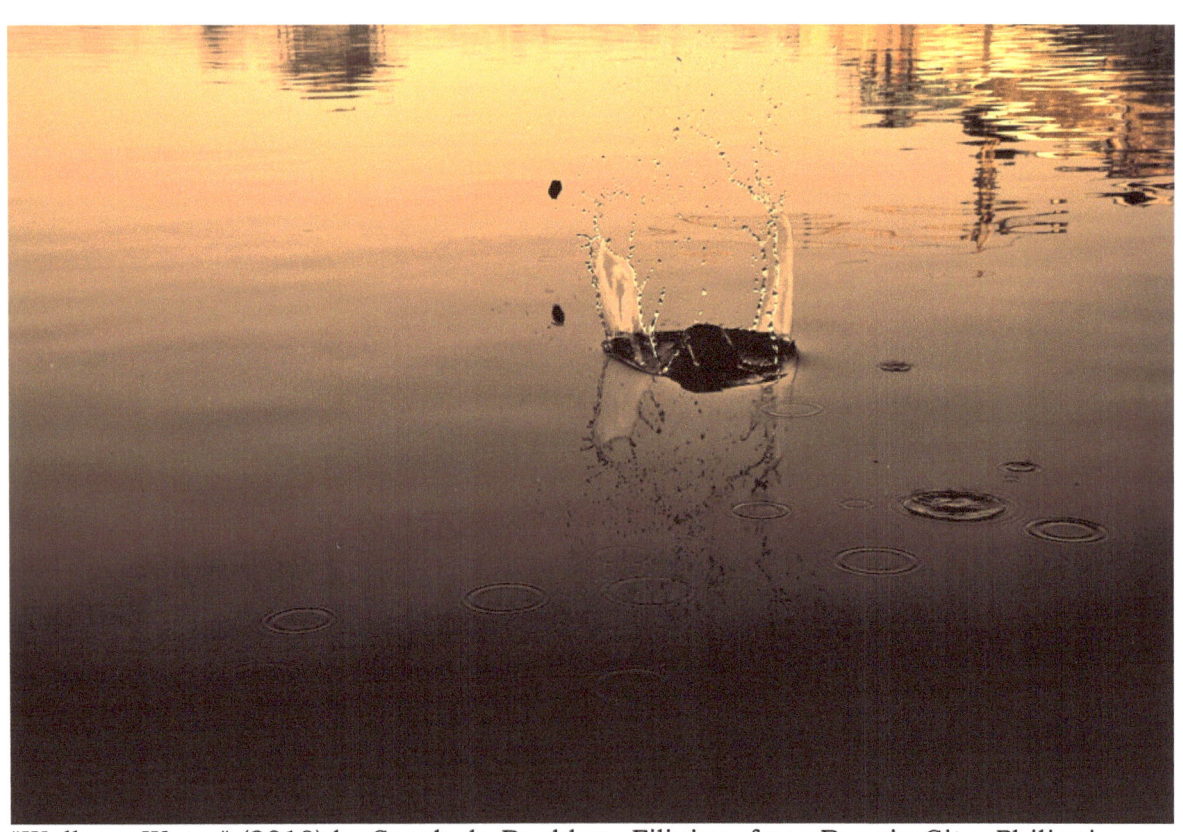

"Walk on Water" (2010) by Sarah de Doelder, Filipino, from Baguio City, Philippines – photograph. "Credits to my fiancé, Phylord Paul Dayag IV, the stone skipper."

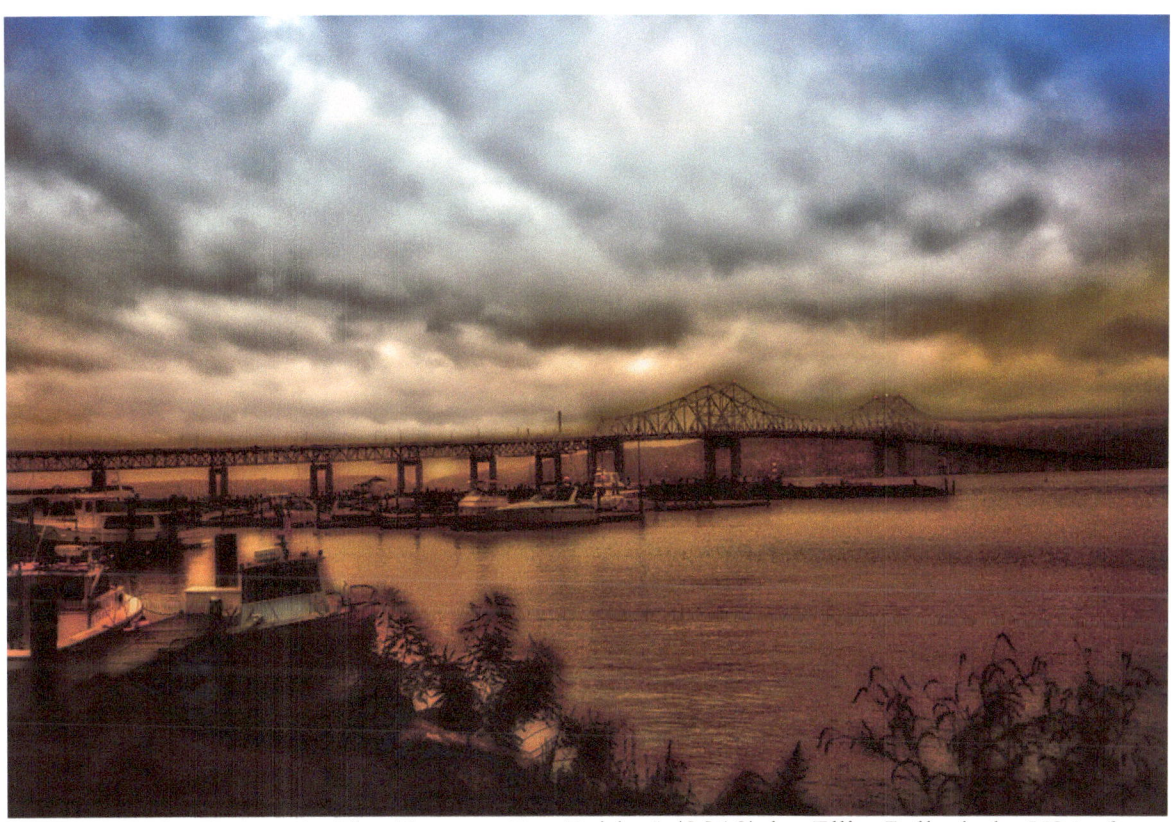

"Awaiting The Storm At The Tappan Zee Bridge" (2010) by Ellin Pollachek, USA, from New York, New York – photograph. "Storms disrupt and enhance our world. As a photographer I try to capture that disruption and find a way to enhance it on my own. Looking out at the color of the light it is impossible not to recognize the calm before the storm."

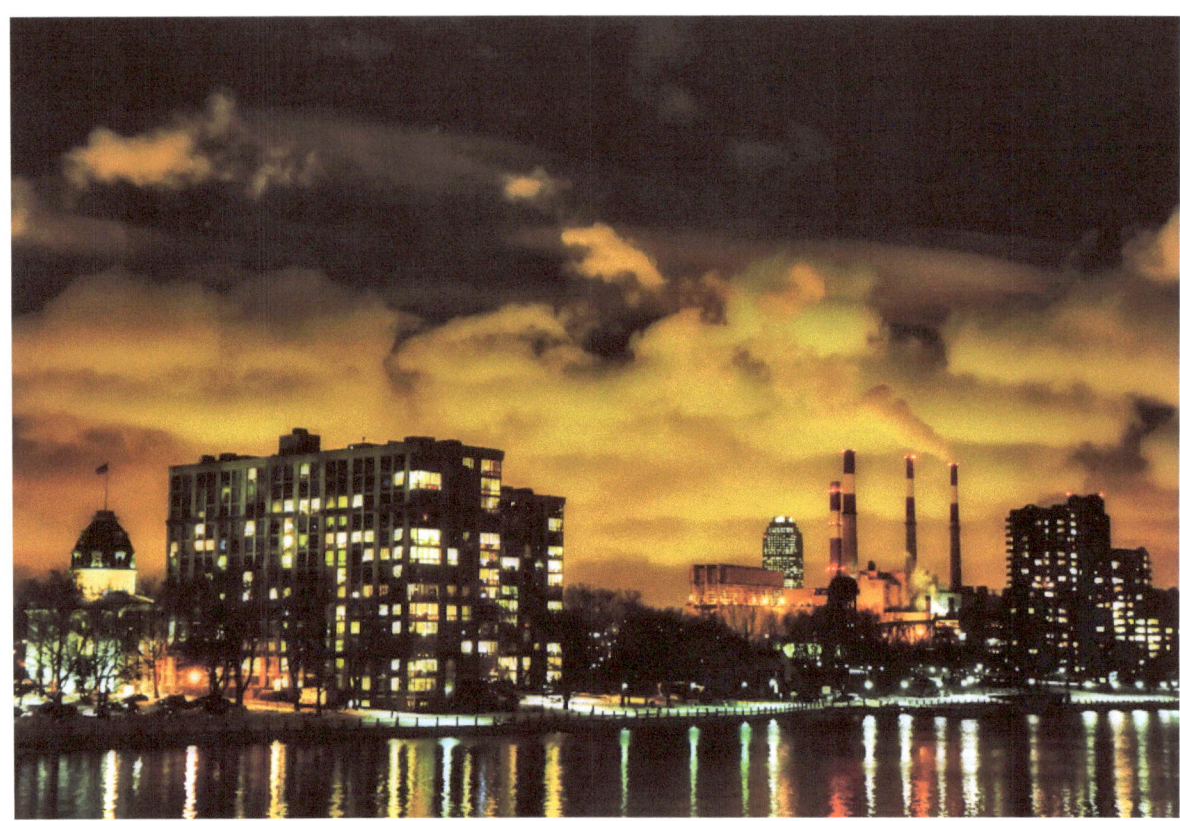
"Across the East River" (2010) by Ellin Pollachek, USA, from New York, New York – photograph. "Manhattan is an island with the East River on one side and the Hudson River on the other. At night I take my tripod and camera and walk a block and half to the East River and set my sights on the magnificent. Across the East River is Roosevelt Island."

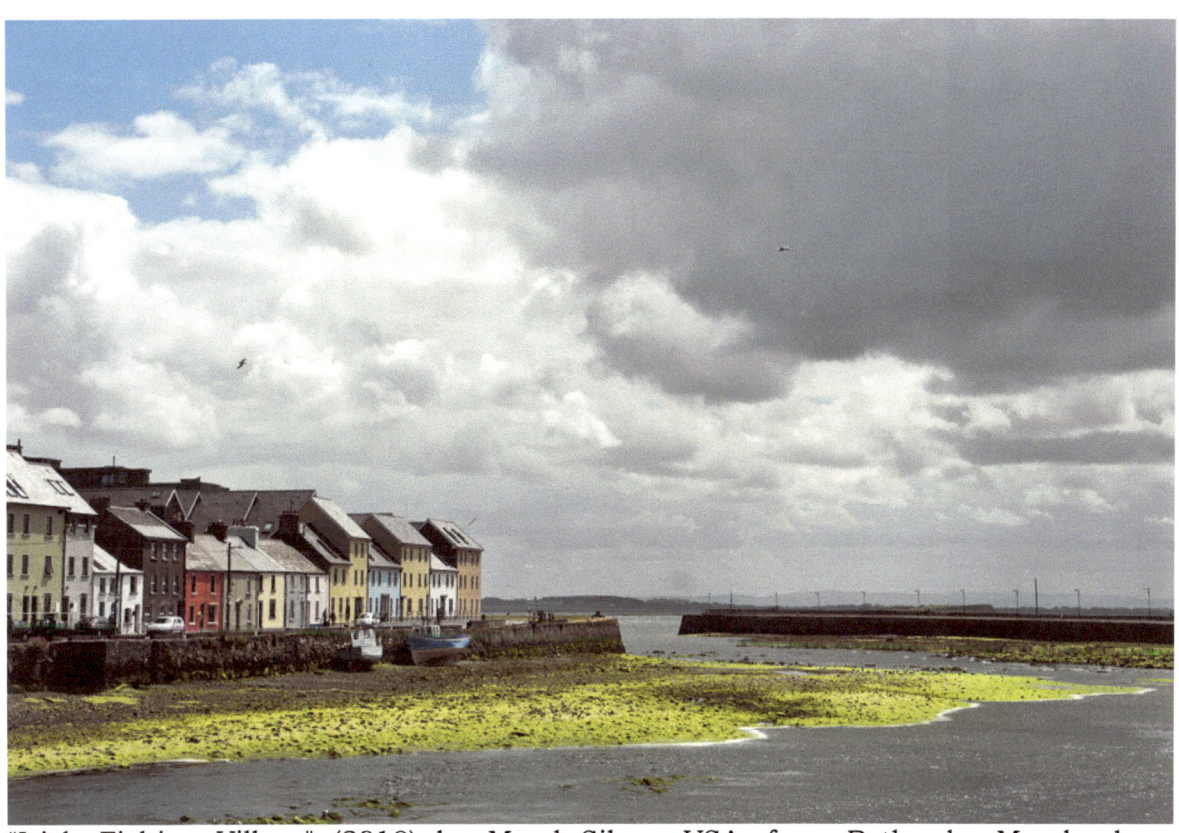
"Irish Fishing Village" (2010) by Meryl Silver, USA, from Bethesda, Maryland – photograph. "My work consists of images taken in natural light with little-to-no manipulation. My favorite images, I hope, project a mood and evoke an emotional response. This image is part of a project entitled 'Reflections On Water', where I'm looking at the beauty of water, both directly and as a means to produce unorthodox, yet beautiful images, through reflections."

WATERCOLOR

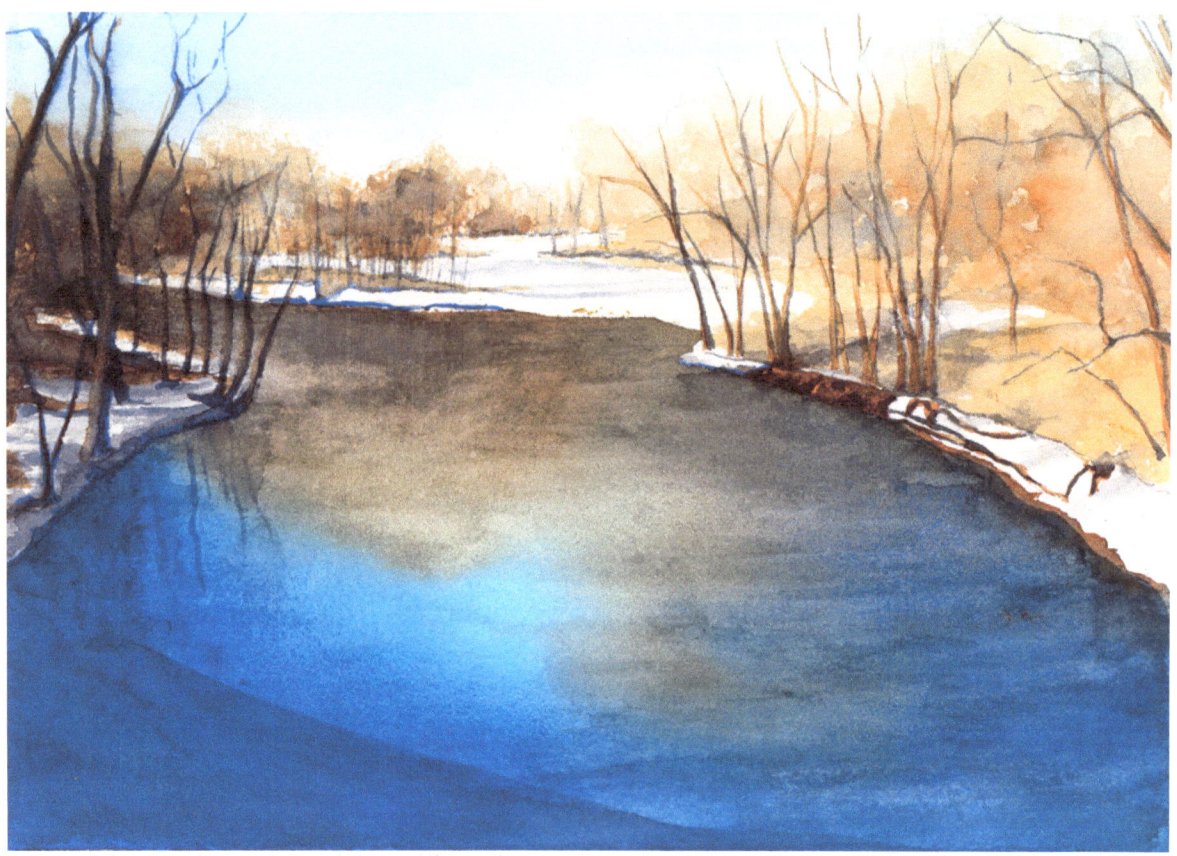

"Desplaines River" (2001) by Alli Farkas, USA, from Dowagiac, Michigan - 1st place in the Watercolor category. "I delight in painting rural Americana--especially winter scenes with water. Maybe I think winter is so fascinating because I spent over four decades in Southern California where there isn't much change of seasons to speak of. There is something about the apparent solitude and silence of snow and ice that quiets my spirit and gives me peace. If I were of a different mind, I could have included boisterous people playing in the snow, or even animals poking about in the trees. But somehow I prefer to paint as if I were the only living being at the scene. A winter hermit, perhaps?"

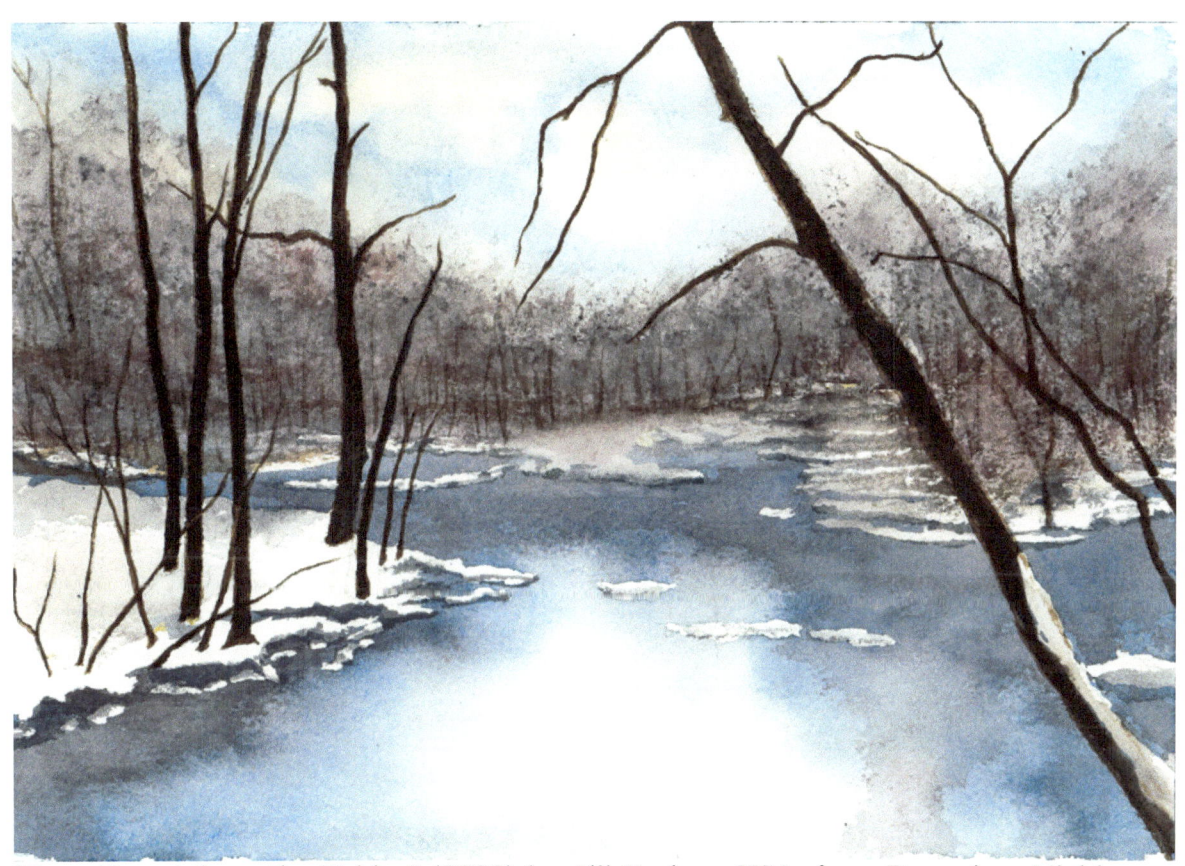
"Russ Forest from the Bridge" (2009) by Alli Farkas, USA, from Dowagiac, Michigan - watercolor.

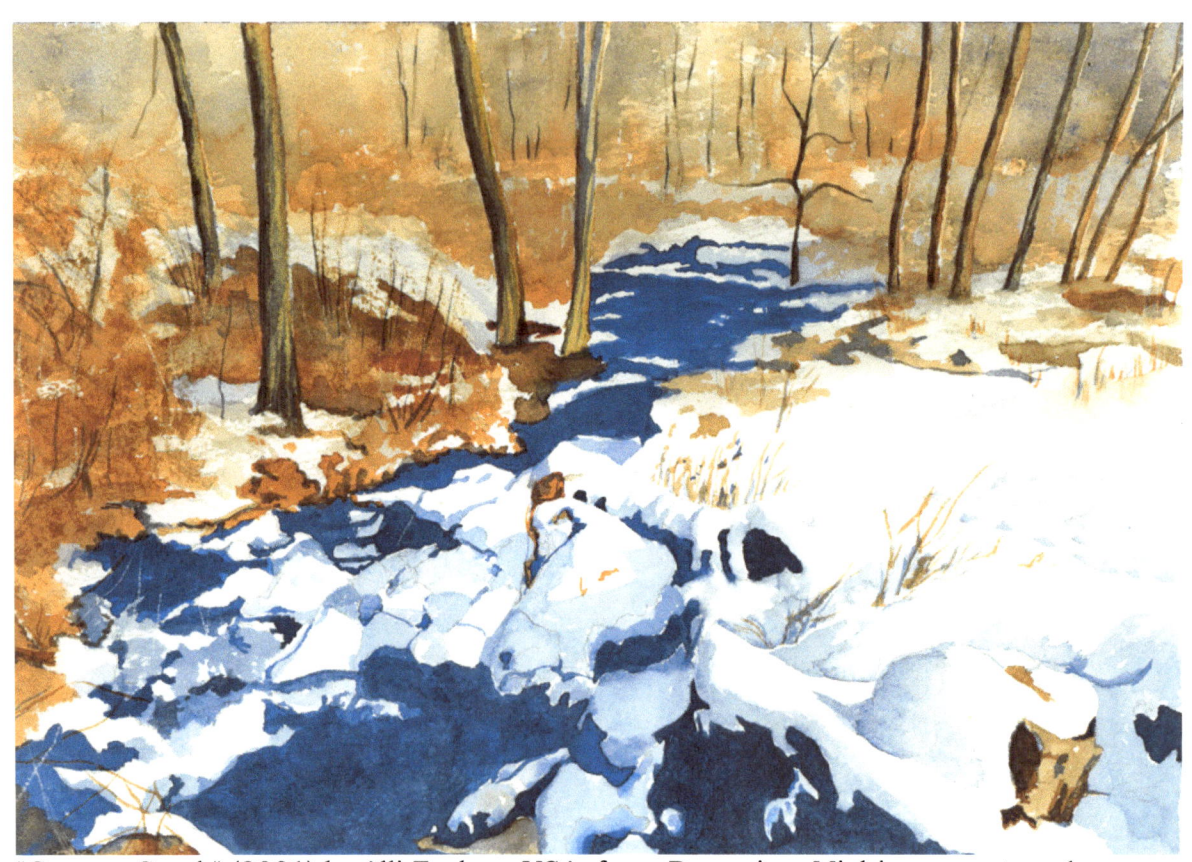
"Geneva Creek" (2001) by Alli Farkas, USA, from Dowagiac, Michigan - watercolor.

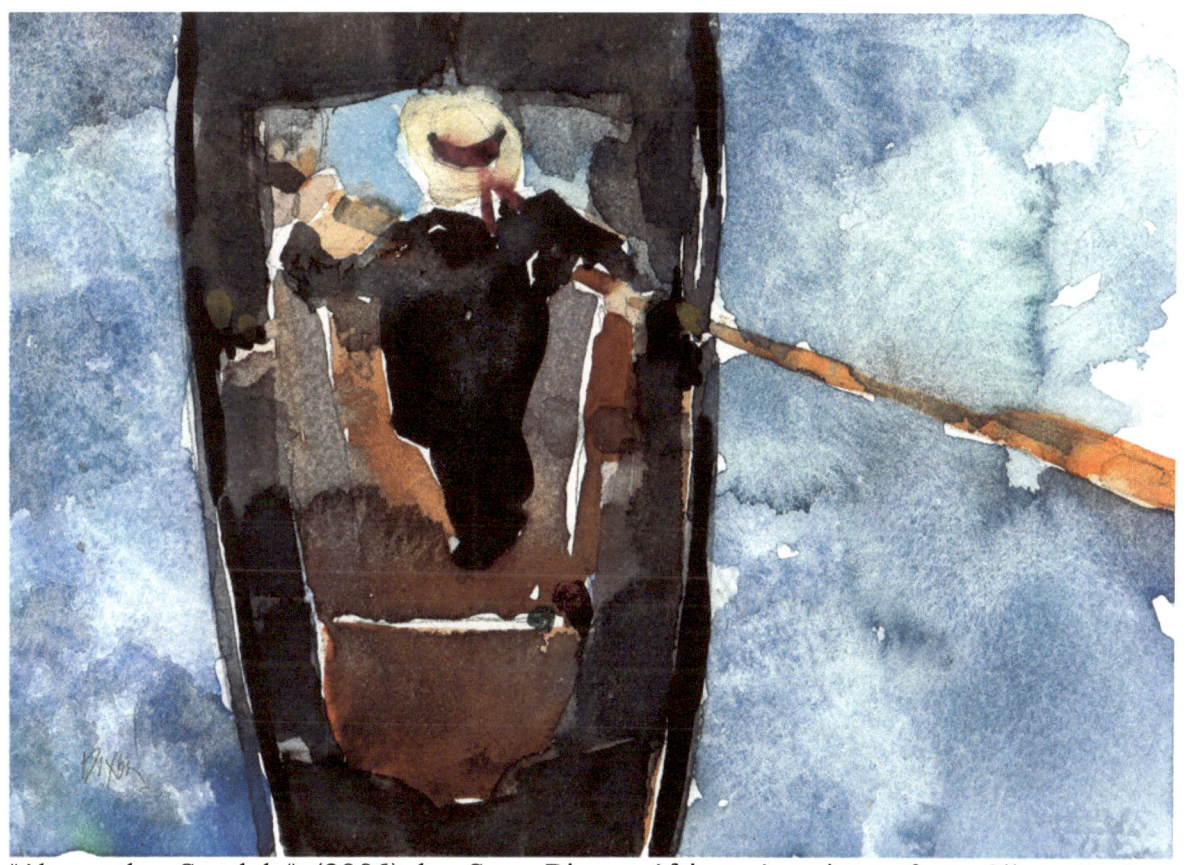

"Above the Gondola" (2006) by Sam Dixon, African-American, from Silver Spring, Maryland – watercolor. "The creative spirit, may it always be represented by the beauty of the mark."

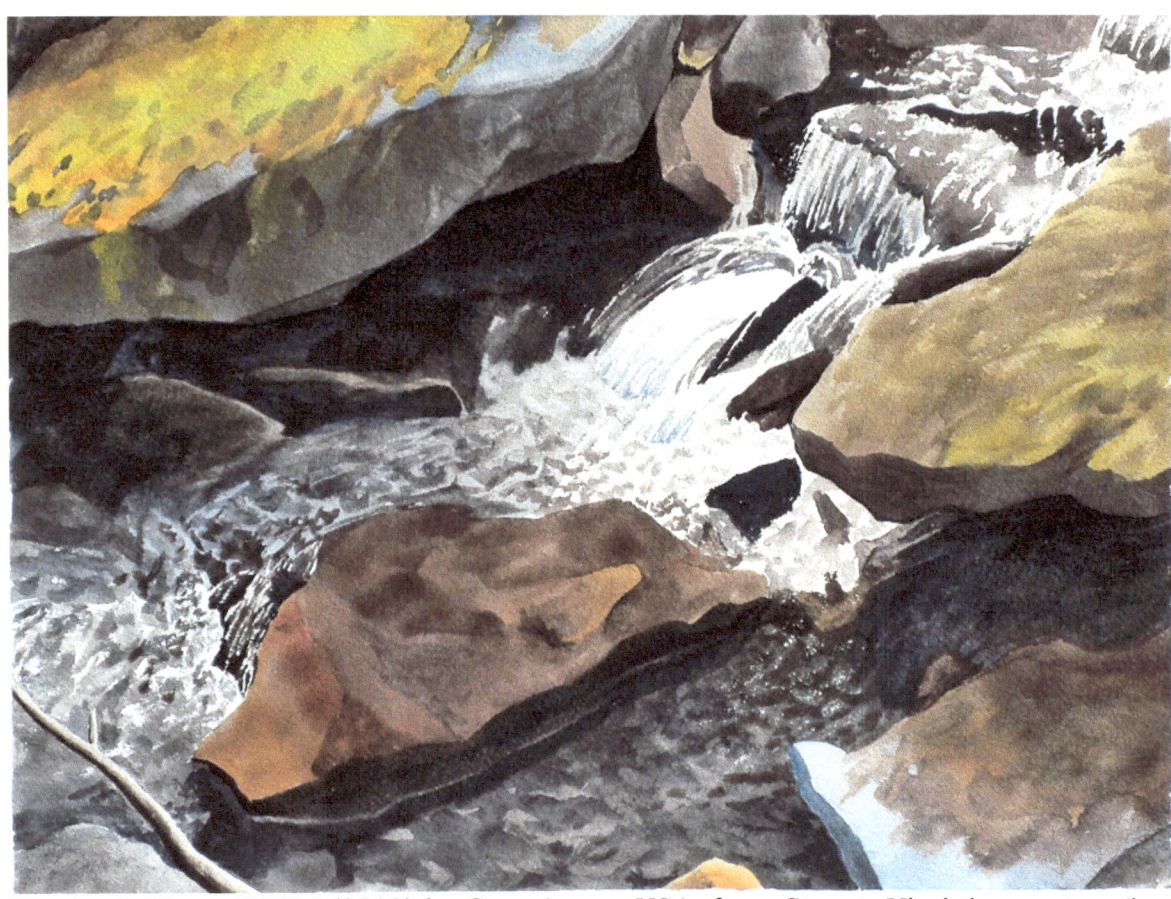

"Rocks & Water XXIII " (2010) by Greg Arens, USA, from Stuart, Virginia – watercolor. "Rocks & Water XXIII" was painted plein aire in less than a day, while visiting my parents in the Cumberland Plateau in Tennessee. It depicts part of a small unnamed stream whose waters eventually flowed into the Obed River. It's the latest in a long series of paintings of Rocks & Water, done on numerous streams, which have been a lifelong subject (obsession?) for me."

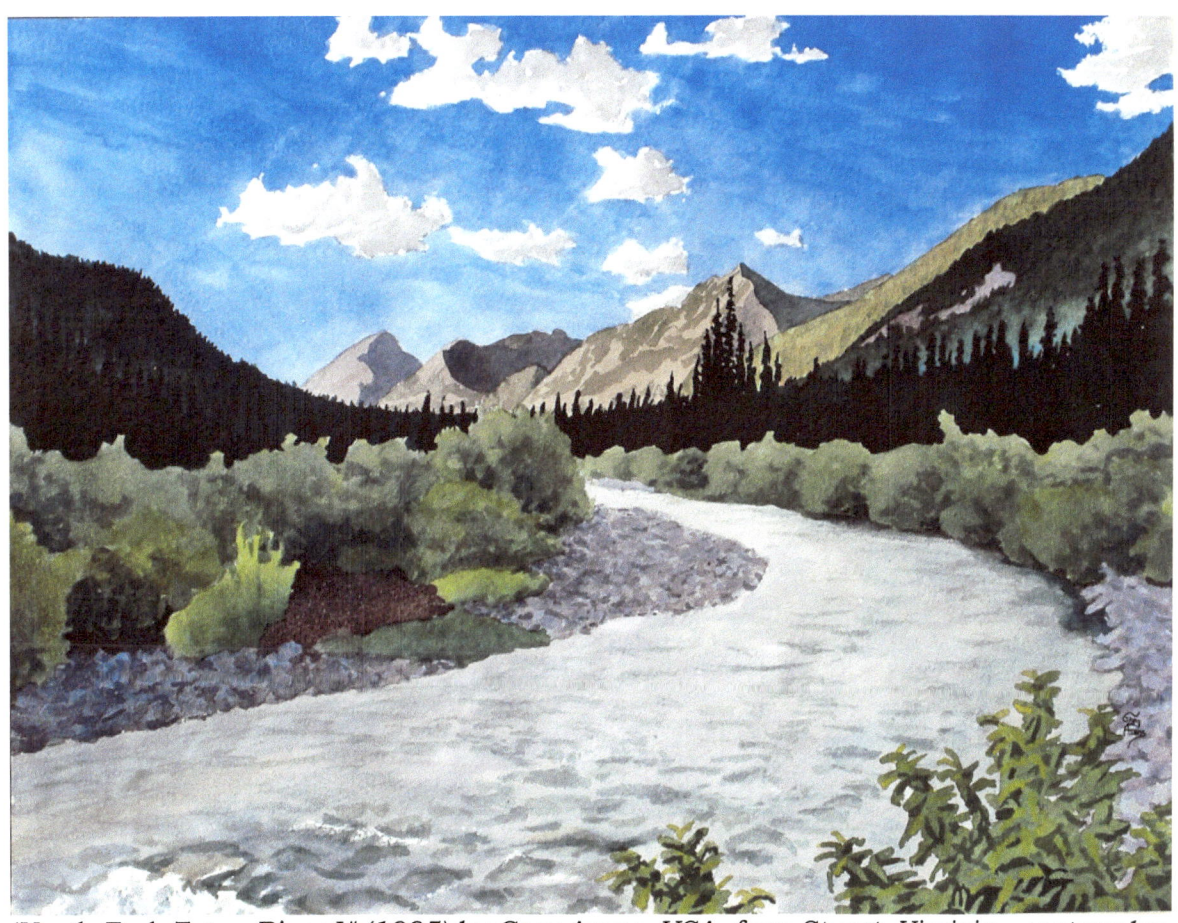

"North Fork Teton River I" (1995) by Greg Arens, USA, from Stuart, Virginia – watercolor.
"North Fork Teton River I' was painted plein aire in the Front Range of the Montana Rockies, on the first of two painting expeditions I made to the Teton River watershed. It was done over 2 or 3 evenings, in an attempt to capture the late afternoon light, when the sky turns a deep blue. This was executed while I was camping nearby, in some truly spectacular territory."

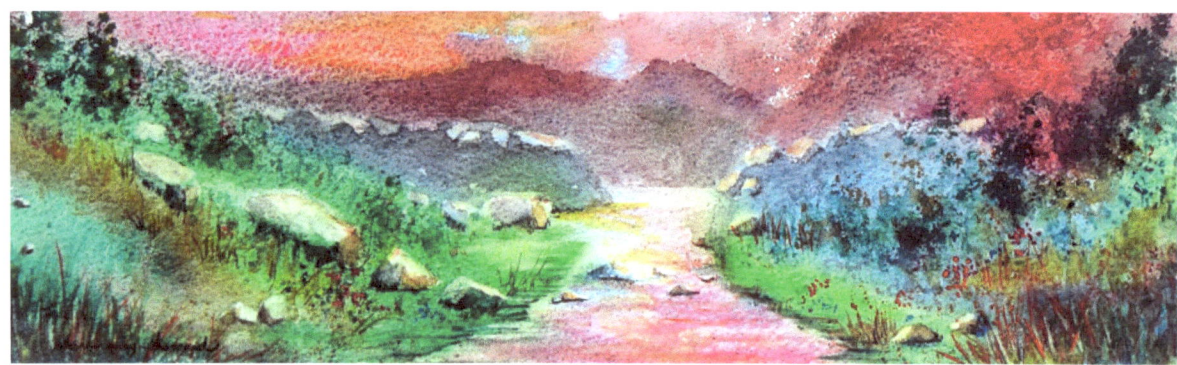
"Dreamscape: The Rose River" (2008) by Sharon Way-Howard, USA, from Sayville, New York – watercolor. "Watercolor is a wonderful medium to experiment with and this work was started as wet washes of color, After the initial washes had dried, I explored the various shapes that had been created, and letting my imagination work, developed these shapes into a flowing river, with rocks, hills and grasses, pushing the colors to reflect a dream-like atmosphere."

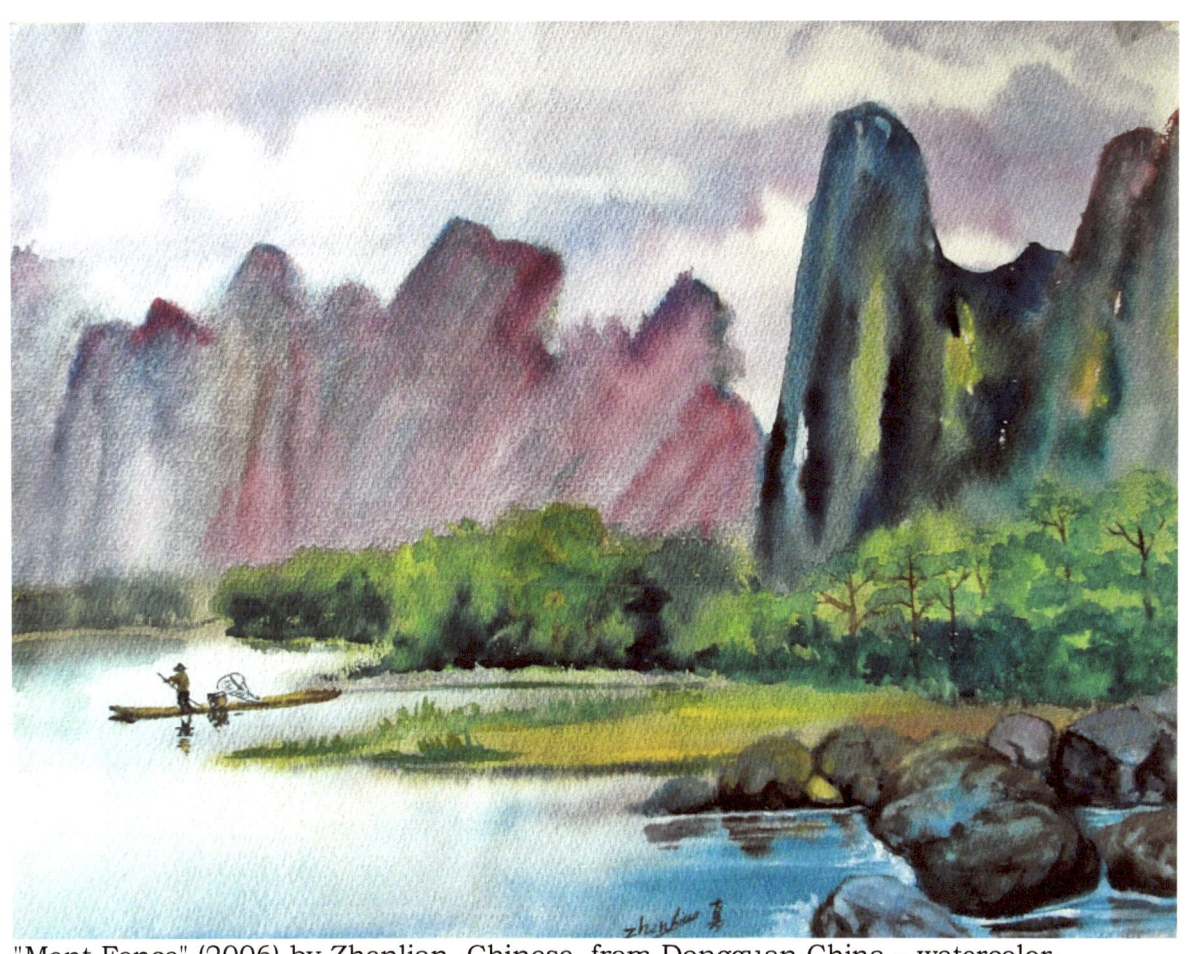
"Mont Fence" (2006) by Zhenlian, Chinese, from Dongguan, China – watercolor.

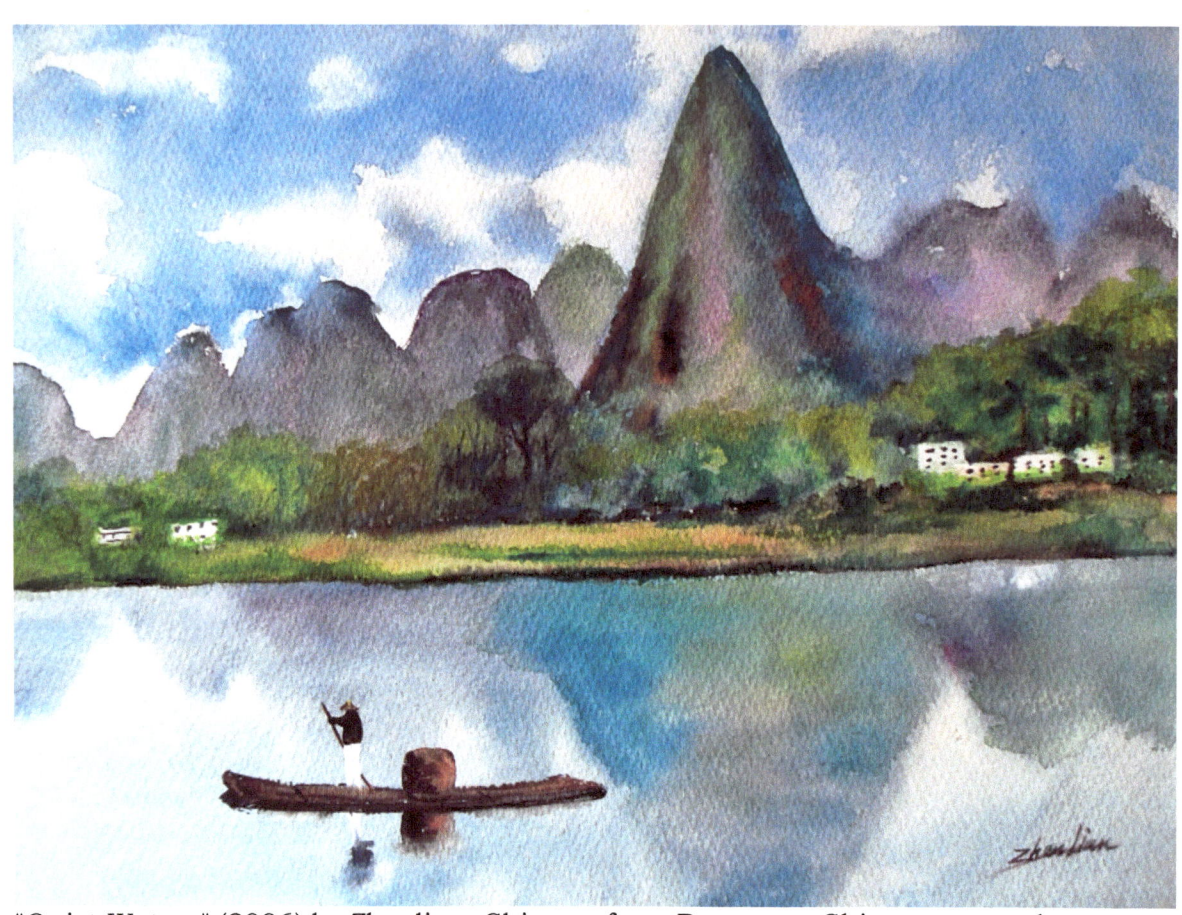
"Quiet Waters" (2006) by Zhenlian, Chinese, from Dongguan, China – watercolor.

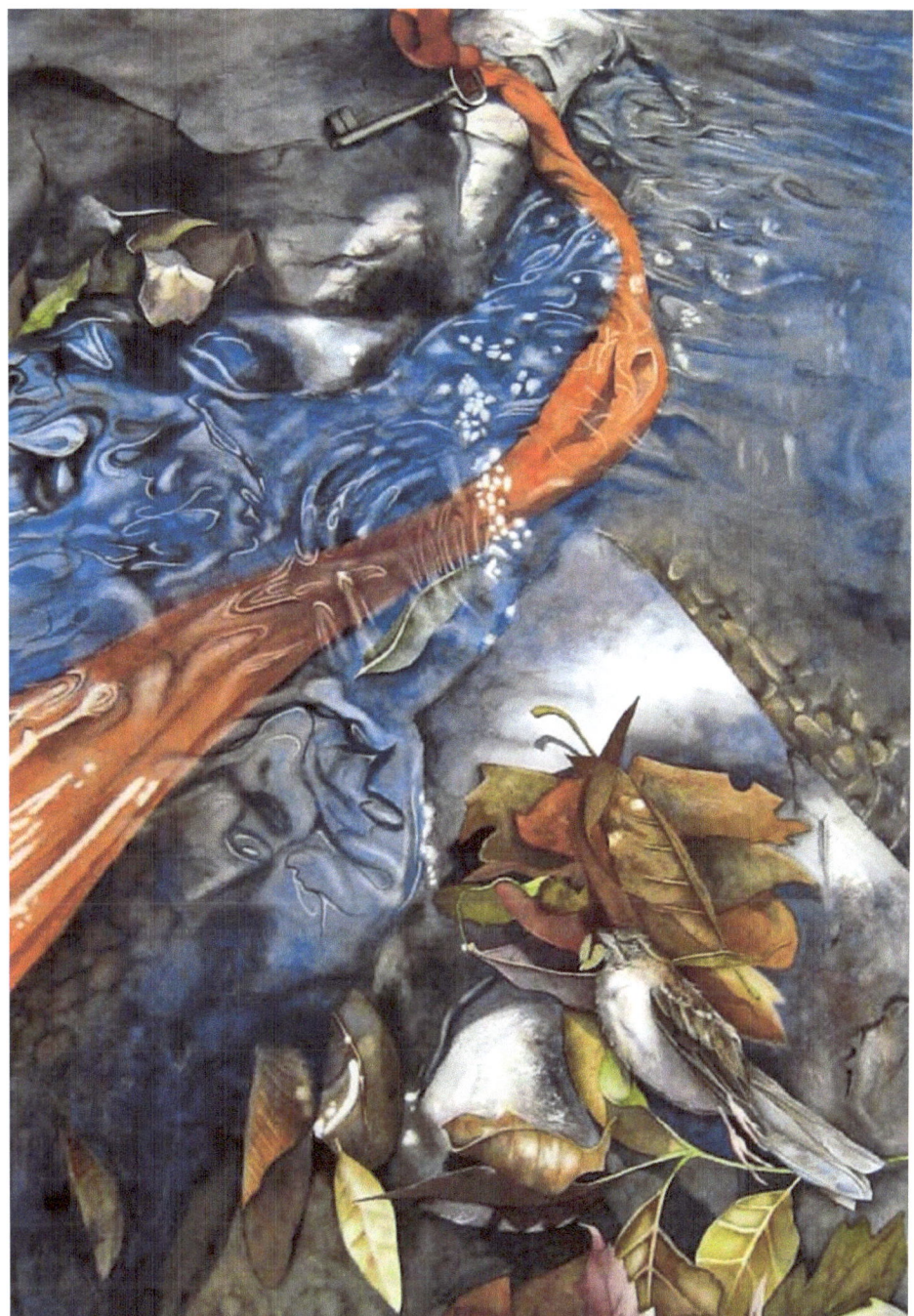

"Eulogy" (2006) by Lauren M. Mulhern, USA, from Chadds Ford, Pennsylvania – watercolor. "Lauren Mulhern is an emerging artist concentrating on large-scale watercolor painting. Her works depict constructed and organic still-lives consisting of found and sculpted objects. She paints in a representational style using many layers of watercolor washes, paying special attention to detail and texture. Lauren paints and resides in Chadds Ford, PA, while diligently working to establish a life-long career as a fine artist."

OTHER

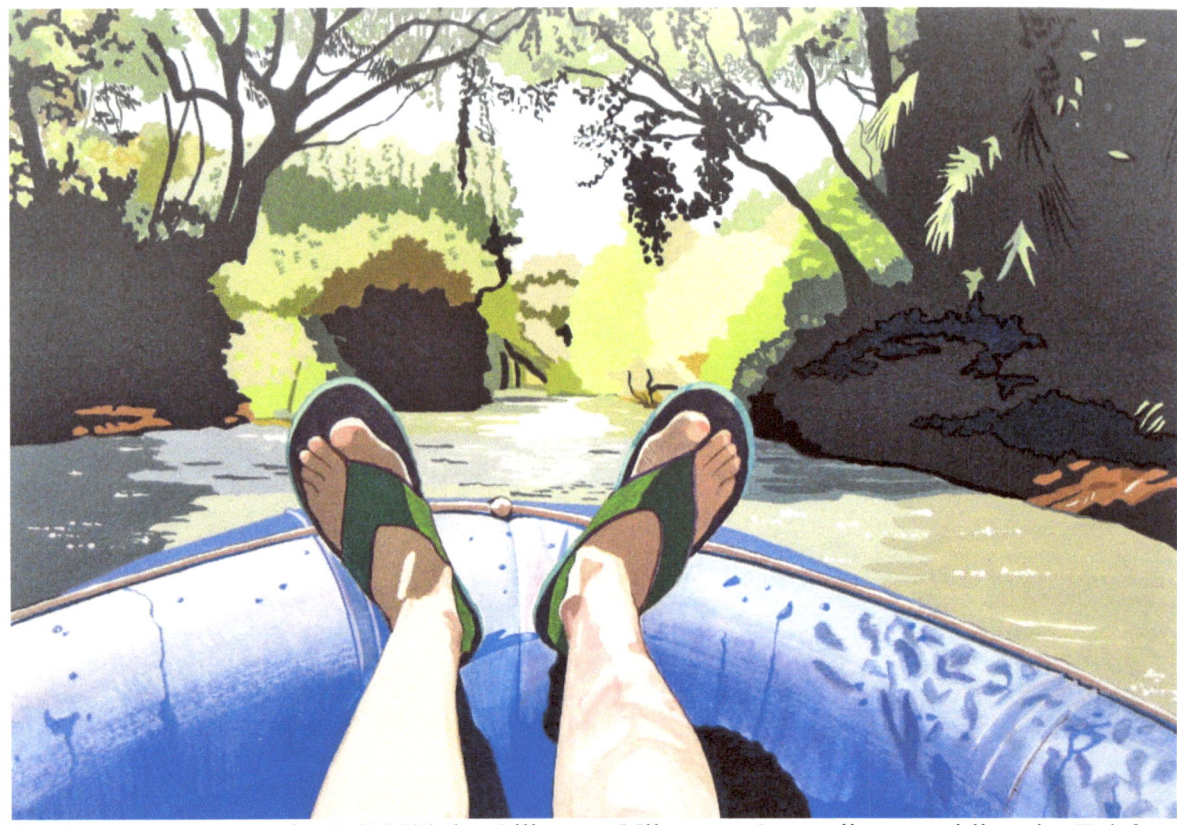

"Rafting on the Jordan" (1997) by Lilianne Milgrom, Australian, residing in Fairfax, Virginia – 1st place in Other category - gouache. "My work is eclectic in subject matter and medium, deriving inspiration from personal experiences or world events. Rafting on the Jordan captures a delightful moment in time during a rafting trip on the Jordan River in Israel where I succumbed to the river's natural course and rhythm."

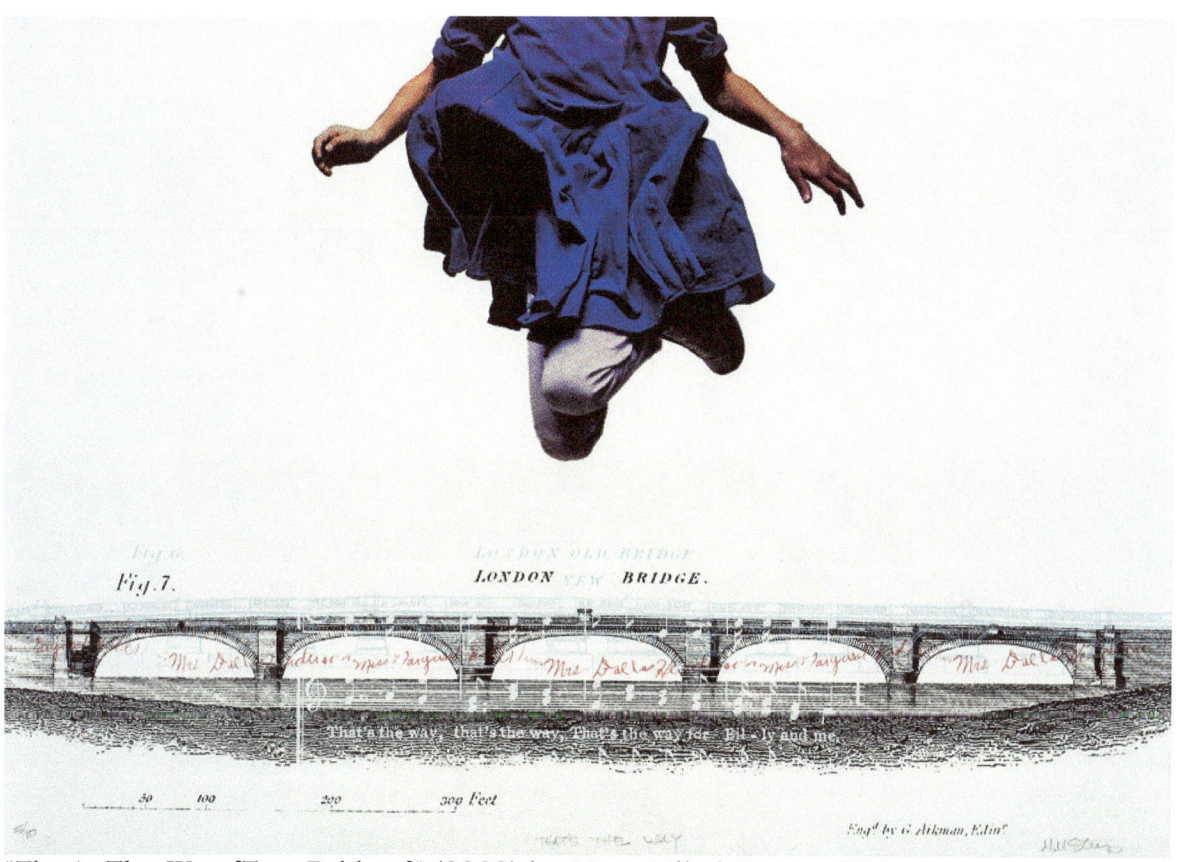

"That's The Way [Two Bridges]" (2009) by Mary Mikel Stump, USA, from Austin, Texas – serigraph. "That's The Way [Two Bridges] uses the river and the bridge as a means of crossing to represent the journey from child to adulthood. The use of imagery from the past/present, personal/technical and natural/built form further refers to the dichotomy that exists between these two states of being. The added ghost image of a re-contextualized traditional English children's song, Billy and Me, further presses the question of the ways in which our relationships change as we progress, developmentally. The river here plays a critical role in the composition as it both grounds the image, formally, and connects the elements, metaphorically."

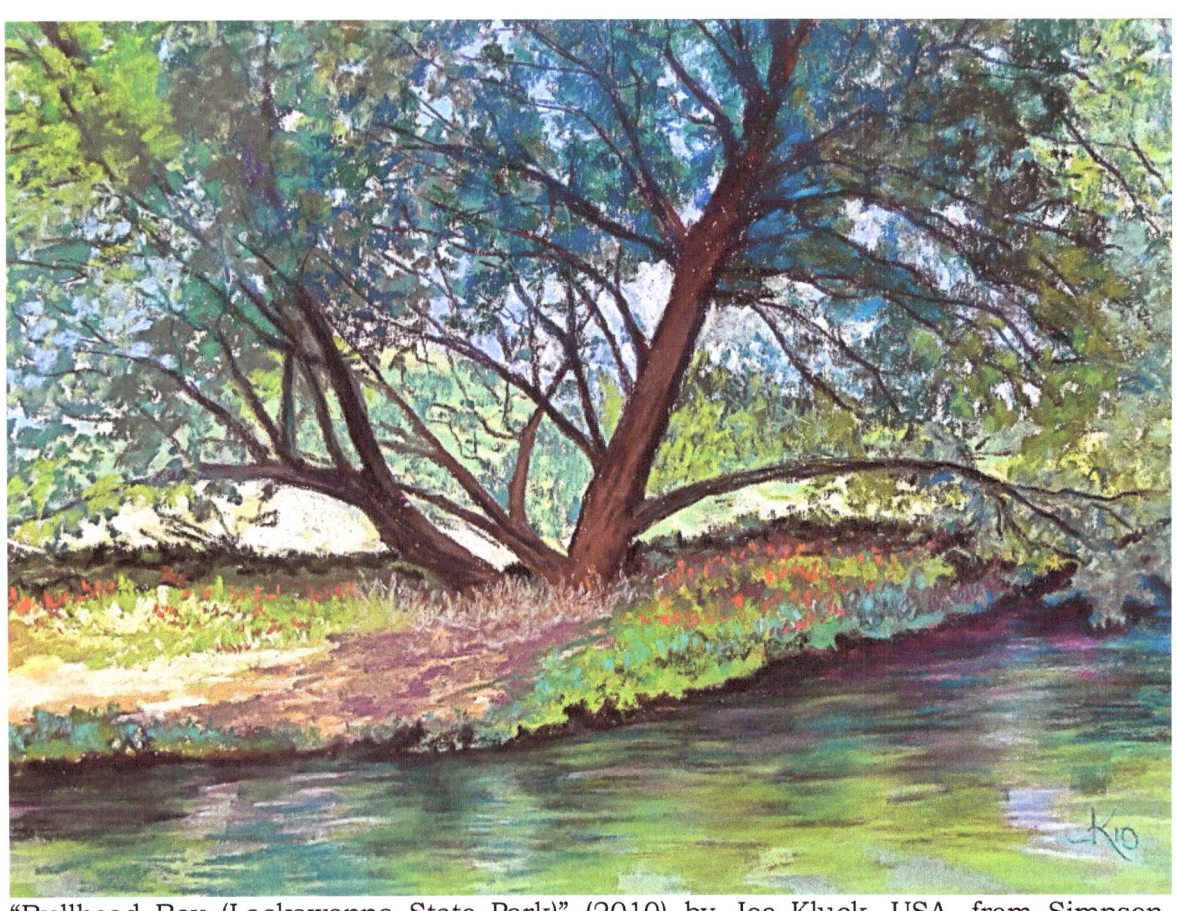
"Bullhead Bay (Lackawanna State Park)" (2010) by Joe Kluck, USA, from Simpson, Pennsylvania – pastel. "This piece is now the property of a private collector in Maryland."

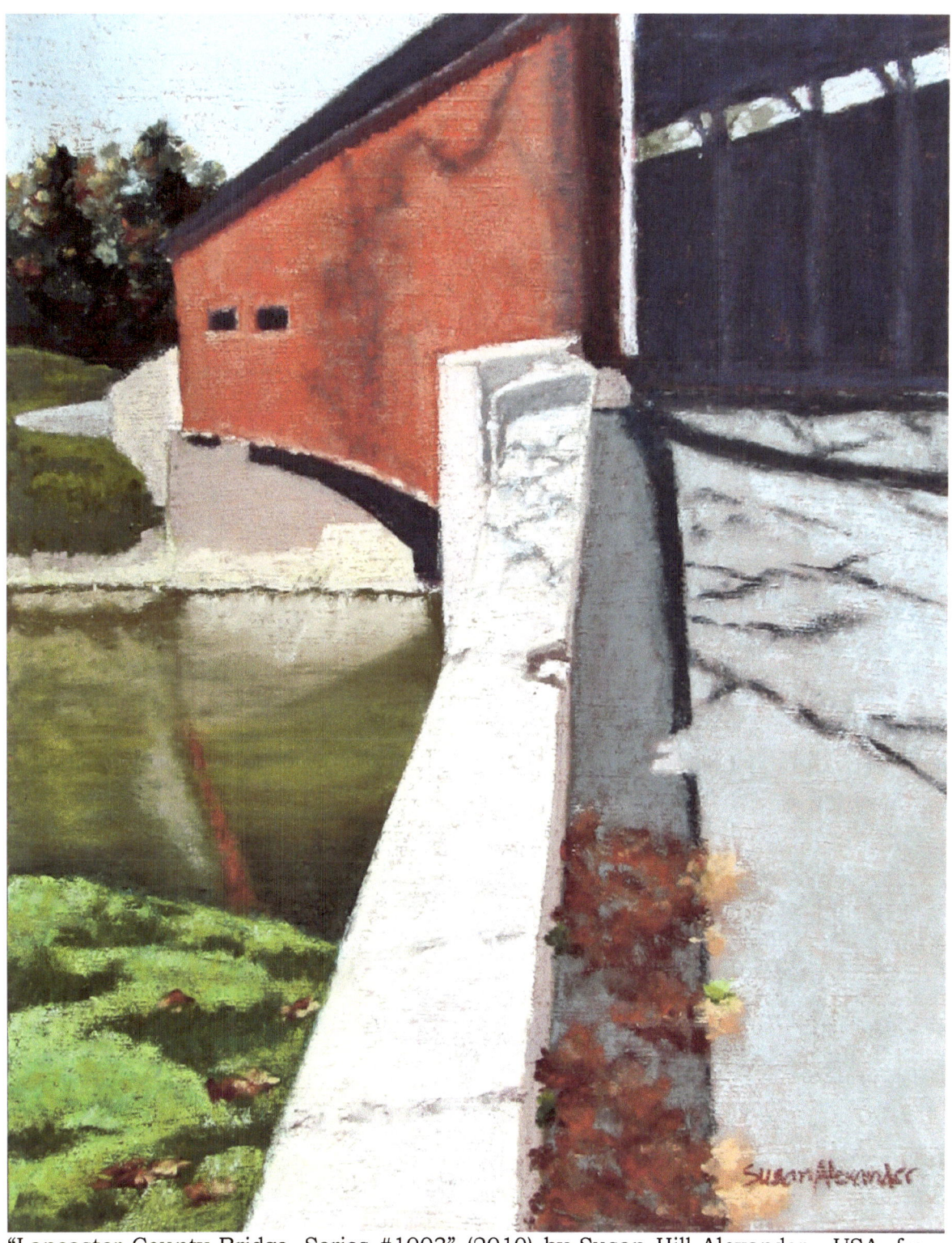
"Lancaster County Bridge, Series #1003" (2010) by Susan Hill Alexander, USA, from Salisbury, North Carolina – pastel.

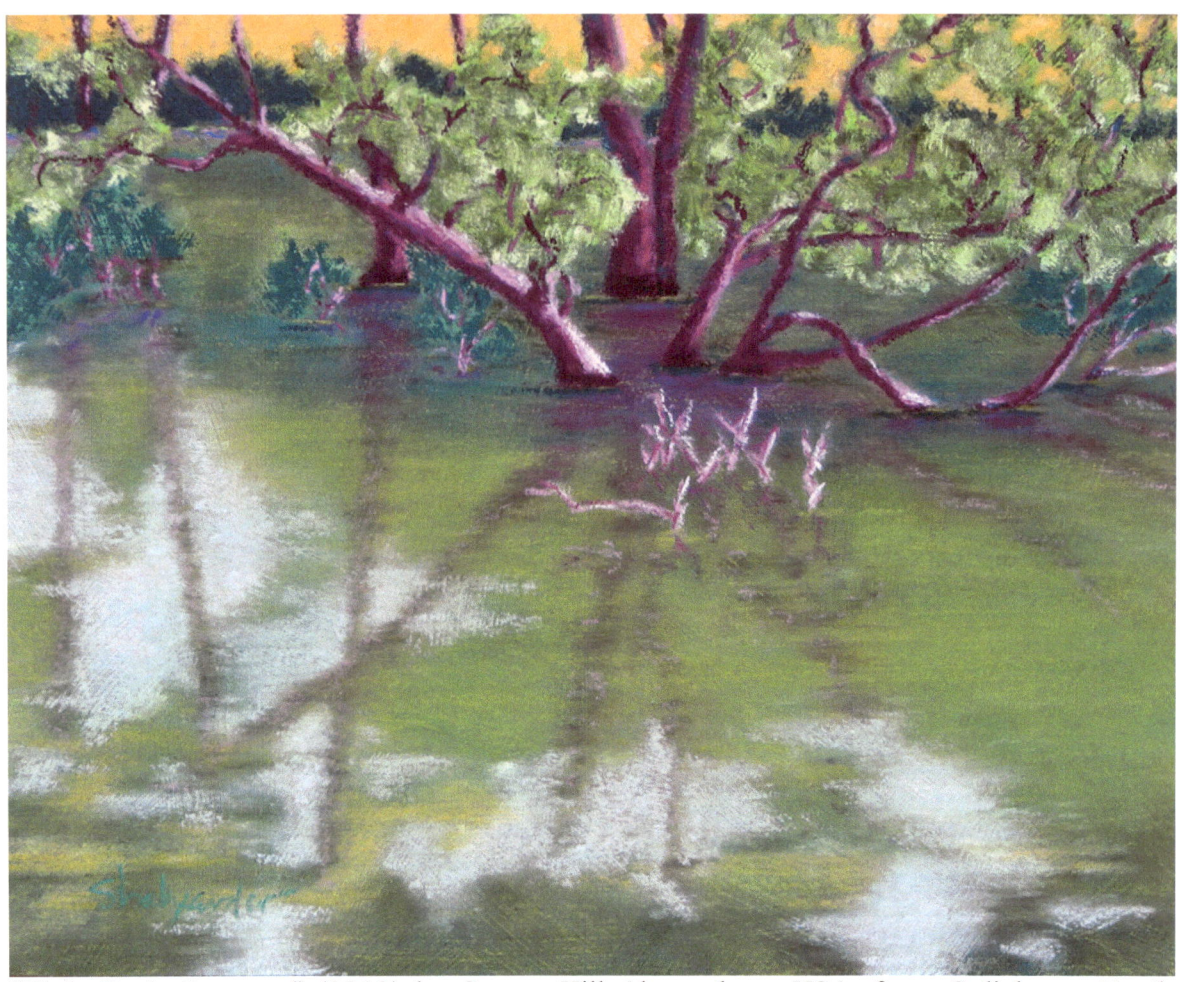

"High Rock Summer" (2010) by Susan Hill Alexander , USA, from Salisbury, North Carolina – pastel. "After taking many years off in order to work and raise a family, I began painting again in the mid 2000's. In college, drawing with graphite pencil was my passion even though I loved color. Several years ago a local artist offered a class in pastel painting and the light went on. The tactile nature of holding the actual pigment in my hand, instead of using a brush for painting, was instant love. My landscape work is done mostly en plein air. I am currently represented by Servello Gallery of Art, Altoona, PA, and I am a member of Plein Air Carolinas and the Piedmont Pastel Society."

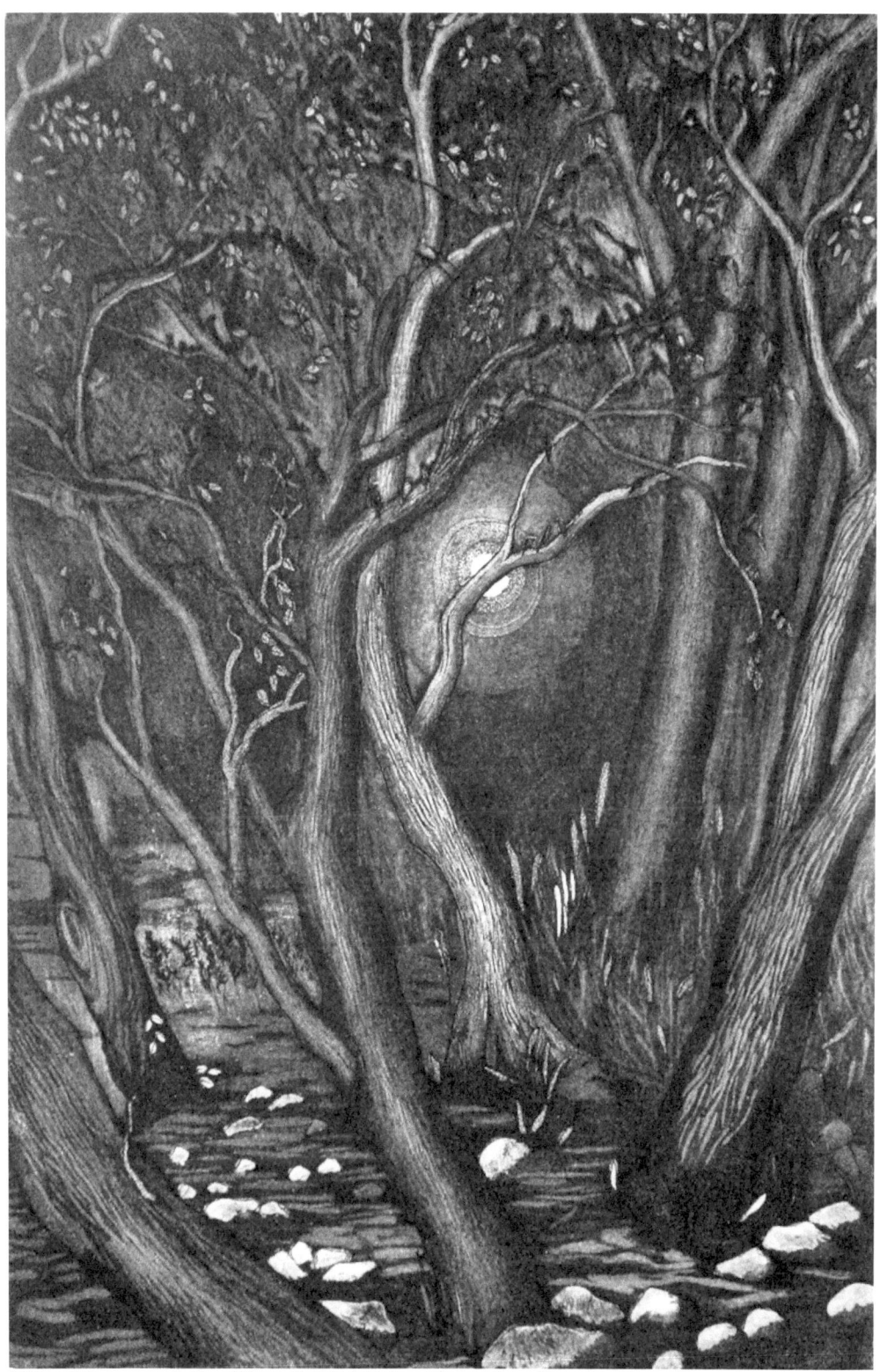
"The River and the Hope" (2010) by Hem Jyotika, Indian, from Delhi, India – etching.

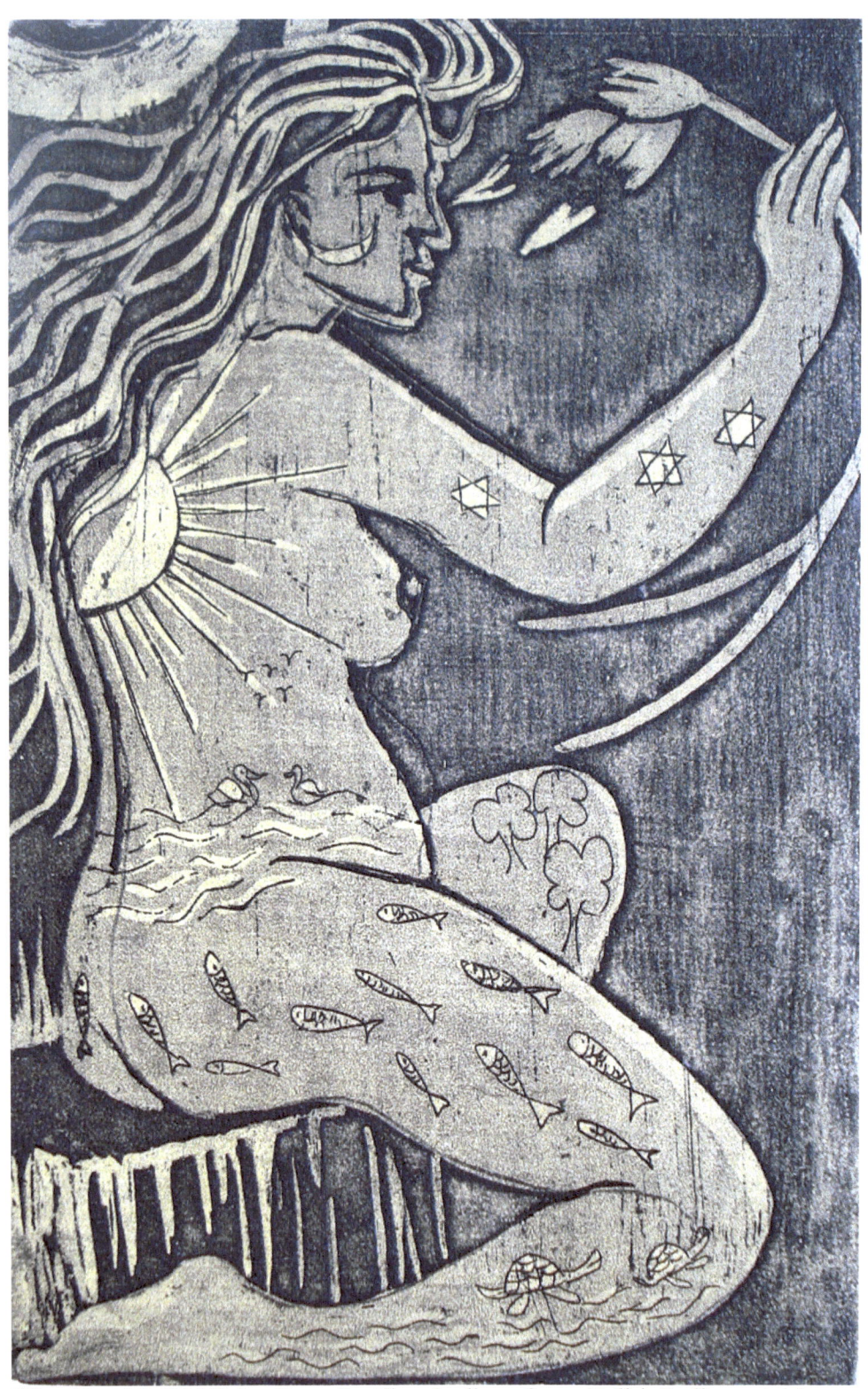
"The Earth" (2010) by Hem Jyotika, Indian, from Delhi, India – etching.

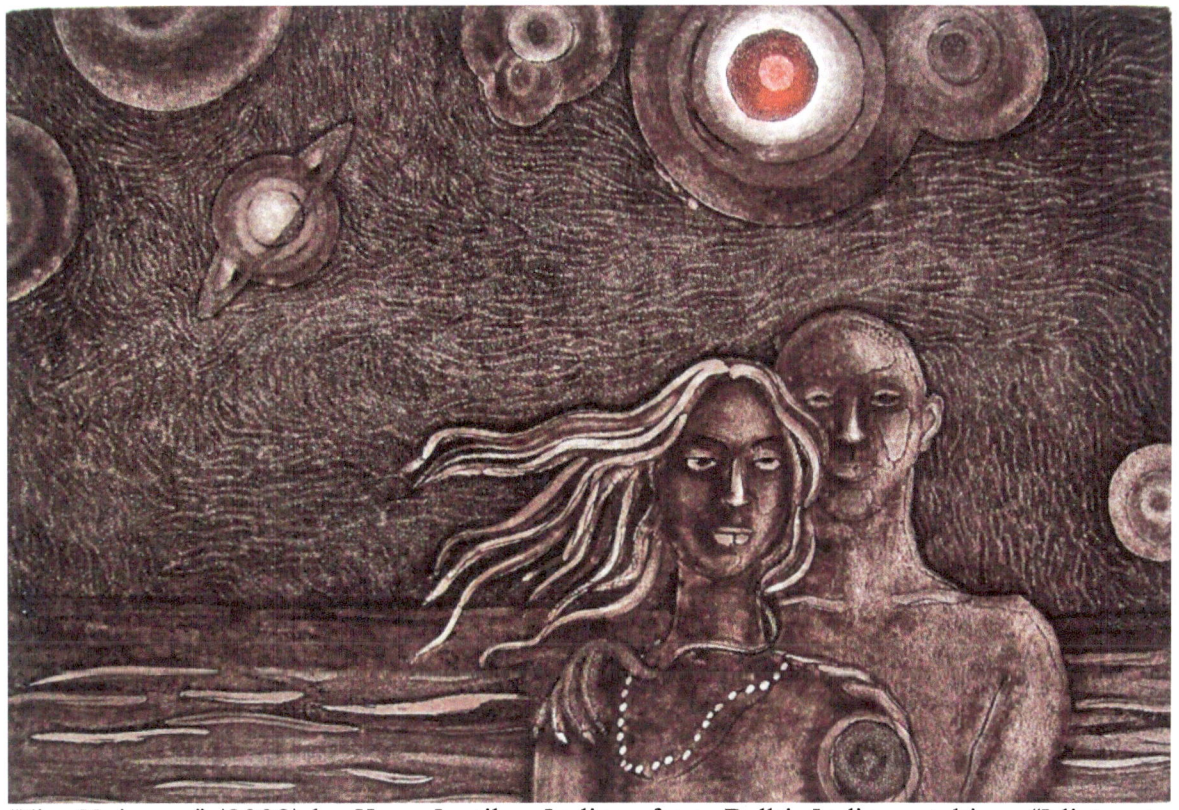

"The Universe" (2009) by Hem Jyotika, Indian, from Delhi, India – etching. "I listen to the composition as it sprouts and stretches. I would like to submit that I relocate figures as I draw them out of utopian realm of manufactured and concocted abstractions of contemporary art factories. Least fashion bound I want to capture the concord between the moment and the era, the man and the woman, the domination and democracy, the autumn and the spring, the linear and the complex, the universal and the personal, the allegory and the prosaic, the elemental and the historical, the surface and the profundity, the space and the color, the transparent and the opaque, the myths and the histories."

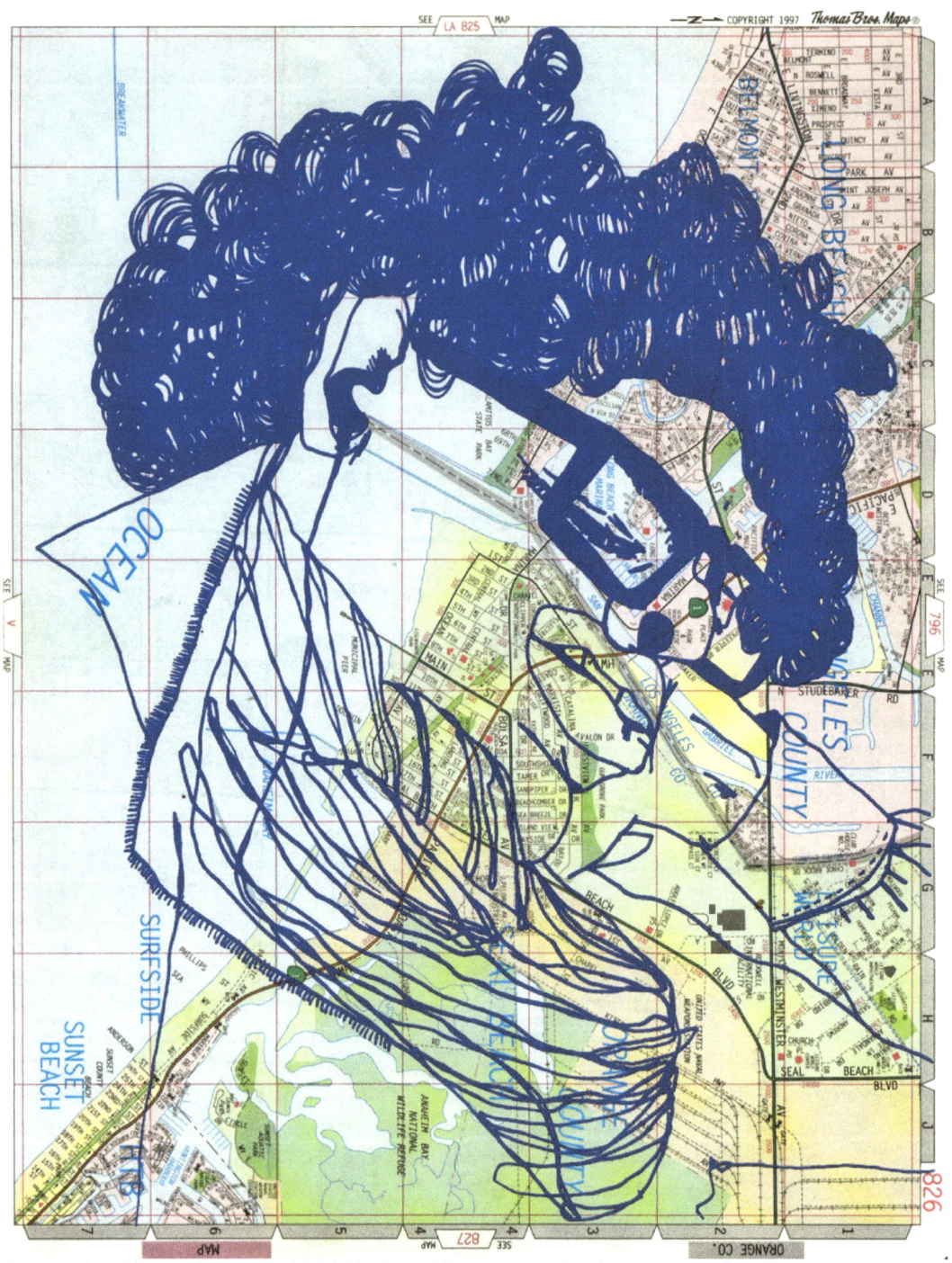

"Lost in Thoughts I" (2010) by Clémence Potier, French, from Brussels, Belgium – silkscreen print. "I used some sketches I did on the bus to make the portraits printed on the maps. I do a lot of sketches on the bus, tramway, plane or train. People look like they're thinking and focusing a lot, sometimes peacefully, sometimes not…"

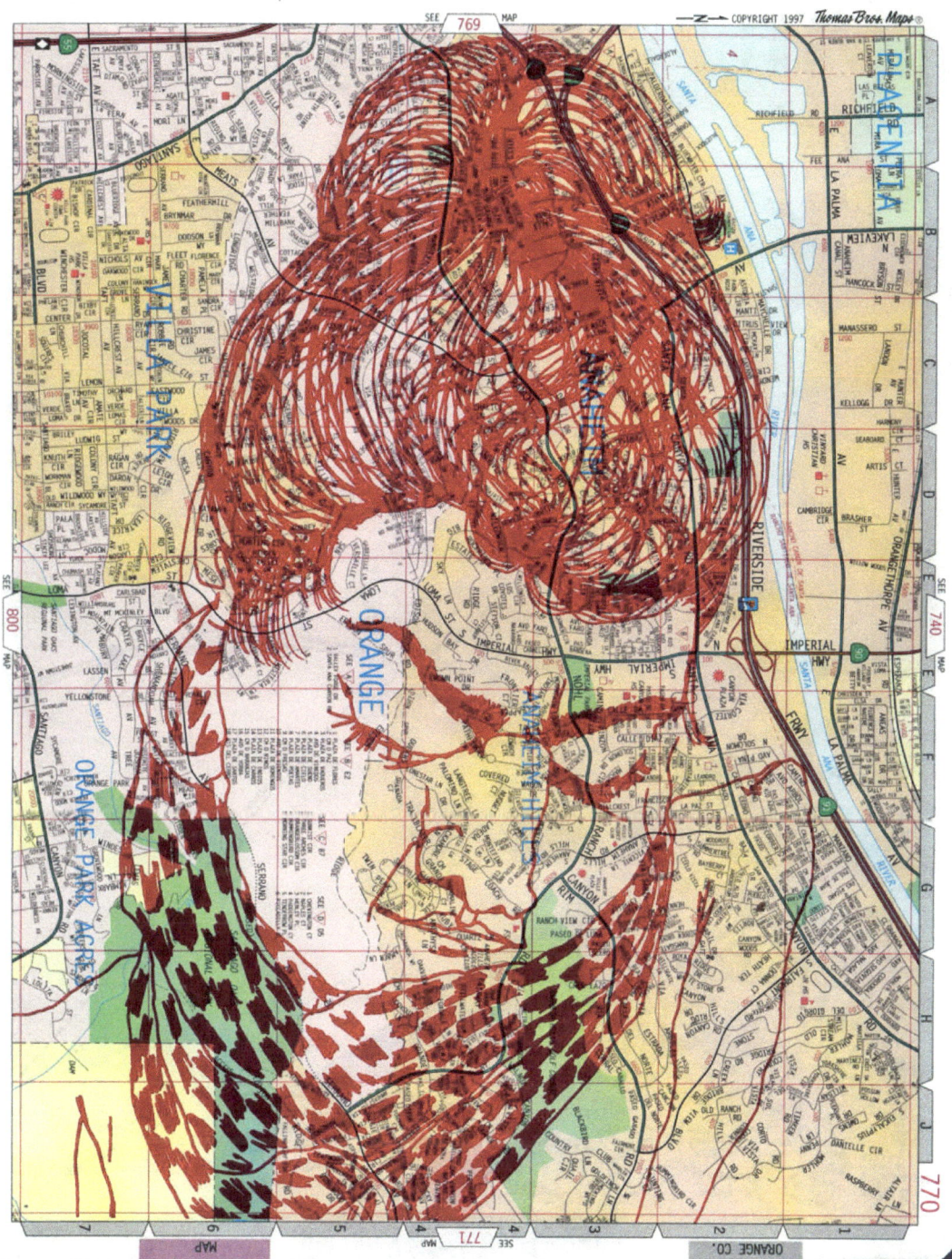

"Lost in Thoughts II" (2010) by Clémence Potier, French, from Brussels, Belgium – silkscreen print. "...I printed the portraits on maps, to make them meld with it, and give an idea of how the persons feel when they're traveling. The rivers we found in the picture, passing thru or near the faces, symbolize the thoughts running freely."

ADDITIONAL OIL & ACRYLIC

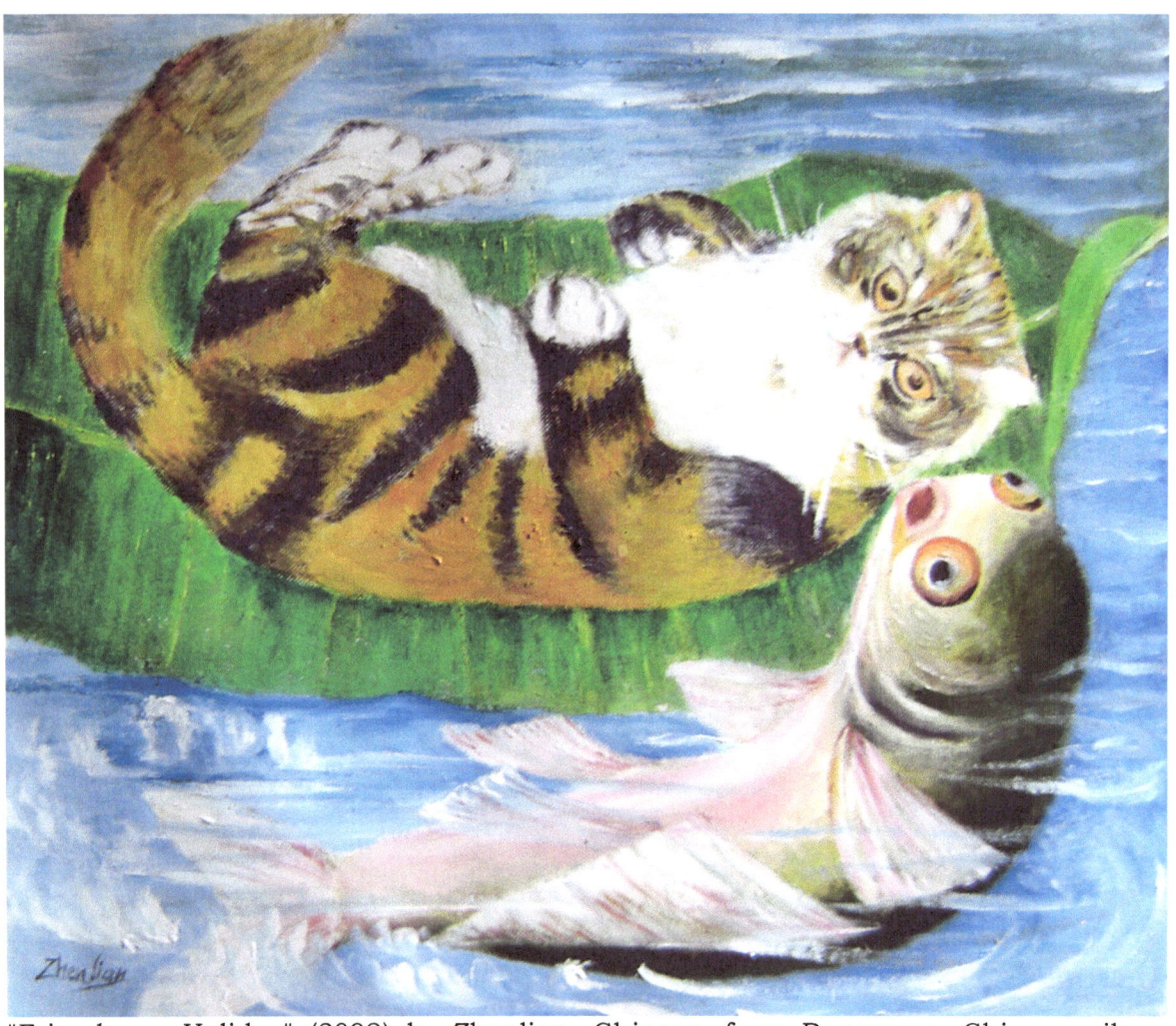

"Friends on Holiday" (2008) by Zhenlian, Chinese, from Dongguan, China – oil on canvas.

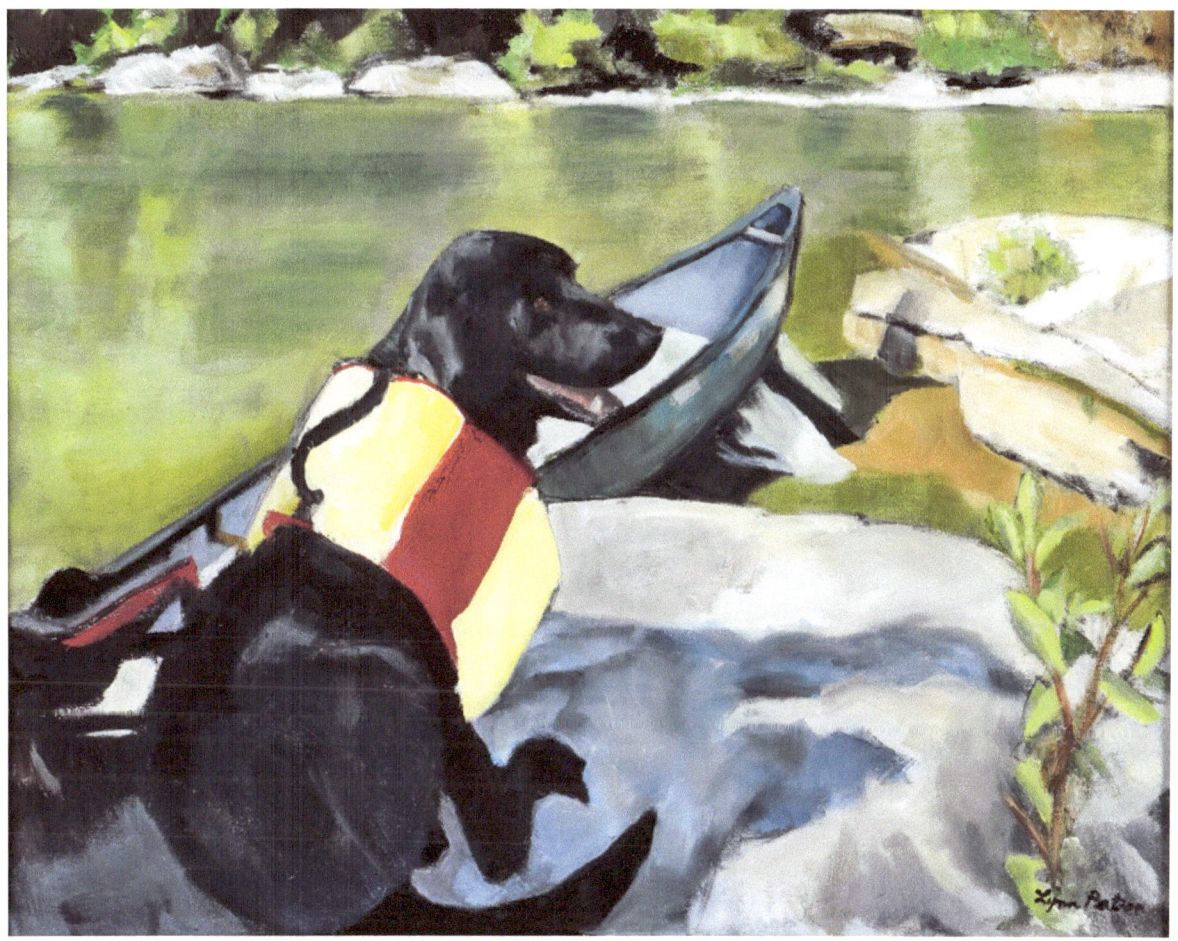

"A Day on the River" (2006) by Lynn Patron, USA, from Miami Beach, Florida – oil on canvas. "My trademark is the uninhibited strong, bold, yet soft, use of color combinations. Often the color red is used to add a touch of strength or drama. Whether whimsical, sensuous, or serious, the use of strong shapes, contrasted with unconventional combinations of colors, produce works that are simplistically understated, yet powerful, and that tell a harmonious story. In my paintings, features are deliberately not exacting, instead, just defined enough to capture the subject's essence so that the viewer can experience the real conversation of the subject."

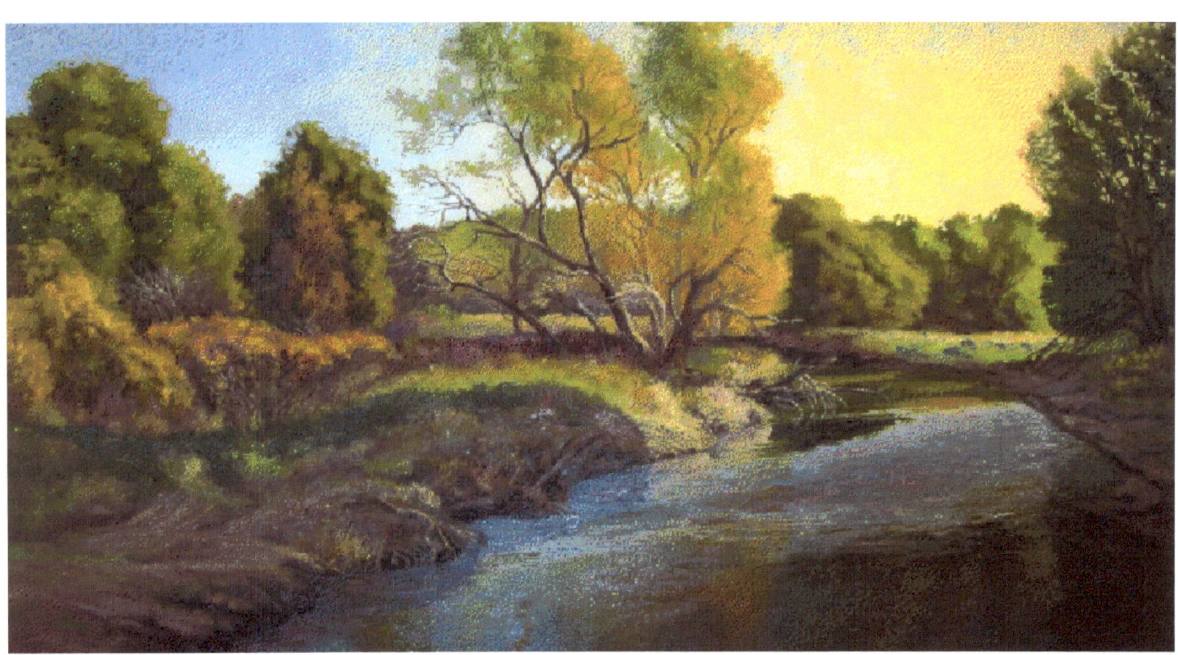

"Almost Autumn" (2009) by William Marvin, USA, from Skokie, Illinois – oil on canvas. "This scene is of the Des Plaines River in Northern Illinois. These old Willows were bathed in the glow of a setting sun and the light held steady for about 2 hours. I had to perch on a hummock in the middle of the river to get this view and a light breeze blew in my face as I did the 8" x 16" sketch. The breeze died down and I was immediately swarmed by a million mosquitoes. The final size of the studio painting is 24" x 48". I was captivated by how the glancing light illuminated the trees and brought out all the colors and textures along the river bank."

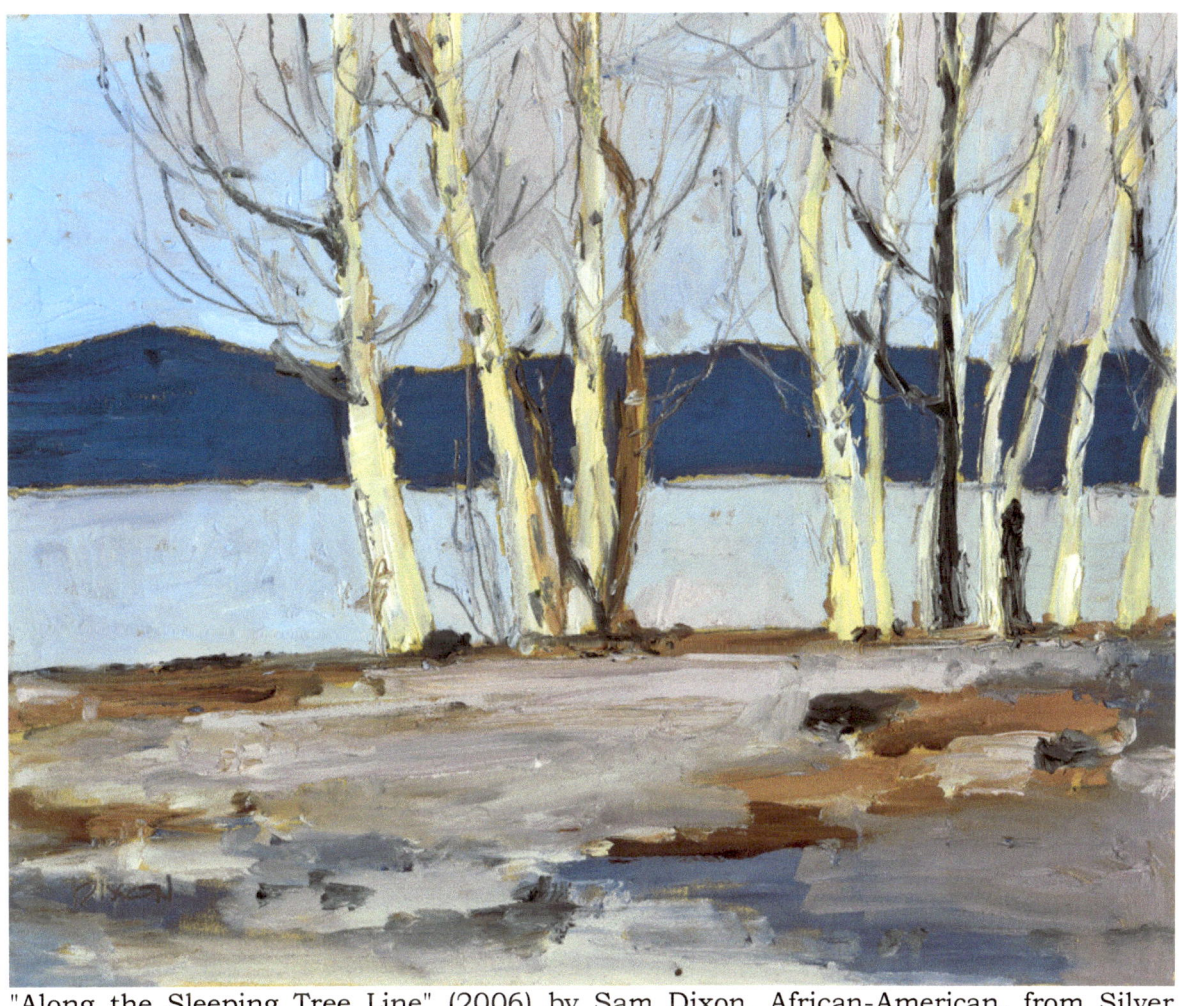
"Along the Sleeping Tree Line" (2006) by Sam Dixon, African-American, from Silver Spring, Maryland – oil.

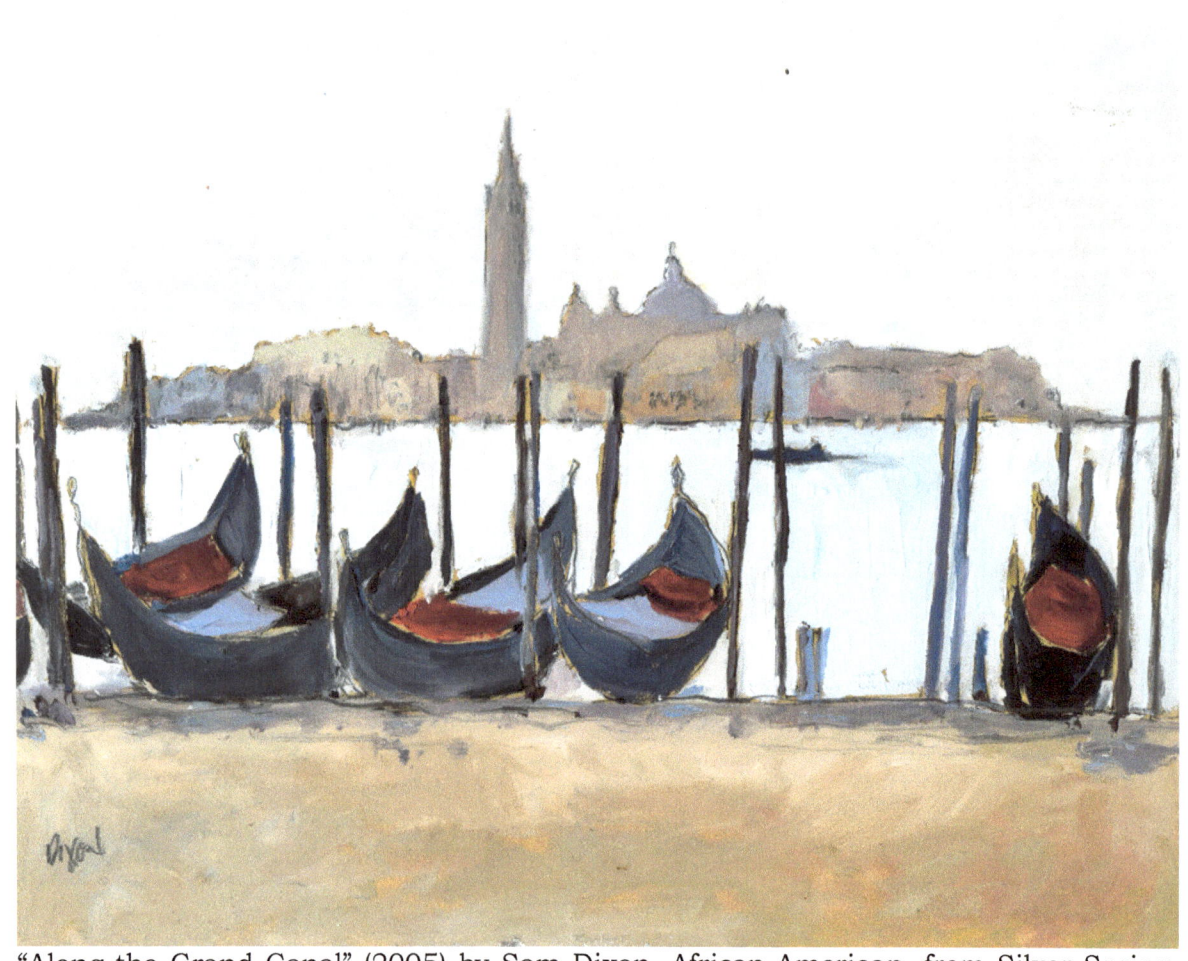

"Along the Grand Canal" (2005) by Sam Dixon, African-American, from Silver Spring, Maryland – oil. "My paintings are in many private collections in the United States and abroad. My main focus is on shapes and abstractions through an impressionist approach."

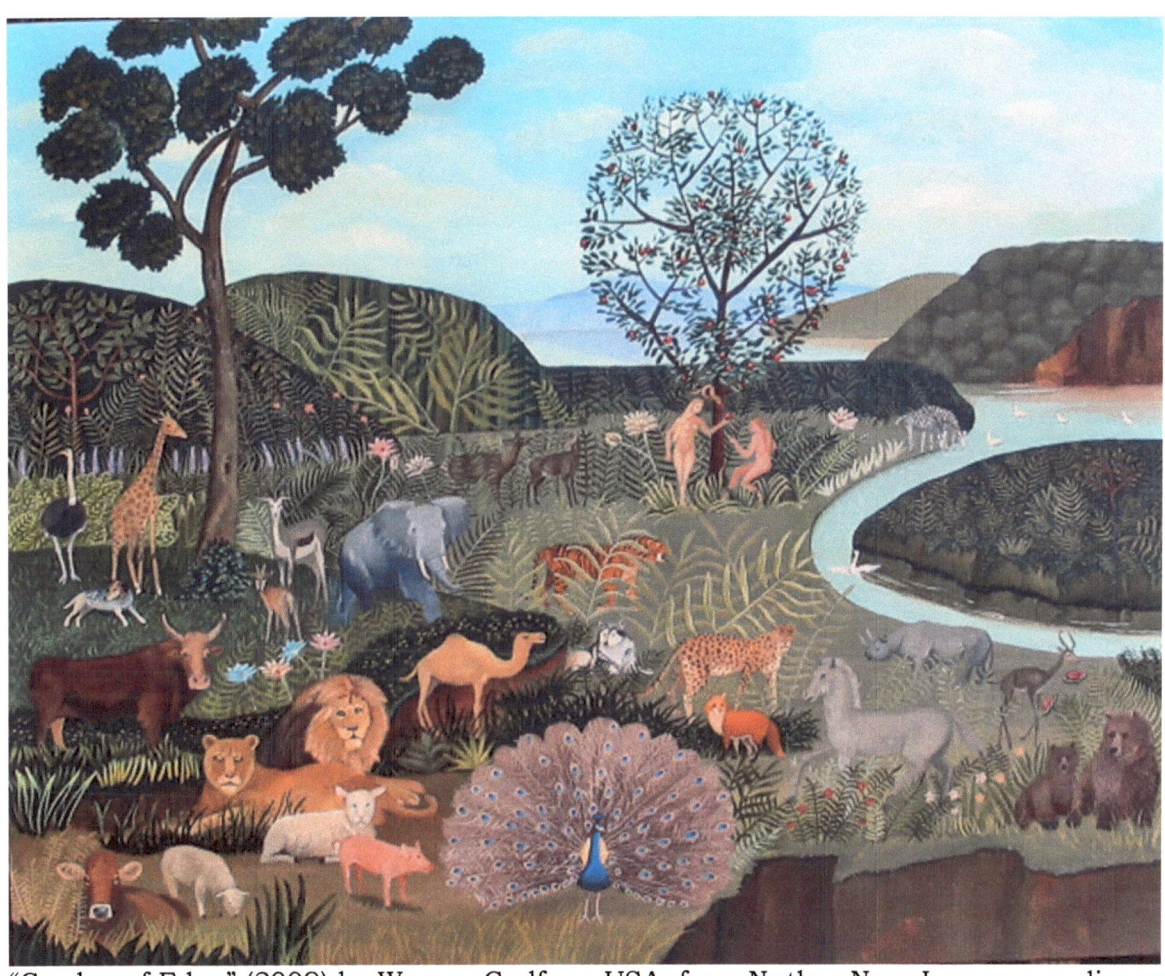

"Garden of Eden" (2009) by Warren Godfrey, USA, from Nutley, New Jersey – acrylic on canvas. "Folk art style painting has been my passion for more than 35 years, 'The Garden of Eden' gave me a chance to reflect the influences of Edward Hicks and Henri Rousseau - two of my favorite primitive painters. As a self-taught artist, I like to keep things simple and enjoy the details that go into creating a painting."

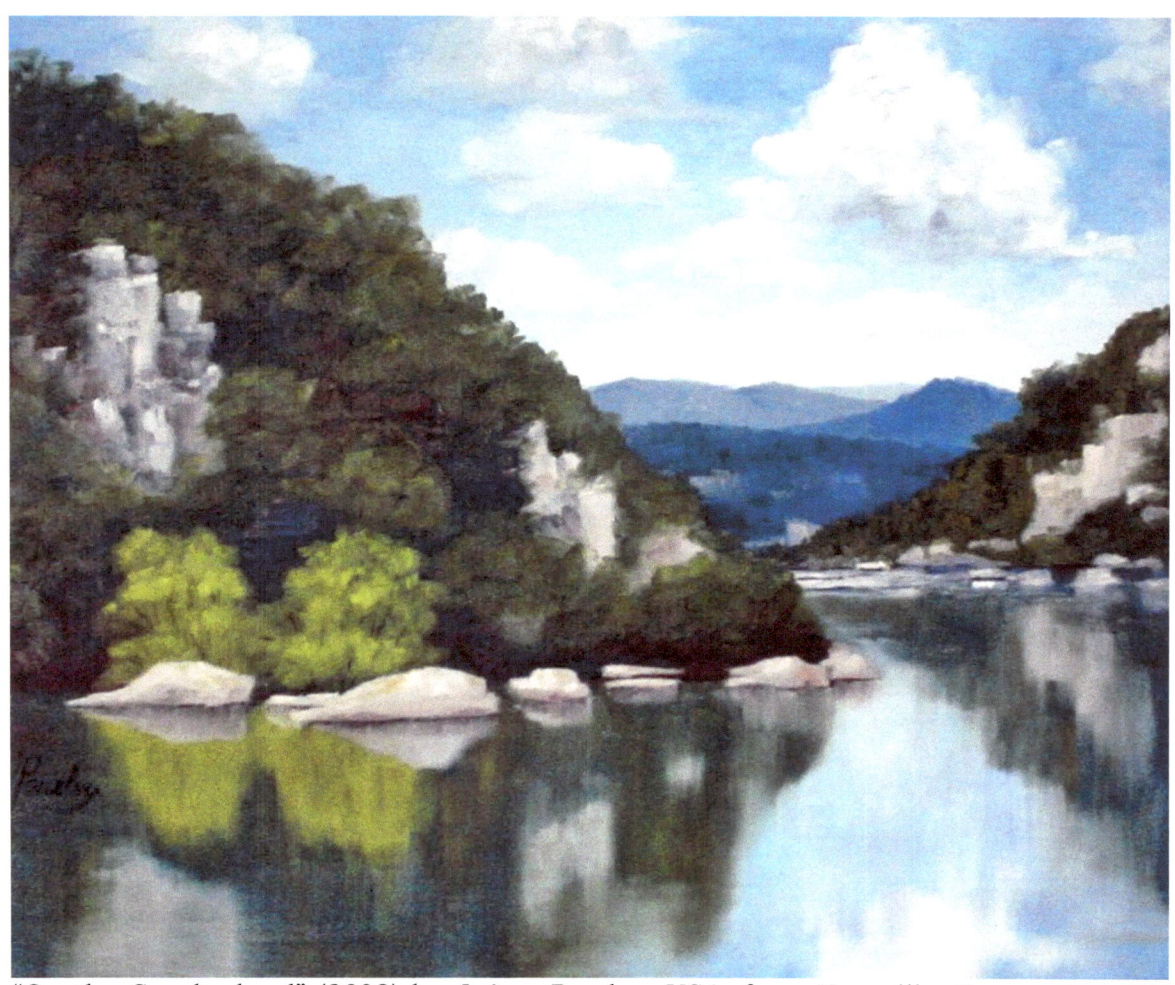
"On the Cumberland" (2008) by JoAnn Parsley, USA, from Knoxville, Tennessee – oil. "This painting was a work in progress for several years, since every time I visited the scene there were changes. The actual location is in Cumberland Falls State Park, Kentucky."

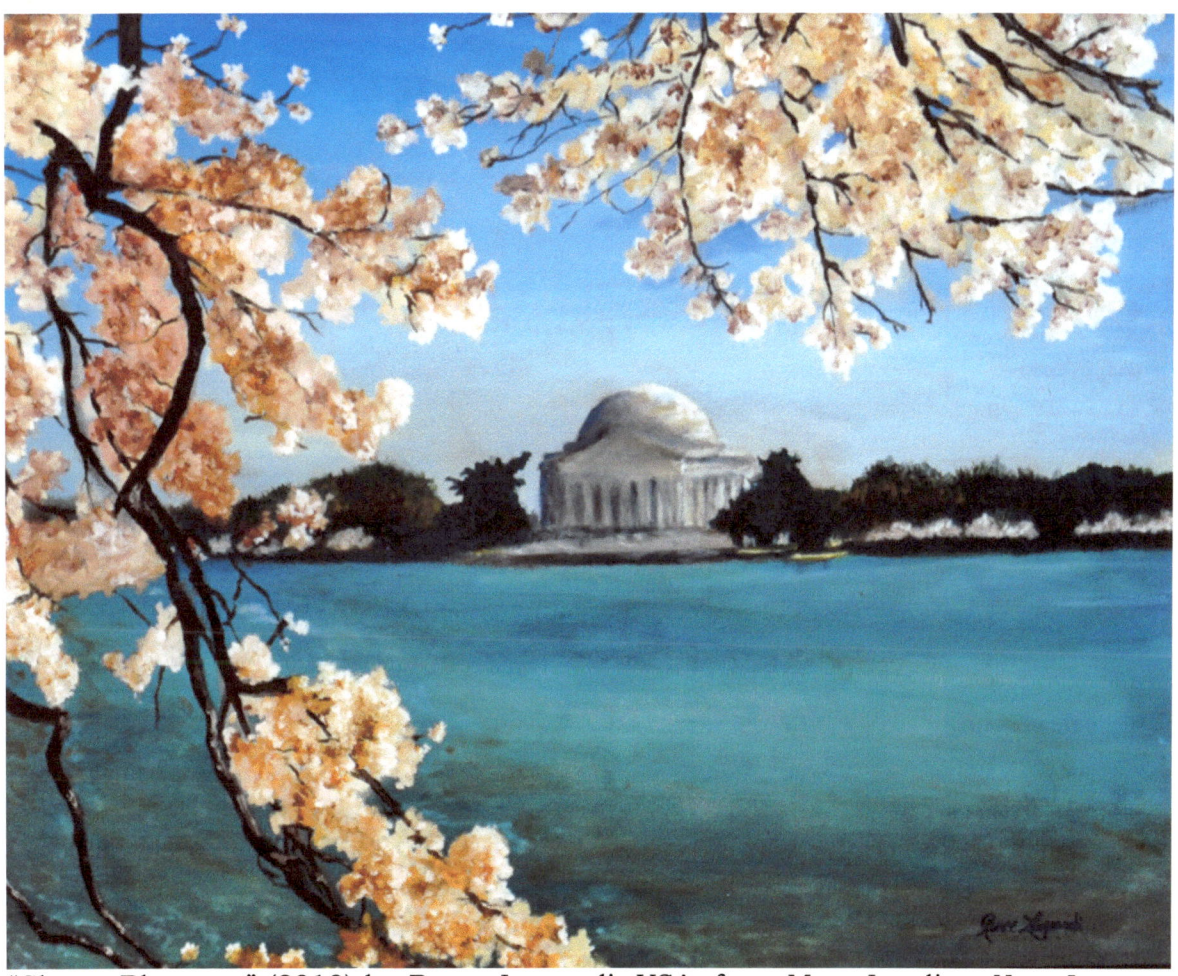

"Cherry Blossoms" (2010) by Renee Leopardi, USA, from Mays Landing, New Jersey – oil. "Thousands of people travel to Washington DC every spring just to enjoy the beauty of the cherry blossoms. This piece is simply meant to capture those few short weeks each year."

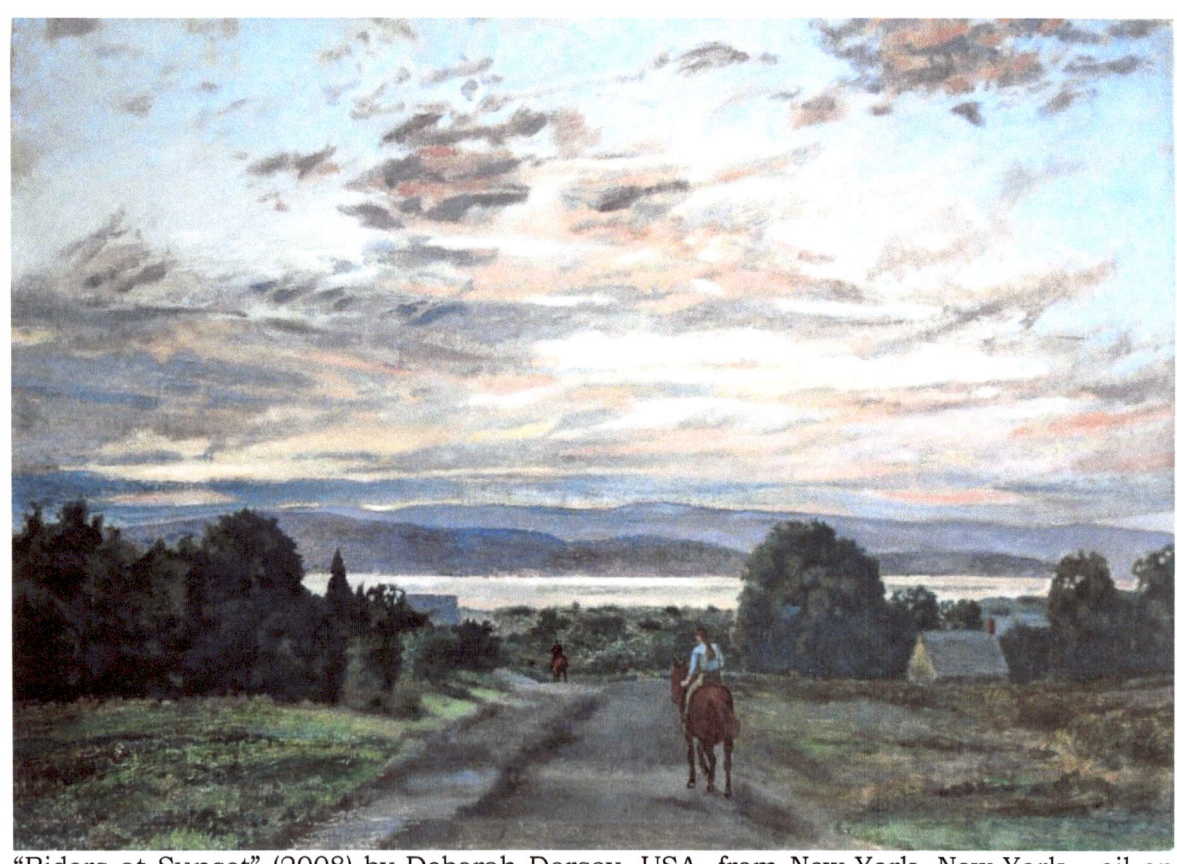
"Riders at Sunset" (2008) by Deborah Dorsey, USA, from New York, New York – oil on linen.

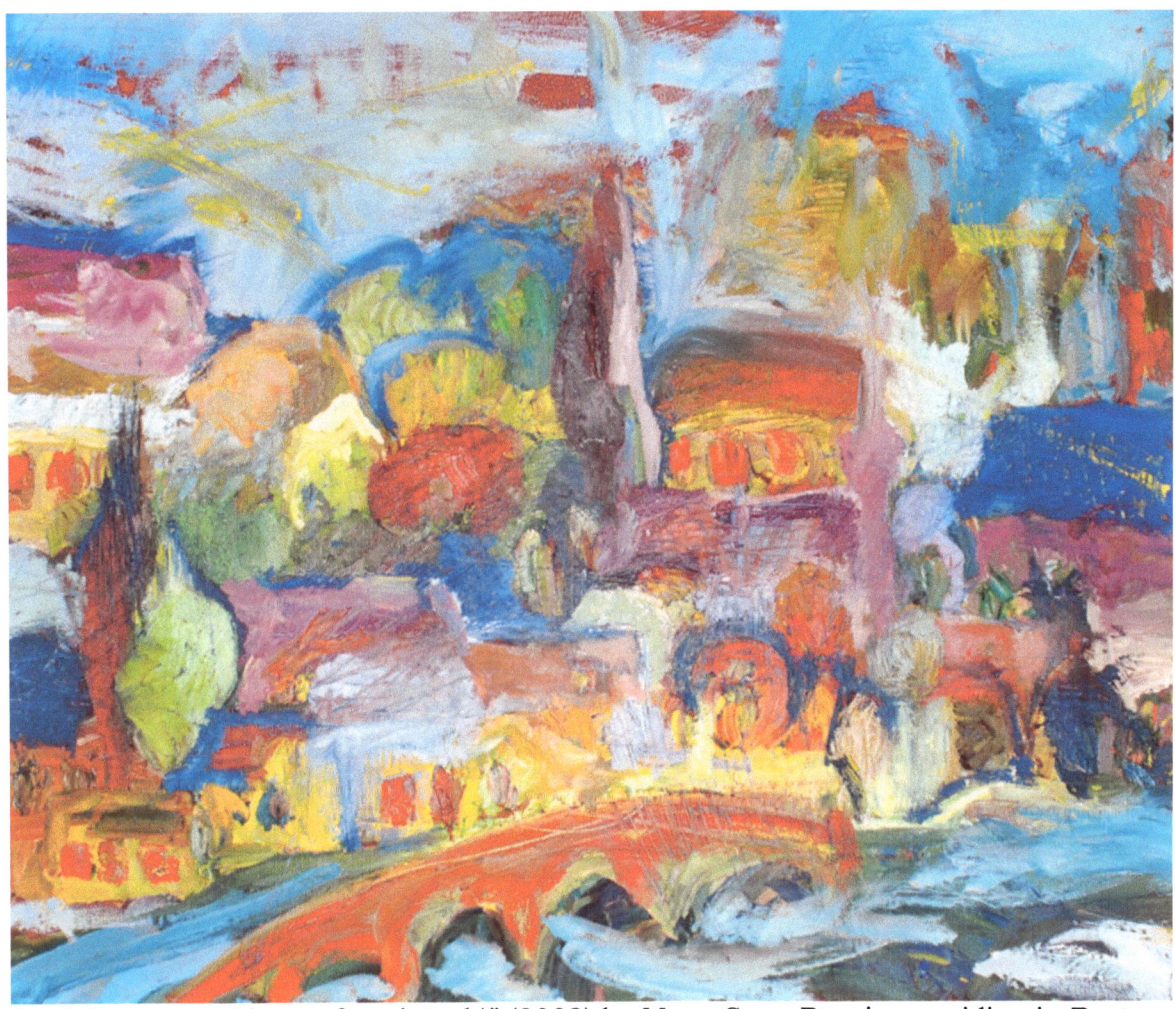

"Child's Dream II (part of a triptych)" (2009) by Maya Gerr, Russian, residing in Boston, Massachusetts – oil on canvas. "My work includes nature, landscapes, and abstractions in paintings and graphics. I use classic media such as oil, acrylic, and watercolors on canvas and paper, usually *a la prima*. These traditional media are, however, combined with non-traditional techniques. My intention is to make the impression of the painting last in time with new shapes and layers of meaning revealing themselves. I frequently hide plants and animals within apparently abstract work and use grotesque expressed through the interplay of color and shape contrasts. The triptych 'Child's Dreams' depicts an imaginary river flowing through an imaginary medieval city. This river has, however, a real prototype, which is Neckar flowing through the town of Heidelberg in Germany, where I once lived."

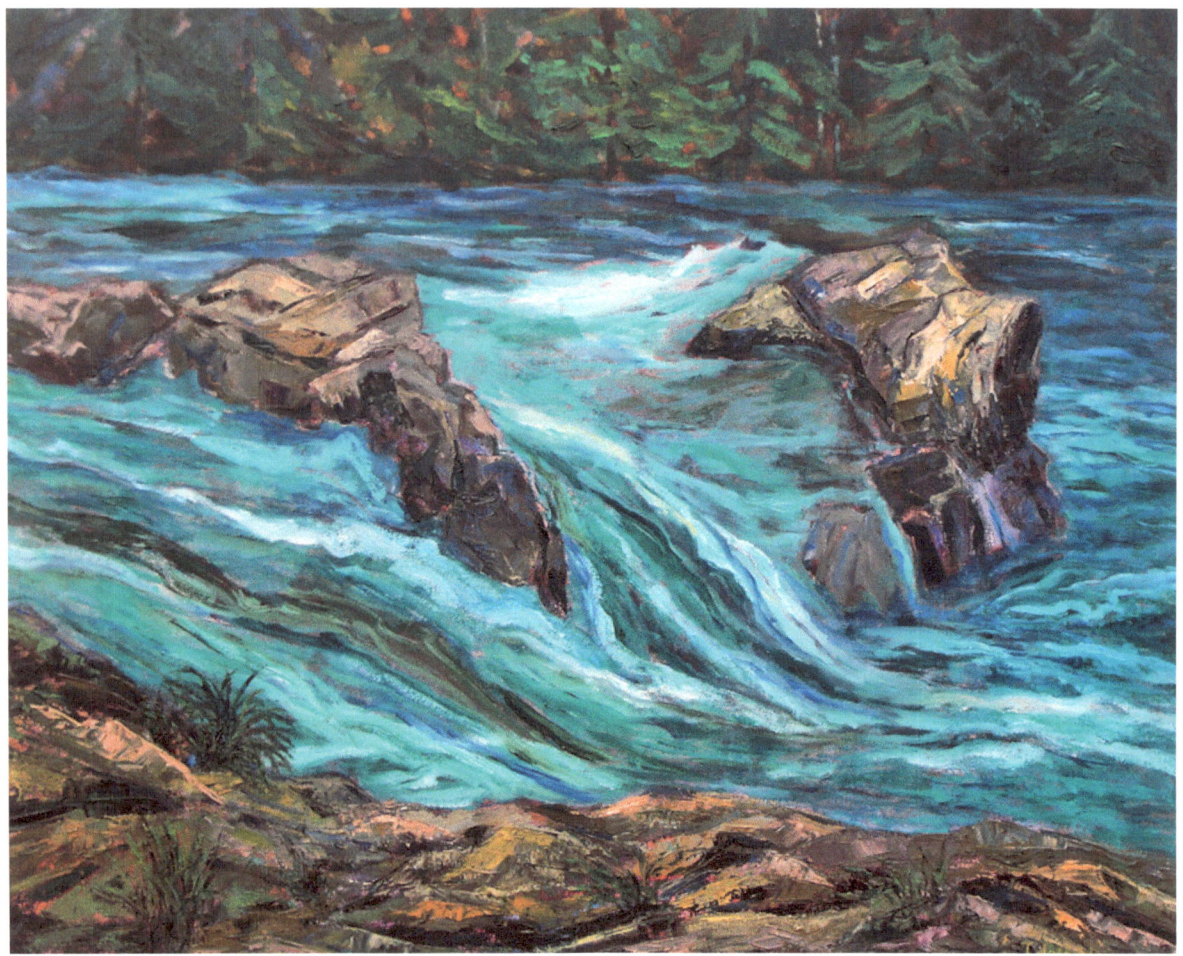

"Coldwater River" (2004) by Idell Weiss, USA, from San Francisco, California – oil on canvas. "In this piece, I tried to convey the shaded coldness of the area and the rapidly flowing river. My work can best be described as 'Landscapes—Representational and Otherwise'. Some pieces, though representational, tend to be somewhat impressionistic. Others are quite abstract. However, all seem to suggest my relationship to the landscape or cityscape, especially as observed from a high vantage point. Because of its tactile and viscous quality, oil paint has tended to remain my favorite medium, although I also work in acrylic, collage, mixed media, and watercolor. I work in any or all of these media simultaneously and become absorbed by whichever medium and style I am currently using on a project."

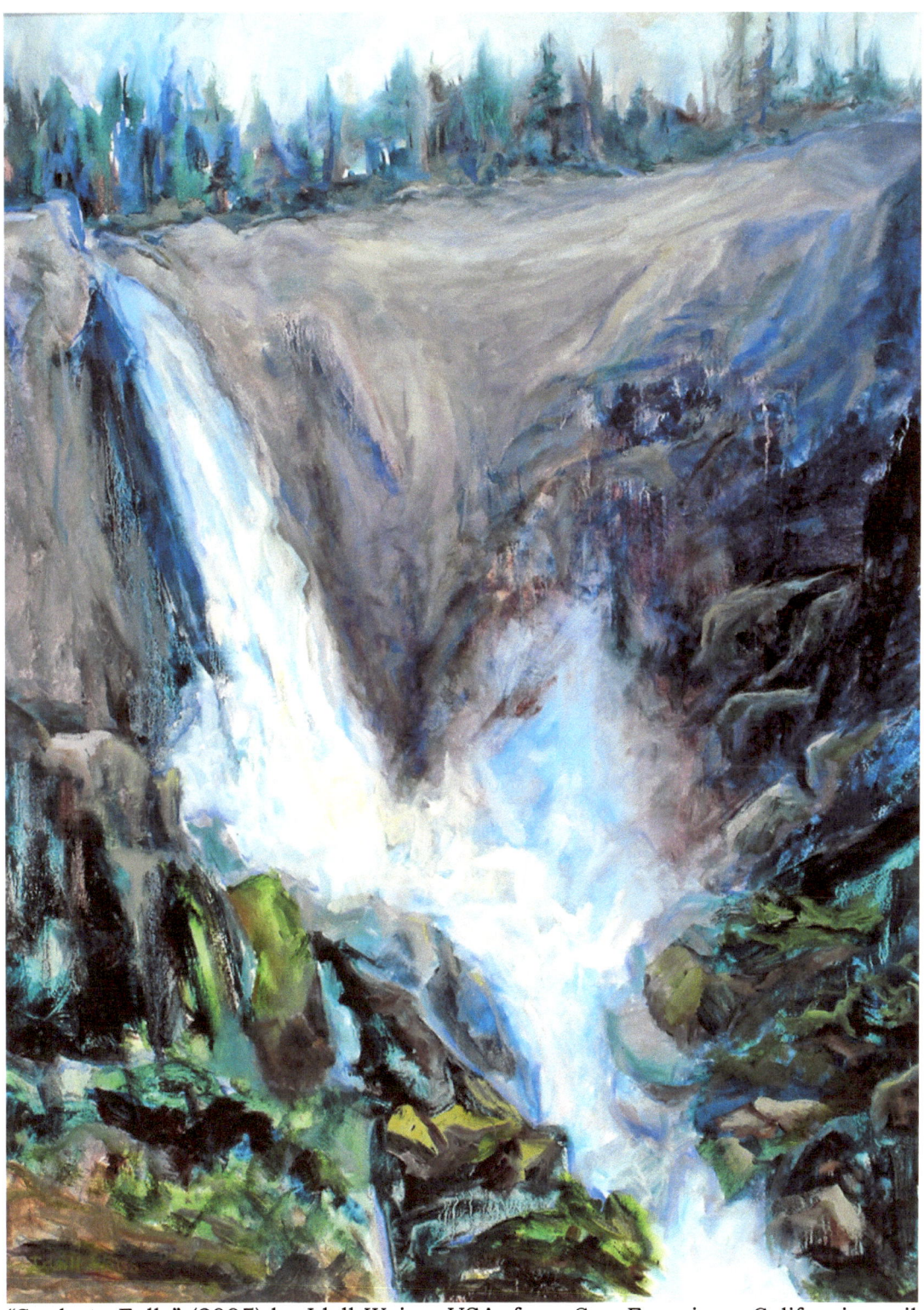

"Spahats Falls" (2005) by Idell Weiss, USA, from San Francisco, California – oil on canvas. "In this painting, I tried to describe the magnitude of the cliffs and the power of the falls pouring into the river."

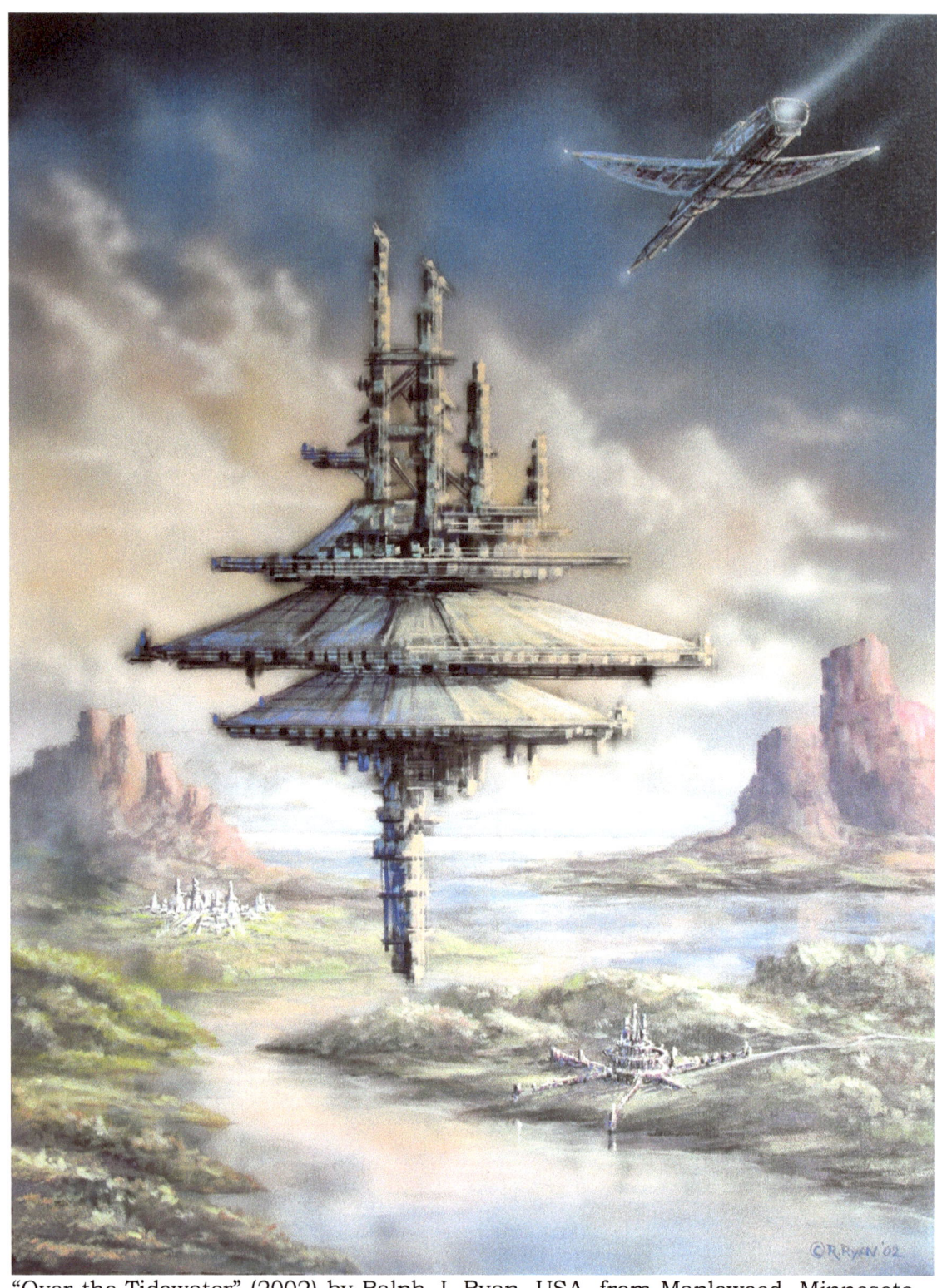

"Over the Tidewater" (2002) by Ralph J. Ryan, USA, from Maplewood, Minnesota – acrylic. "I paint Science Fiction/Fantasy art. My inspirations come primarily from my own imagination."

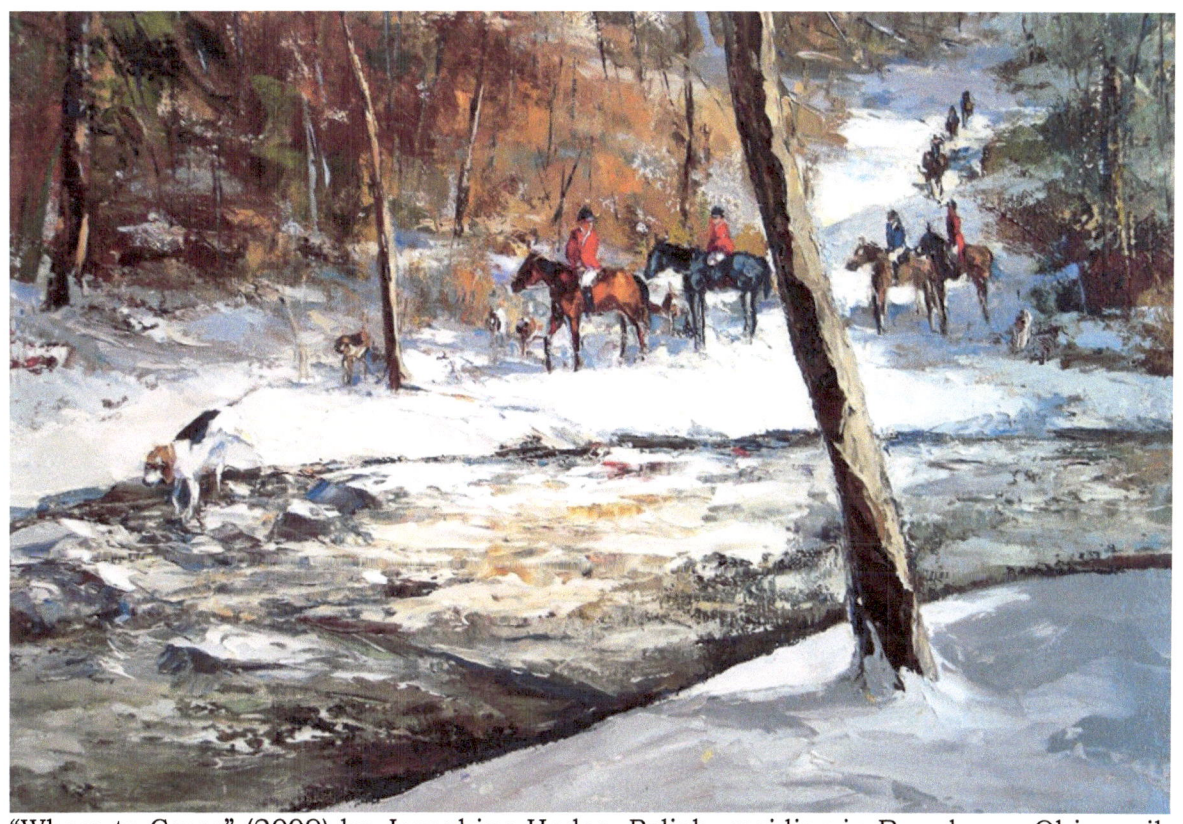

"Where to Cross" (2009) by Josephine Hodos, Polish, residing in Boardman, Ohio – oil. "Using a palette knife gives me that impasto, impressionistic look I want to create in a variety of scenes."

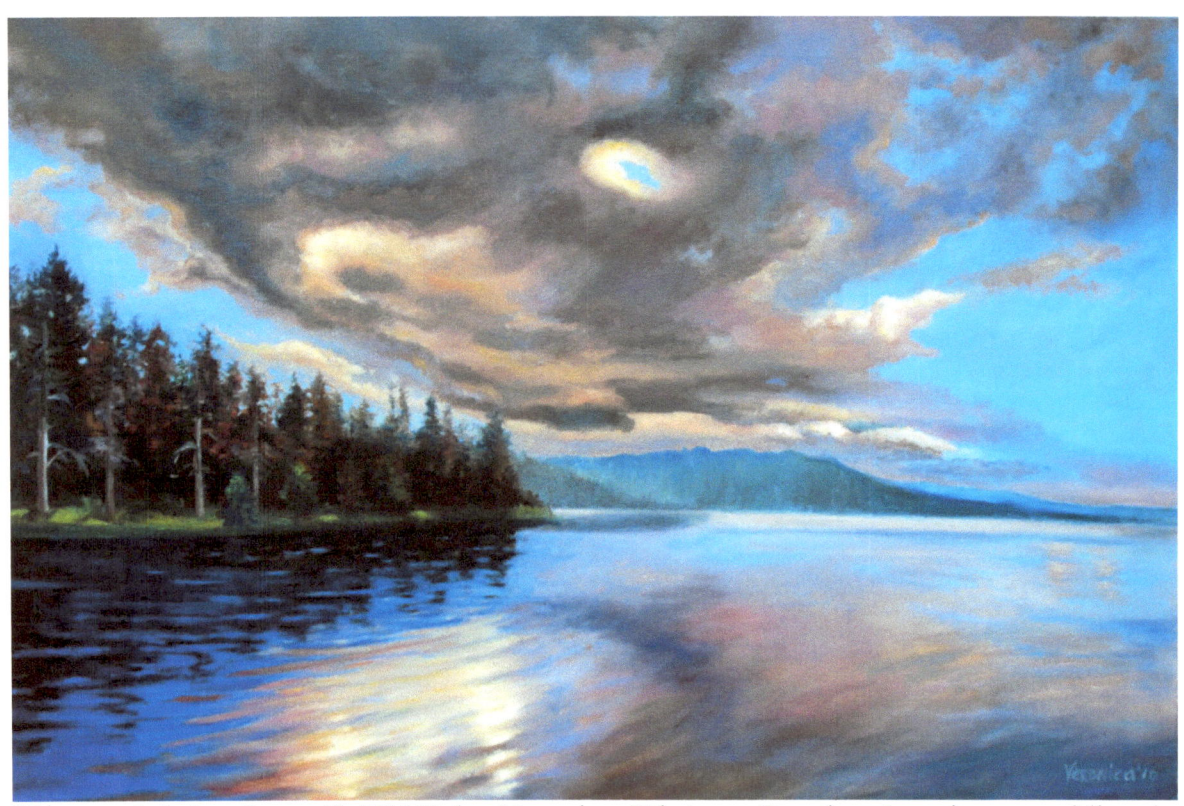

"Diamond Lake Sunset" (2010) by Veronica Winters, Russian-American, residing in State College, Pennsylvania – oil.

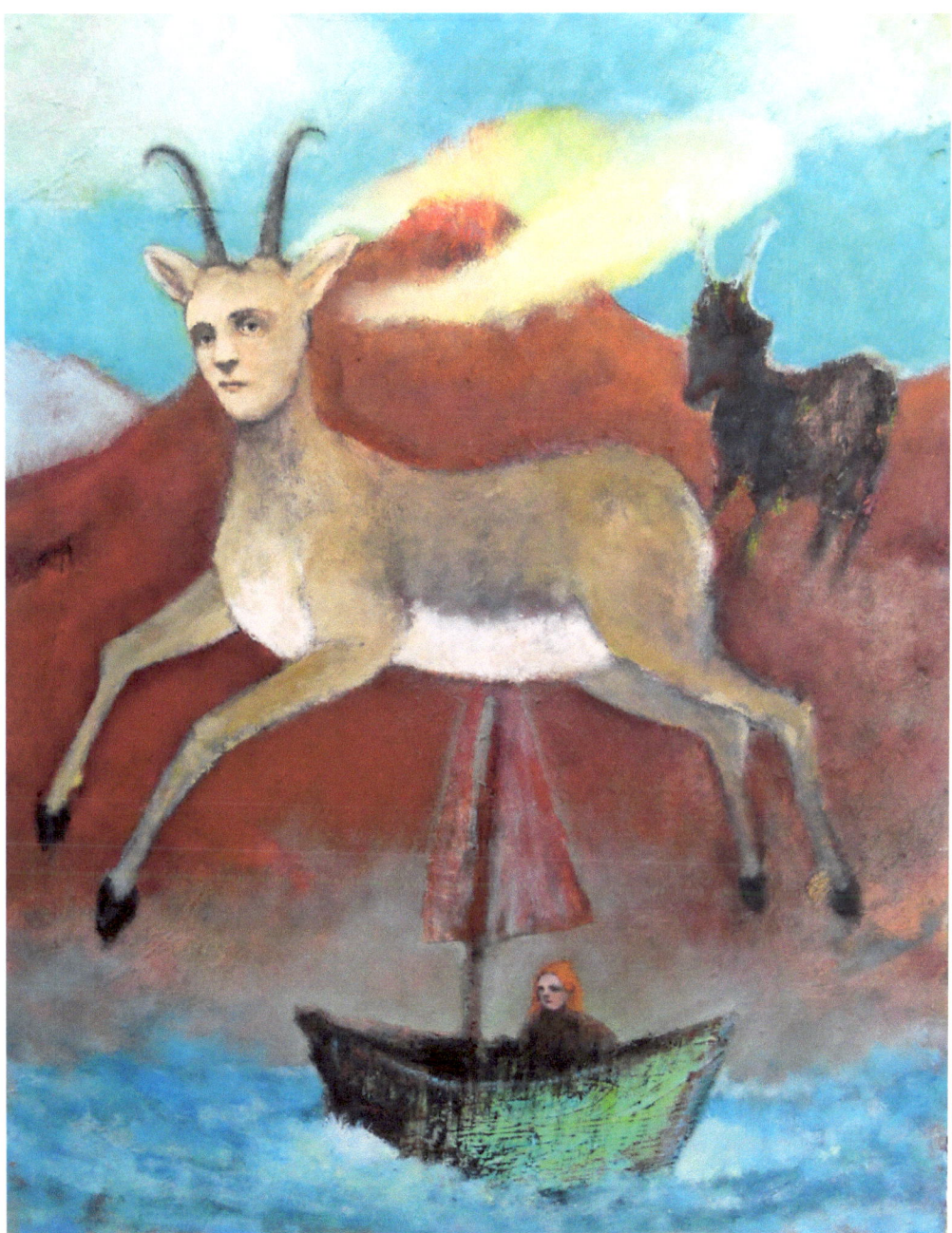

"I Climb, You Sail" (2010) by Shannon Richardson, USA, from Portland, Oregon – oil on board. "This recent collection of paintings focuses on the concealment of memory through imaginative imagery... When memory and fable intertwine I am able to separate myself from the memory to allow objective observation and imaginative interplay to connect reality and fantasy. The work transcends the boundaries between memory and fantasy with an added element of the fantastic; this infuses the works with a sense of romance and reverie. I am able to take some of the severity of life and turn it into something tangible and beautiful, but not quite real."

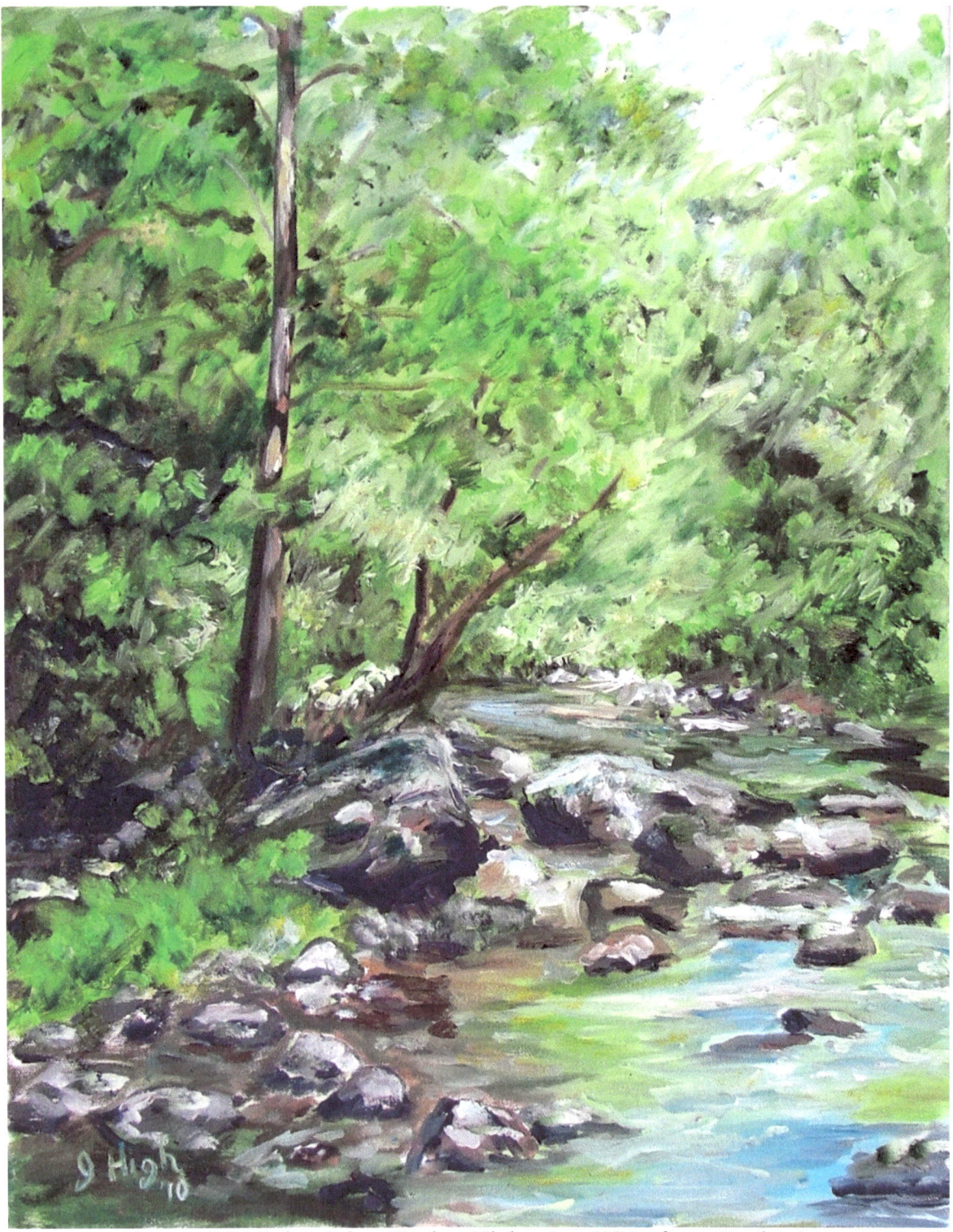

"Pleasant Times" (2010) by John Wesley High, Jr., USA, from Rocky Mount, North Carolina - oil. "John specializes in plein aire landscapes and florals. In addition, his bonds formed with students and colleagues are his greatest legacy."

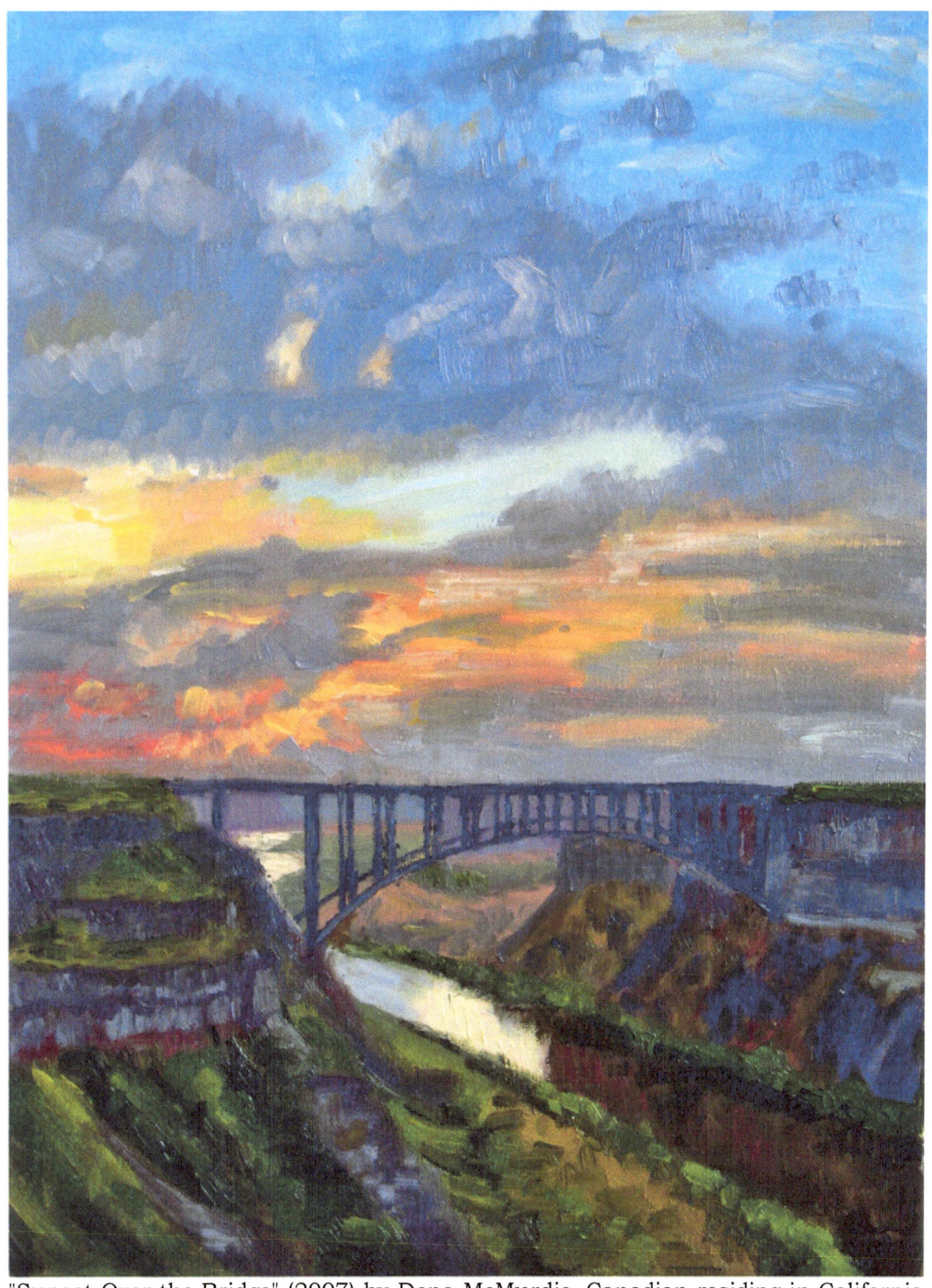
"Sunset Over the Bridge" (2007) by Dena McMurdie, Canadian residing in California – oil on canvas.

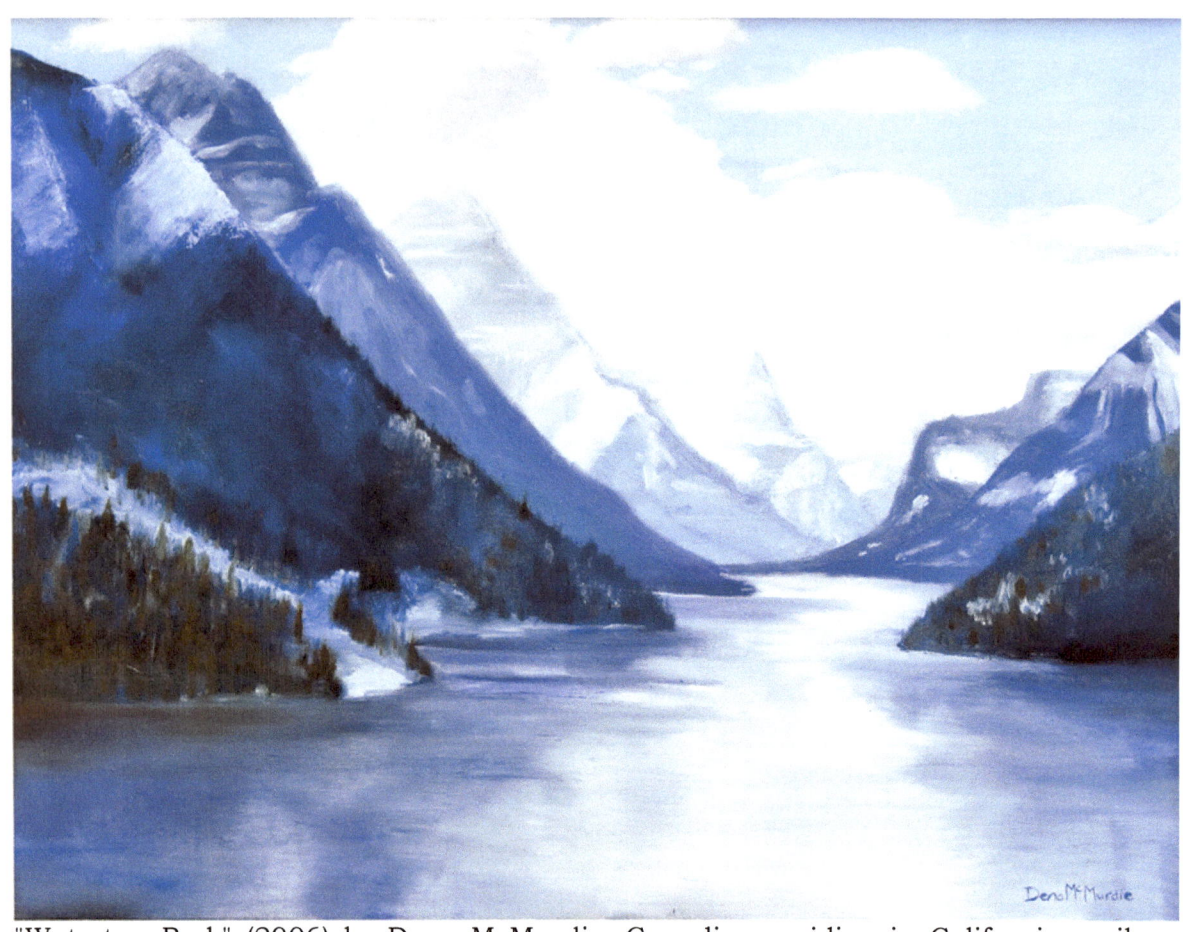

"Waterton Park" (2006) by Dena McMurdie, Canadian residing in California – oil on canvas. "Dena McMurdie grew up in the breathtaking foothills of the Canadian Rockies. It was there that she developed her passion for art and nature. She sees the world as a masterpiece that is made up of millions of paintings just waiting to be captured on canvas. She resides in California with her husband and two children."

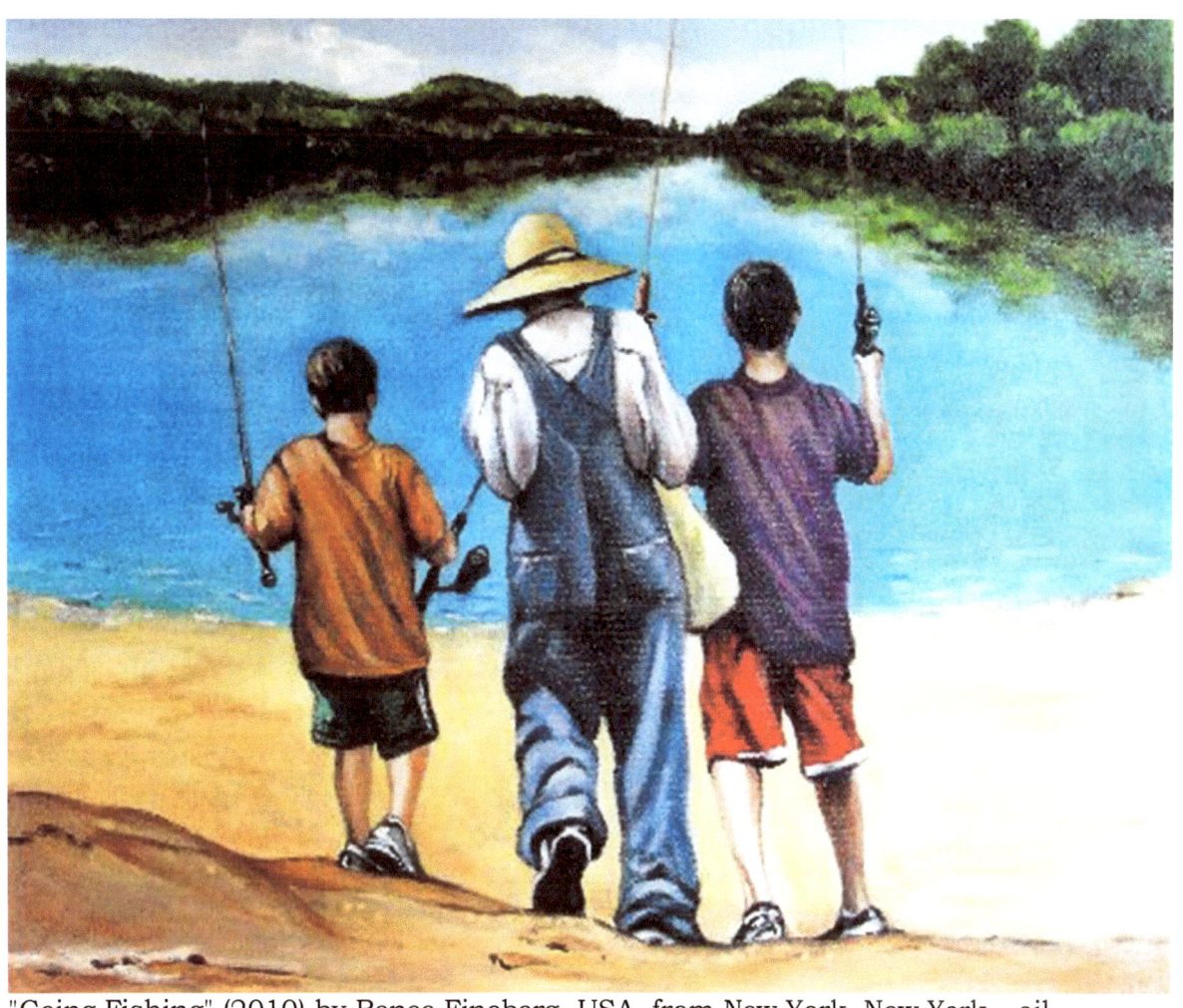
"Going Fishing" (2010) by Renee Fineberg, USA, from New York, New York – oil.

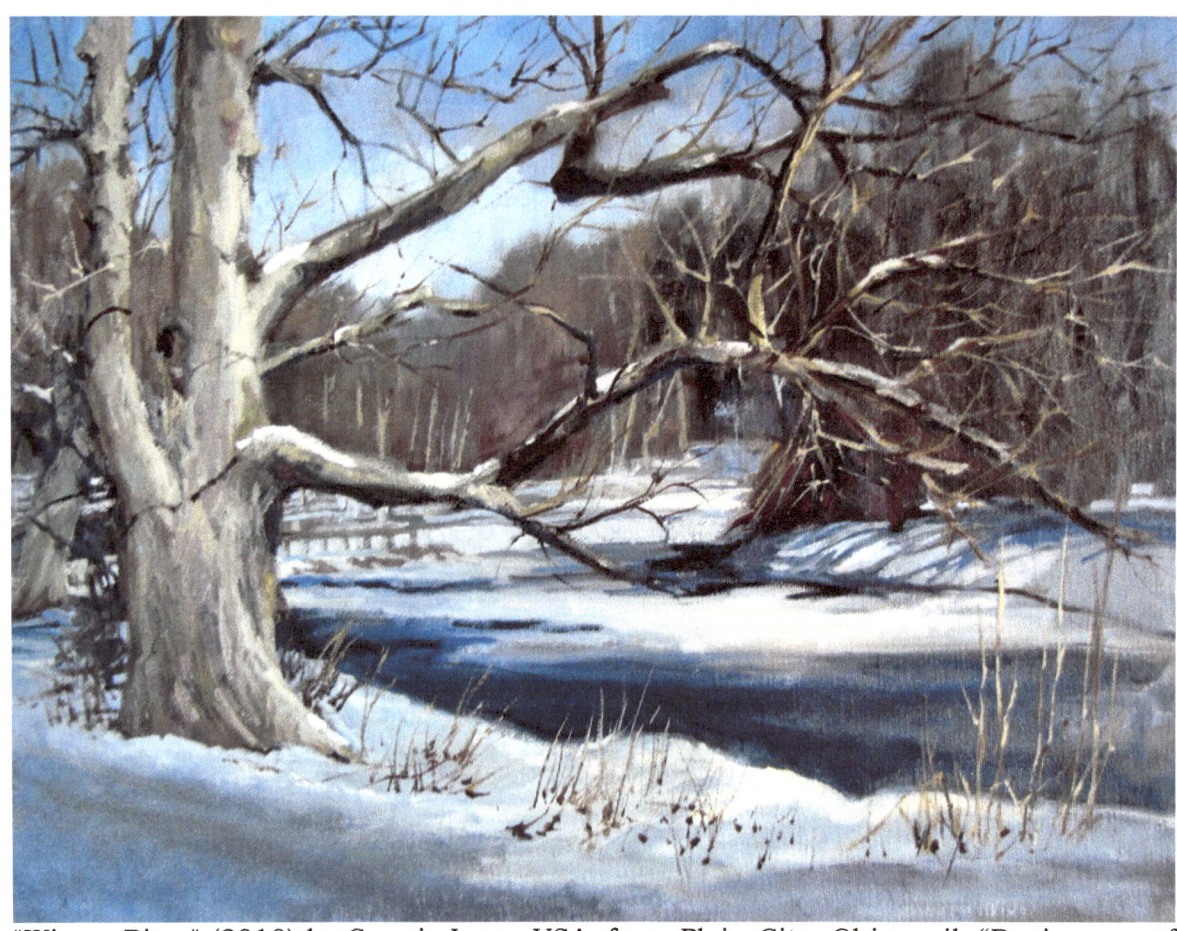
"Winter River" (2010) by Connie Lane, USA, from Plain City, Ohio – oil. "During one of many day trips from home, I came across this lovely spot. A mile or so upstream, there were historic buildings lining the river that gave a hint of the industrial past that helped develop northeast Ohio. The beautiful trees depicted here, are along the Chagrin River near Chagrin Falls on a cold winter day. The serene stillness and quiet of this area after a fresh snow fall, was something I tried to capture. When things get hectic in my life, this painting is a refreshing change of pace to which I can escape."

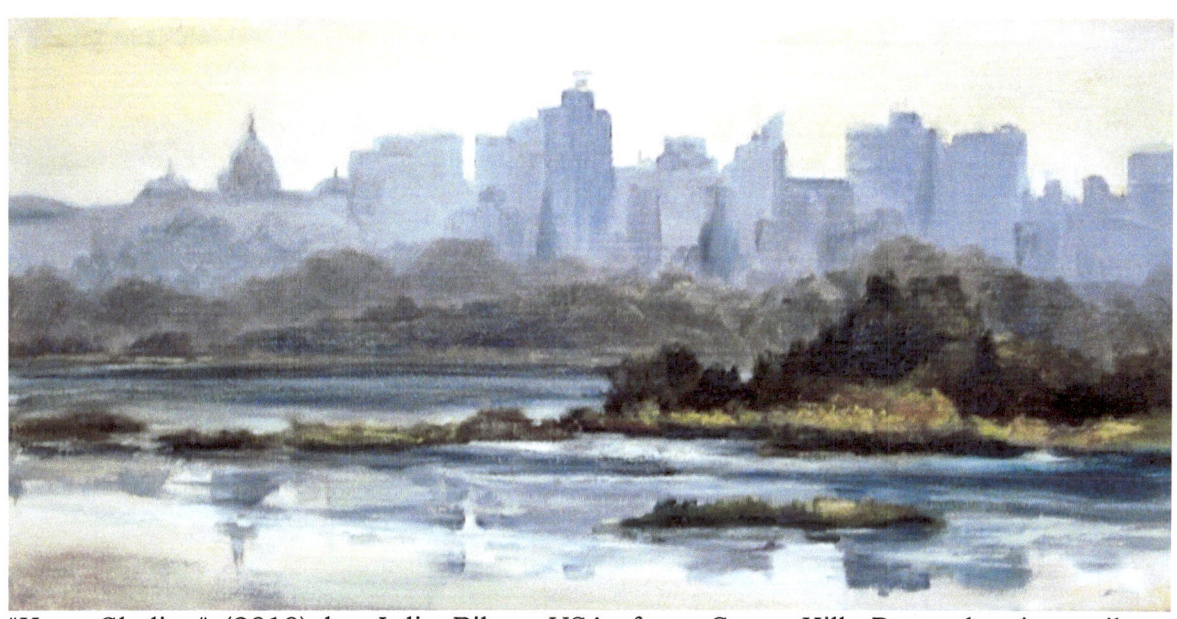

"Hazy Skyline" (2010) by Julie Riker, USA, from Camp Hill, Pennsylvania – oil on canvas. "This was painted in West Fairview, PA looking across the Susquehanna to the state capitol in Harrisburg. The overcast day reduced the skyline to beautiful shades of gray."

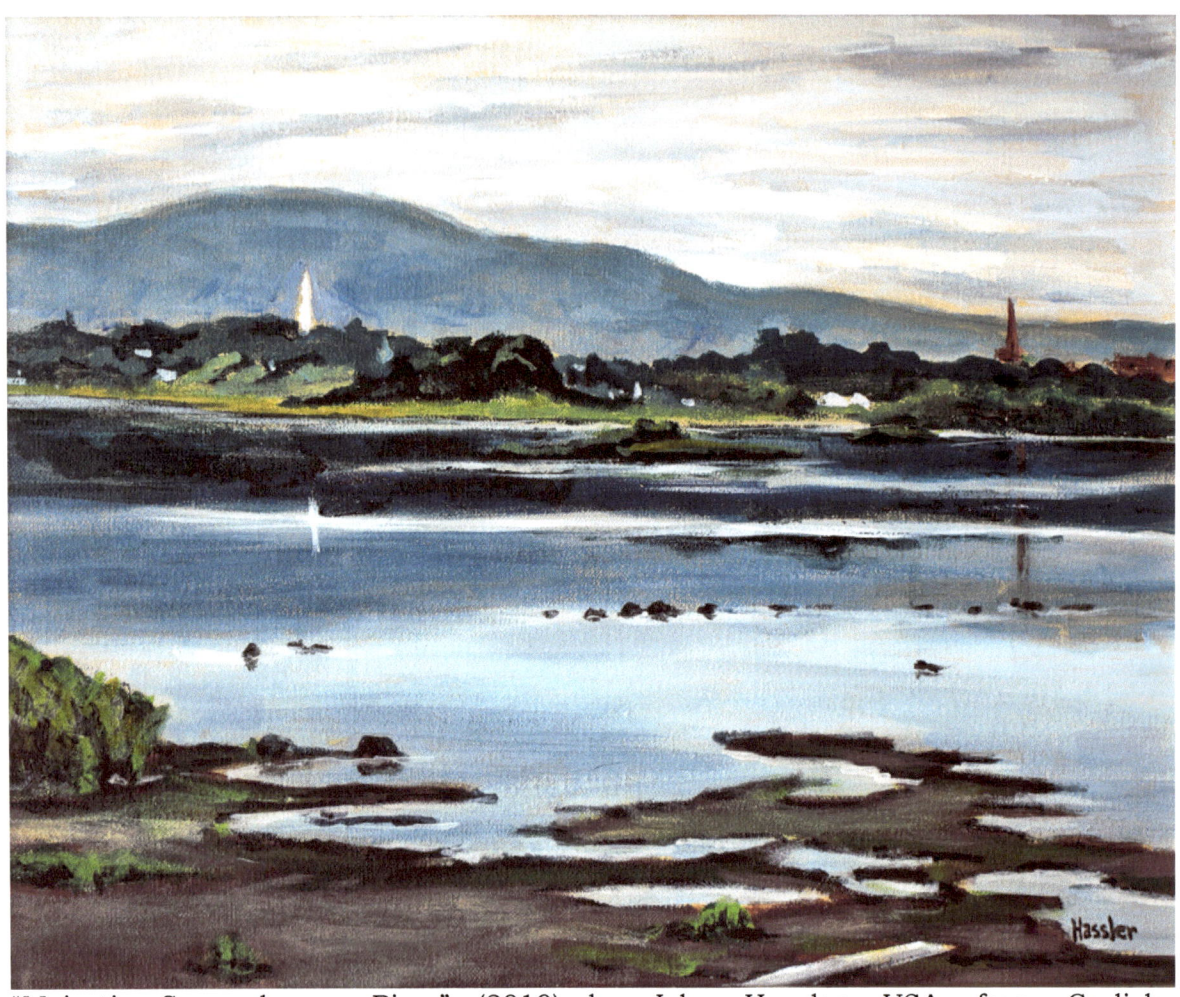
"Majestic Susquehanna River" (2010) by John Hassler, USA, from Carlisle, Pennsylvania – acrylic. "This painting is a pure plein air painting done on a beautiful day along the west side of the river."

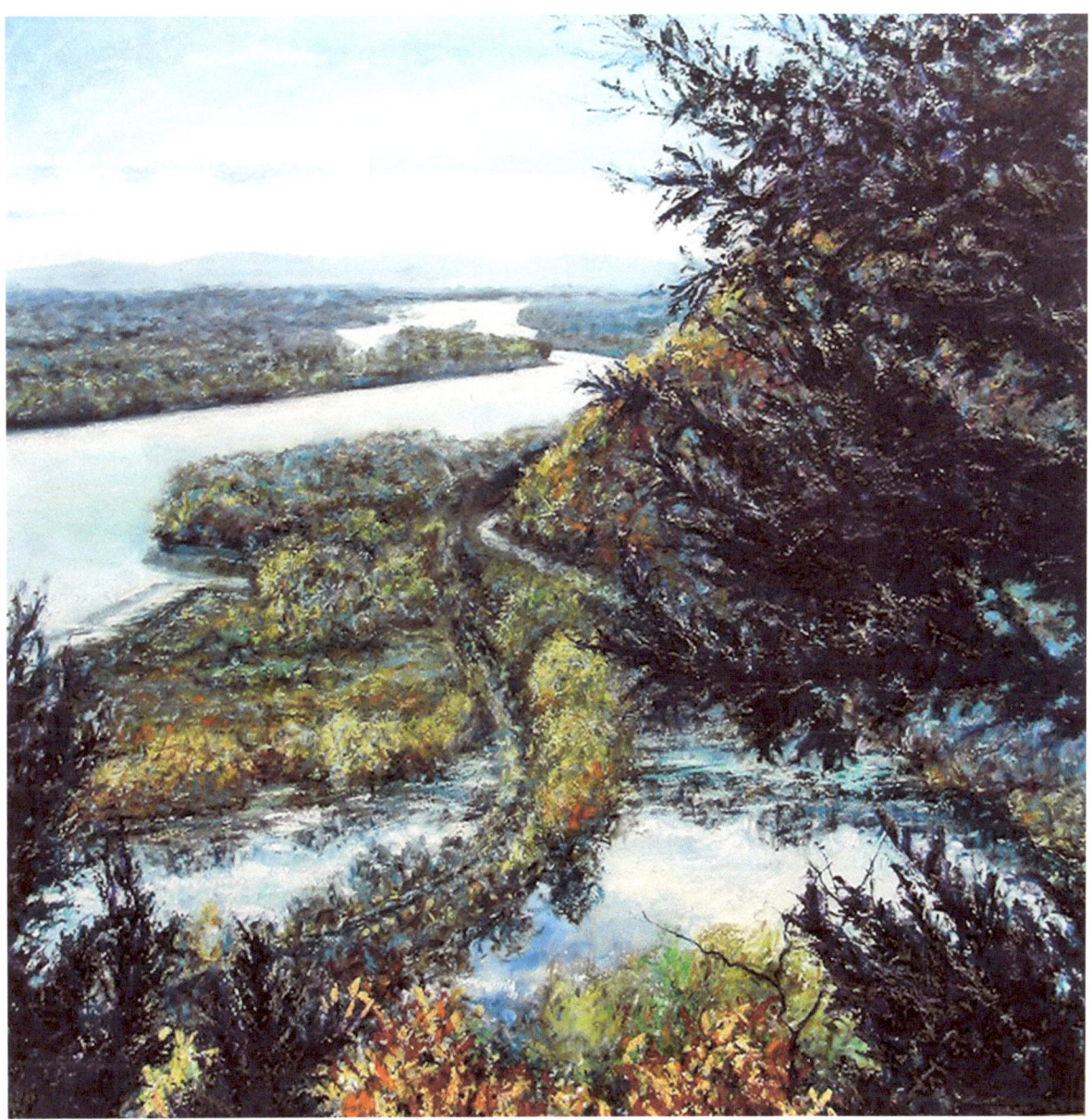

"Iowa River Series" (2009) by Robert Sunderman, USA, from Boone, Iowa – oil on canvas. "As a Fine Artist, I continue to explore the natural world in which we live. Investigating rivers, landscapes and prairie systems are not my only on going passion. I am very comfortable working in natural 3D mediums to digest and express the natural world around us. Crossing disciplines and interacting with other areas of Fine Art is very much on my mind. There is so much we can gain and learning from each other."

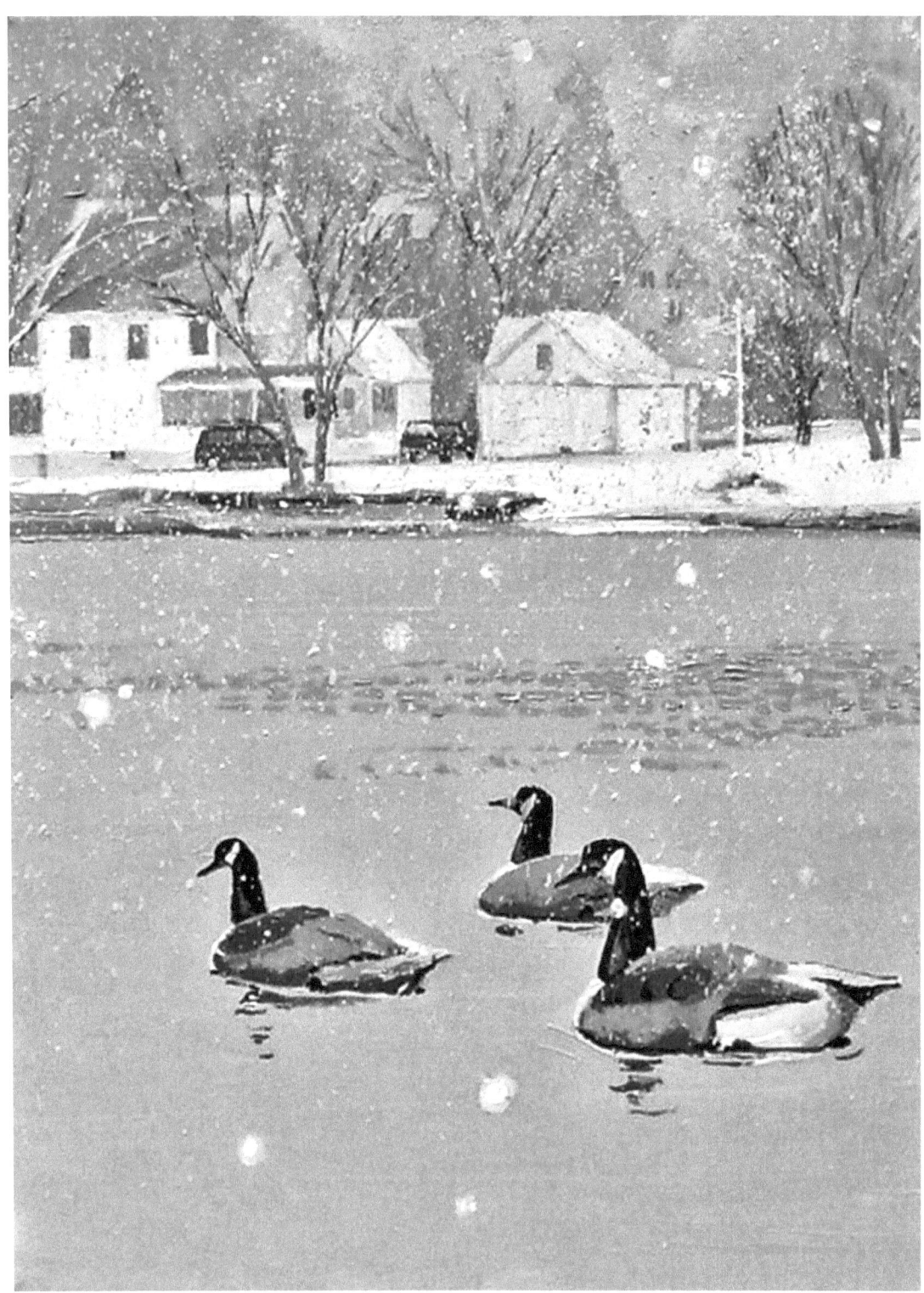

"Geese" (2009) by Paul Hitchen, USA, from Somerset, Massachusetts – oil. "This is a painting of the Lee's River which runs between Somerset and Swansea, Massachusetts USA on a snow February day. The geese are permanent residents."

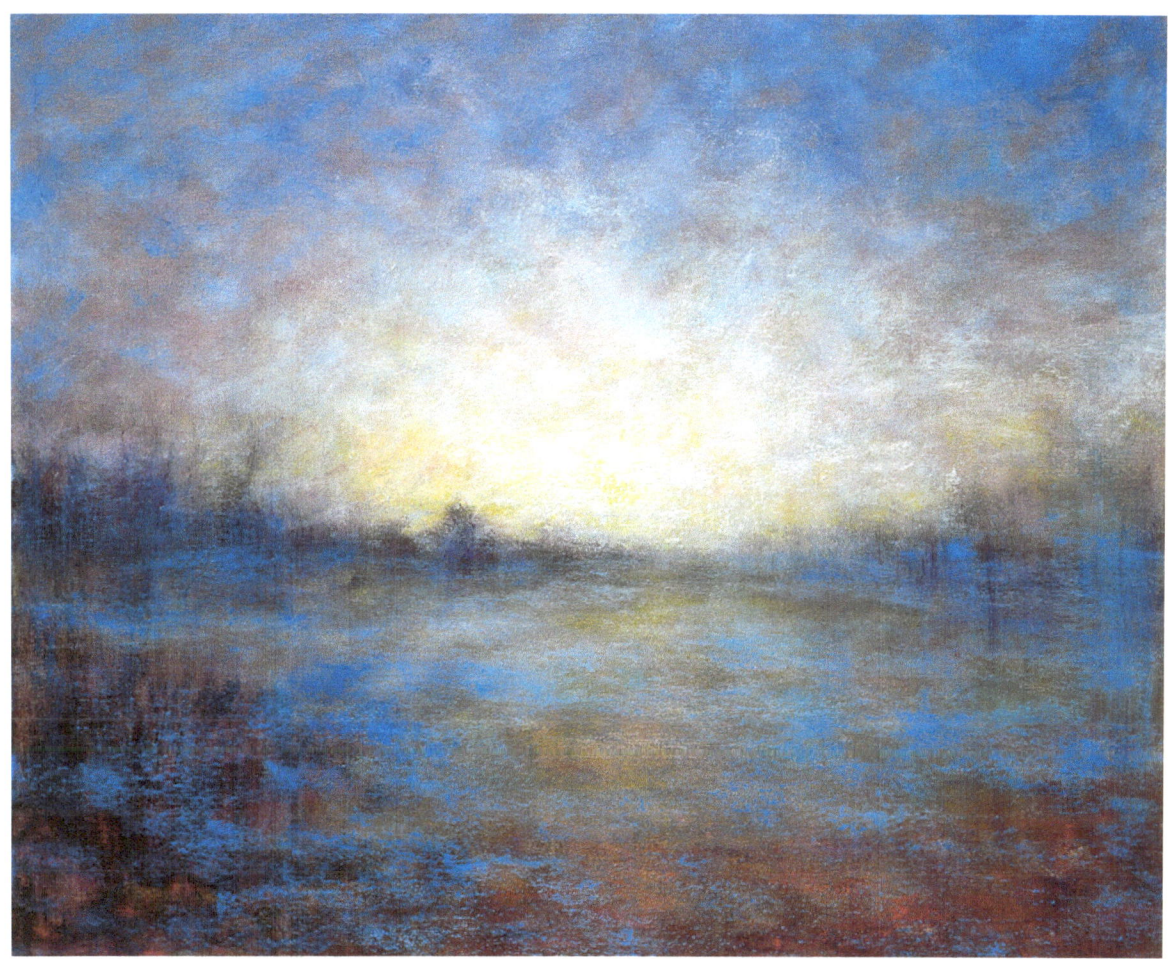

"River Haze" (2010) by Victoria Veedell, USA, from San Francisco, California – oil on canvas. "My paintings are based on nature, fashioned from memory and imagination, and imply landscapes not necessarily seen, but felt. I dissolve the landscape, leaving only what I consider to be the essence of nature. I continually examine the effects of light and form in the natural world. The dramatic effect of light that happens throughout the day sets the mood for each painting. The images created are grounded in a perspective associated with landscape; but rather than mirror the outside world I look inward reflecting on my experiences to find new meaning and relationships between form, light and perspective."

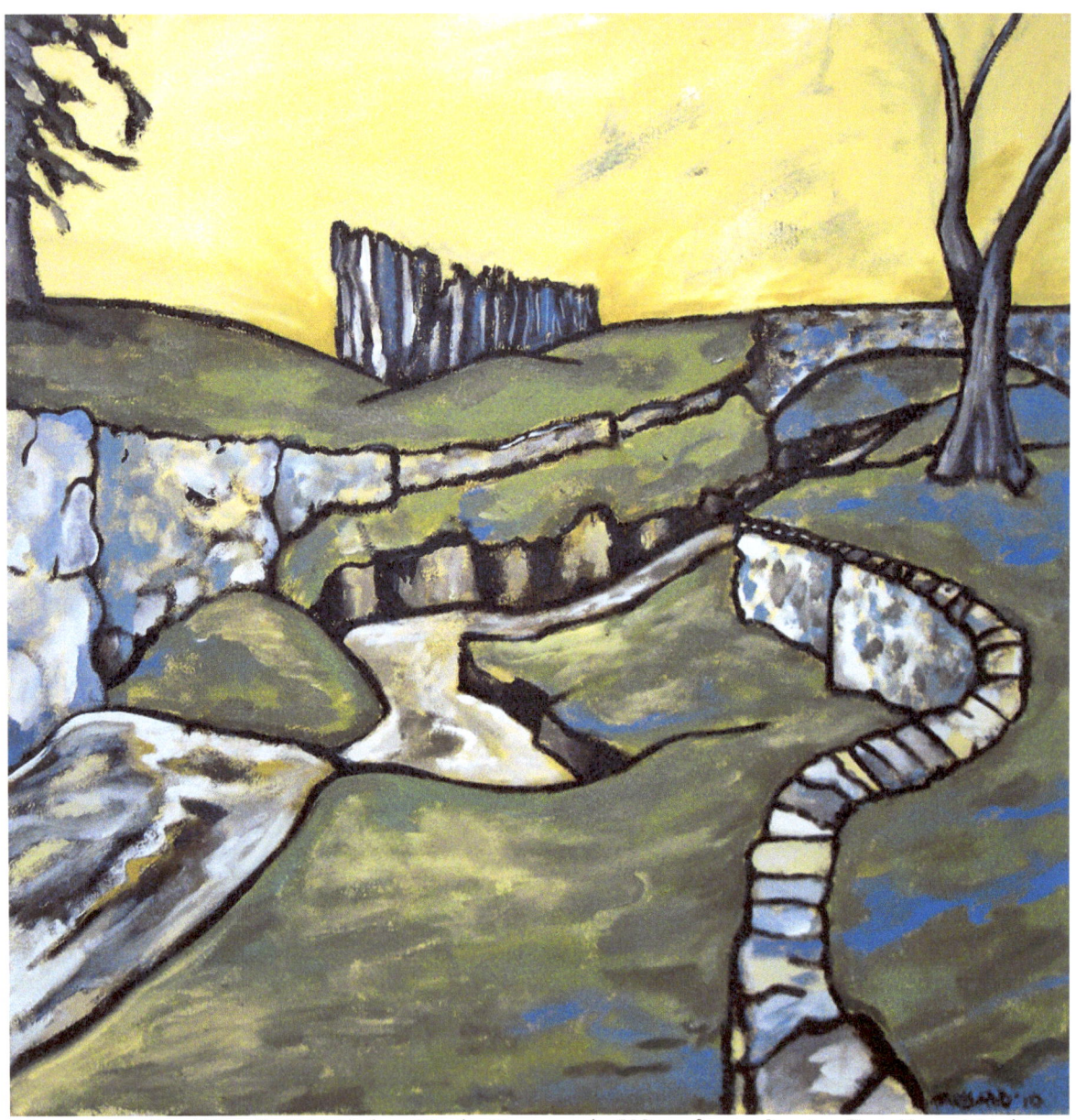

"Crossing the River" (2010) by Mark Frossard, USA, from Santa Fe, New Mexico – acrylic on canvas. "In the Southwest, water is a precious resource. This painting was created to raise awareness of the fragility of the Santa Fe River. While it supports 40% of the city's water needs, it is considered to be one of the most endangered rivers in the United States. Without protection of our natural resources, where do we turn to?"

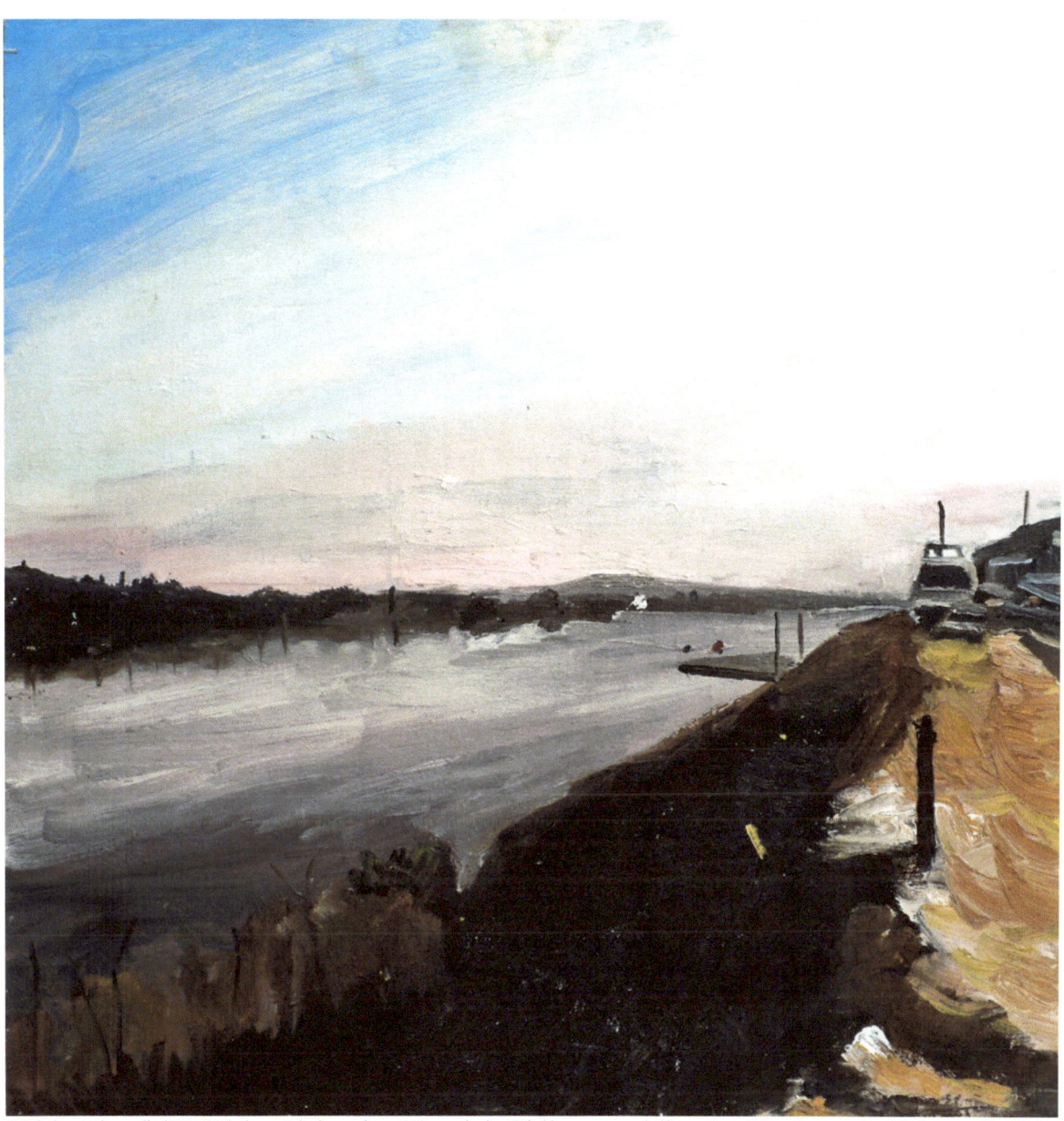

"Ohio River" (2009) by Alejandro Mandel, Chilean residing in Cincinnati, Ohio – oil. "My art expresses my interpretation of environment and the changes it has suffered, which can only be understood through a historical and cultural point of view. Many Latin American artists such as Diego Rivera, Jorge Luis Cuevas and Orozco, and European artists such as Corbet and Goya understood this and they found a balance between the political and the personal, between the aesthetic and the social. My intent is to create art that expresses this balance. Through my landscapes and figurative art I make reference to the changes my surroundings suffered, but when I describe these changes I use an aesthetic vocabulary of the past. In this way I am trying to put this reality in historical perspective."

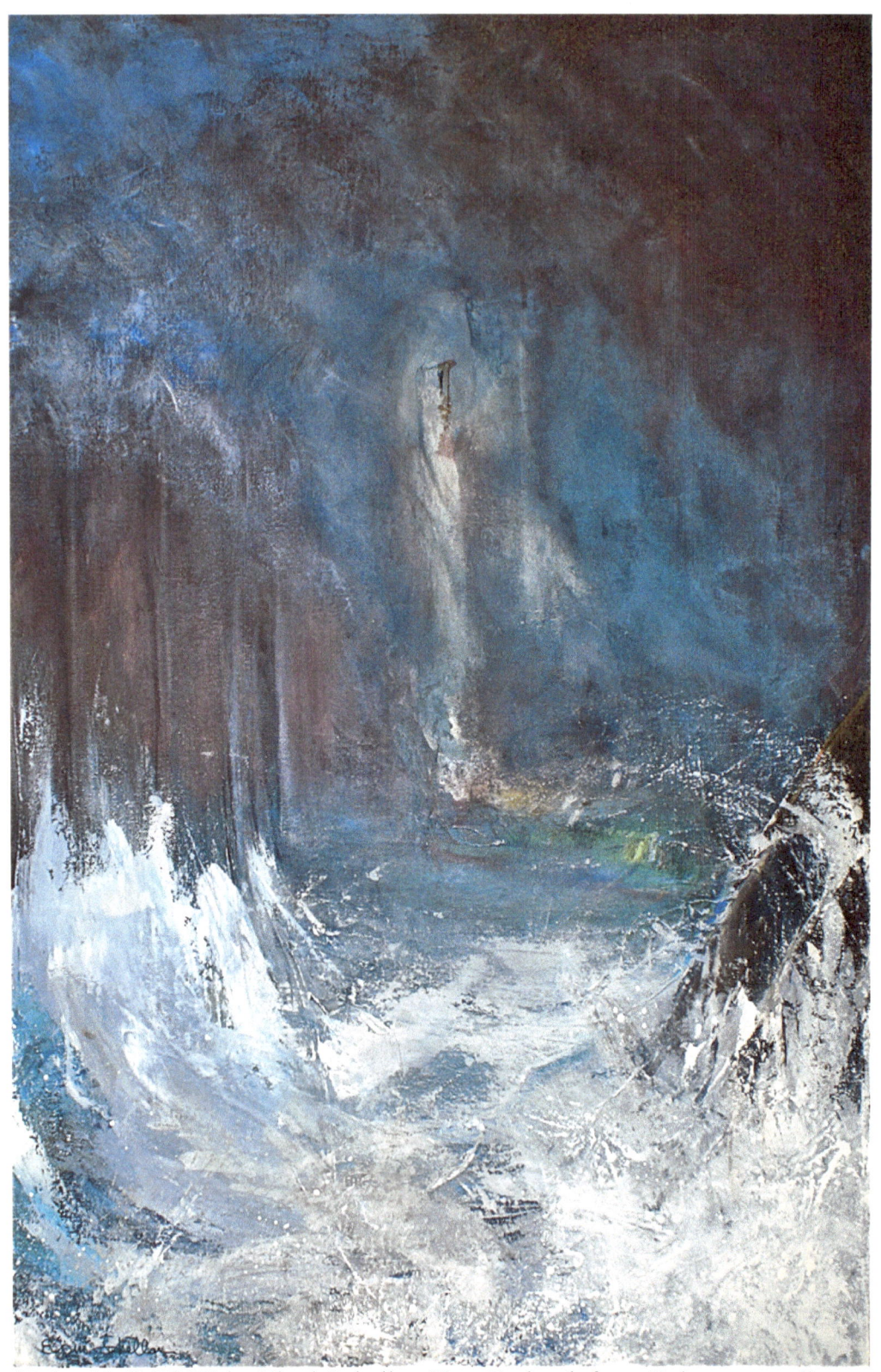
"False Idol" (2007) by Eleni Sakellar, New Zealand, from Nelson – acrylic.

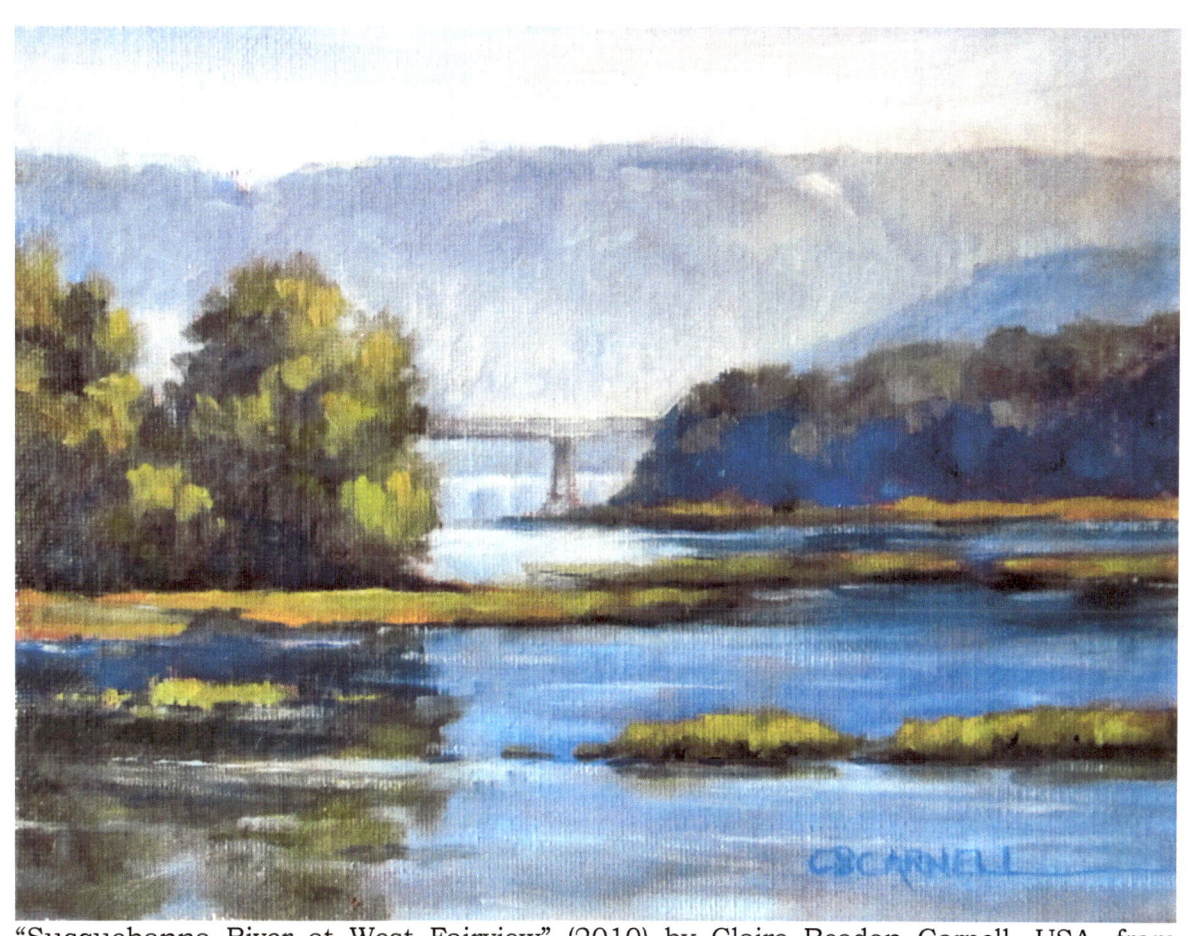

"Susquehanna River at West Fairview" (2010) by Claire Beadon Carnell, USA, from Gardners, Pennsylvania – oil. "Hazy morning light softened the view along the Susquehanna River at West Fairview in Pennsylvania."

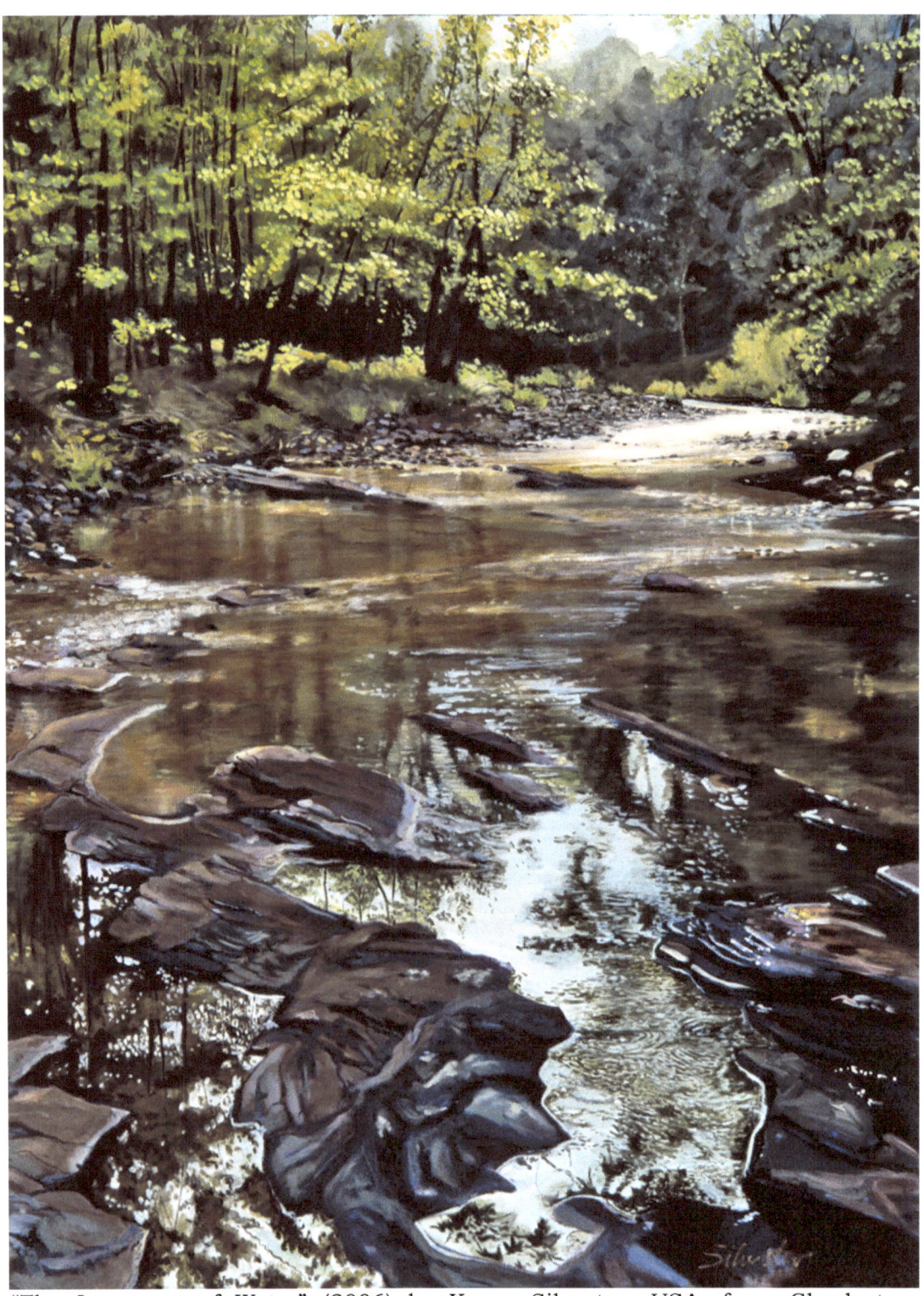
"The Language of Water" (2006) by Karen Silvestro, USA, from Charleston, South Carolina – oil.

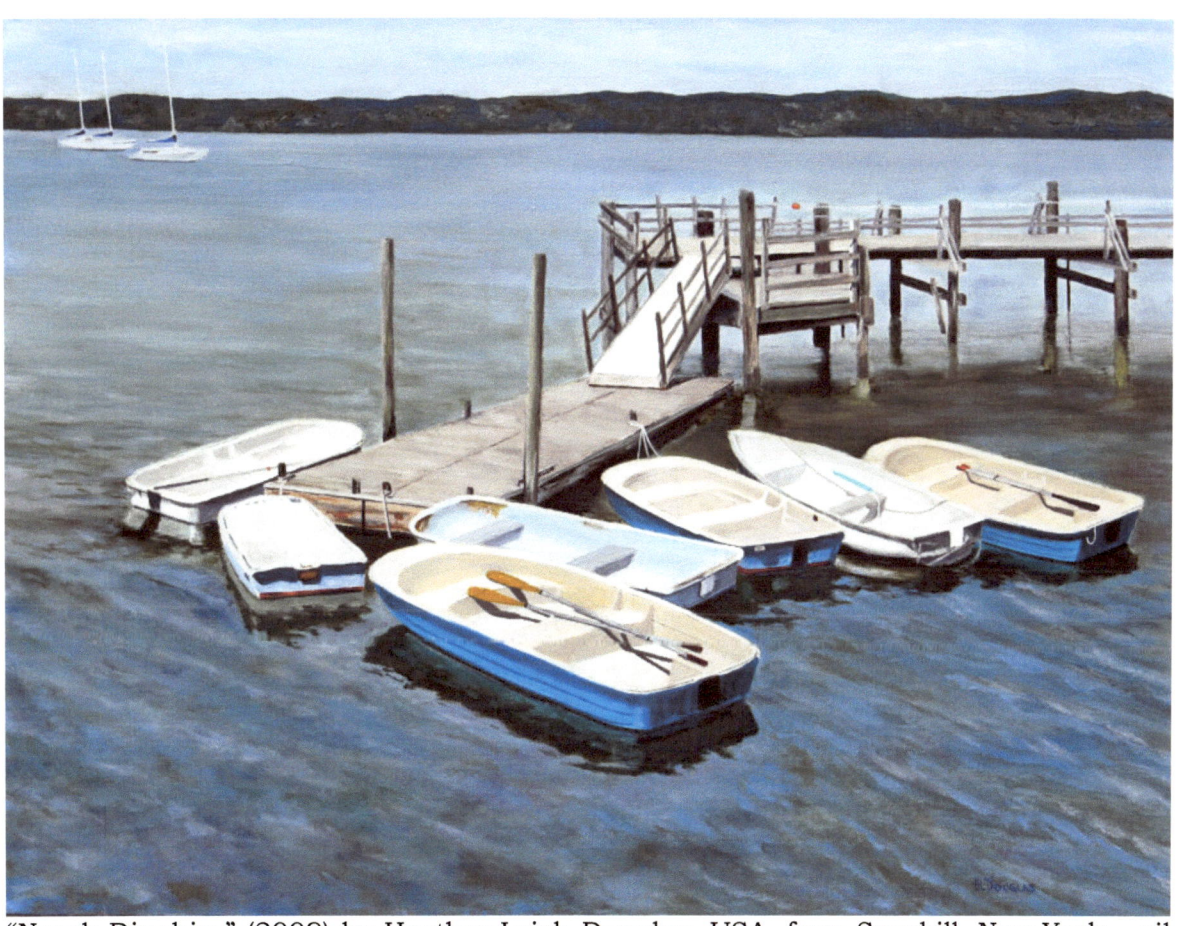
"Nyack Dinghies" (2009) by Heather Leigh Douglas, USA, from Sparkill, New York – oil on canvas. "On a hot summer day I came upon these boats tied up to a dock on the Hudson River in Nyack, New York. I am often drawn to the water. It's a challenging subject and has limitless possibilities for a painter."

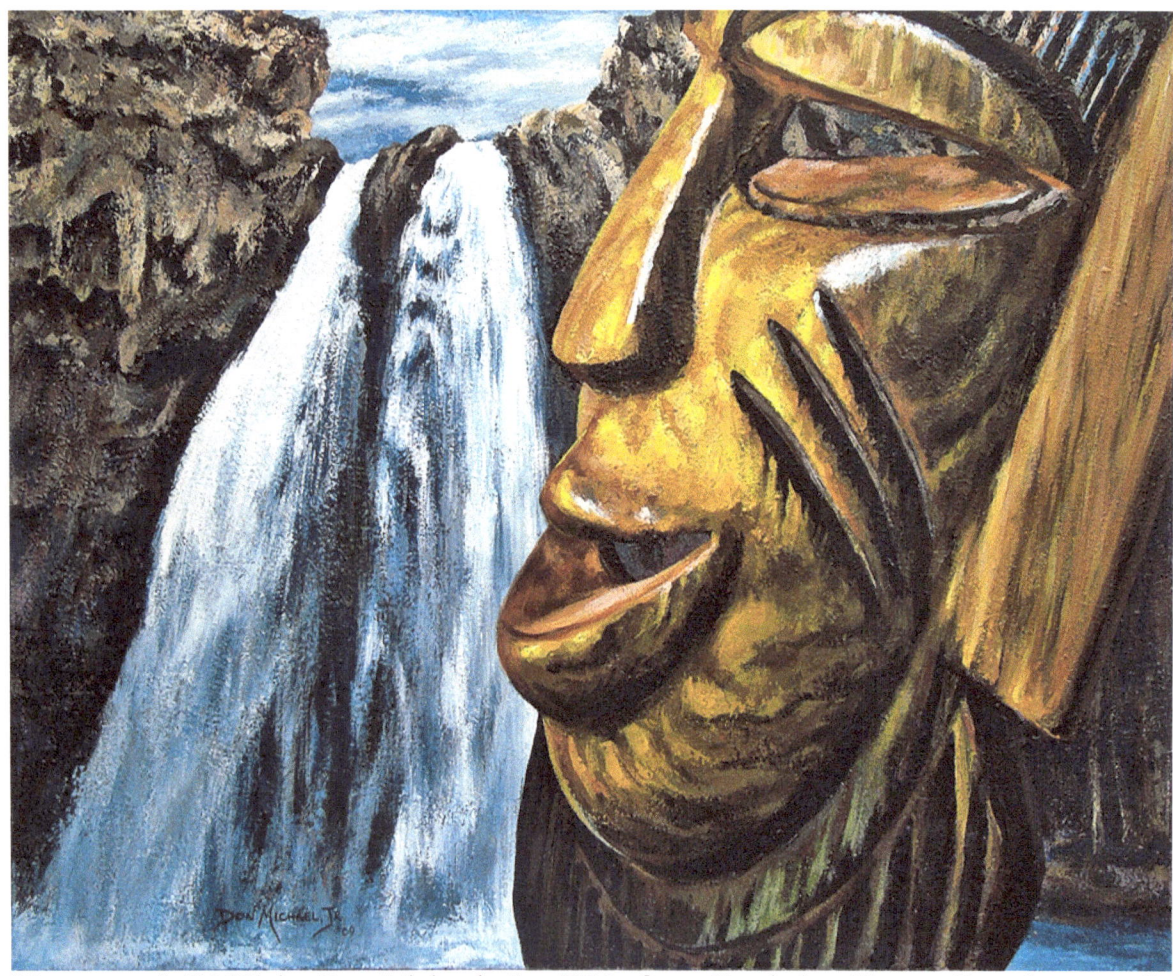
"Sanctuary" (2009) by Don Michael, Jr., USA, from North Las Vegas, Nevada – acrylic on canvas. "We all need a place where we can get away from it all. A place where we feel safe. A place of peace. A place we call 'Sanctuary'. That place for me is in my studio. My mind is free. My spirit is free. The noise of the world cannot get through. There are no worries, there are no fears, there is no doubt, there is no sorrow? There is only peace. If only I could bottle it?"

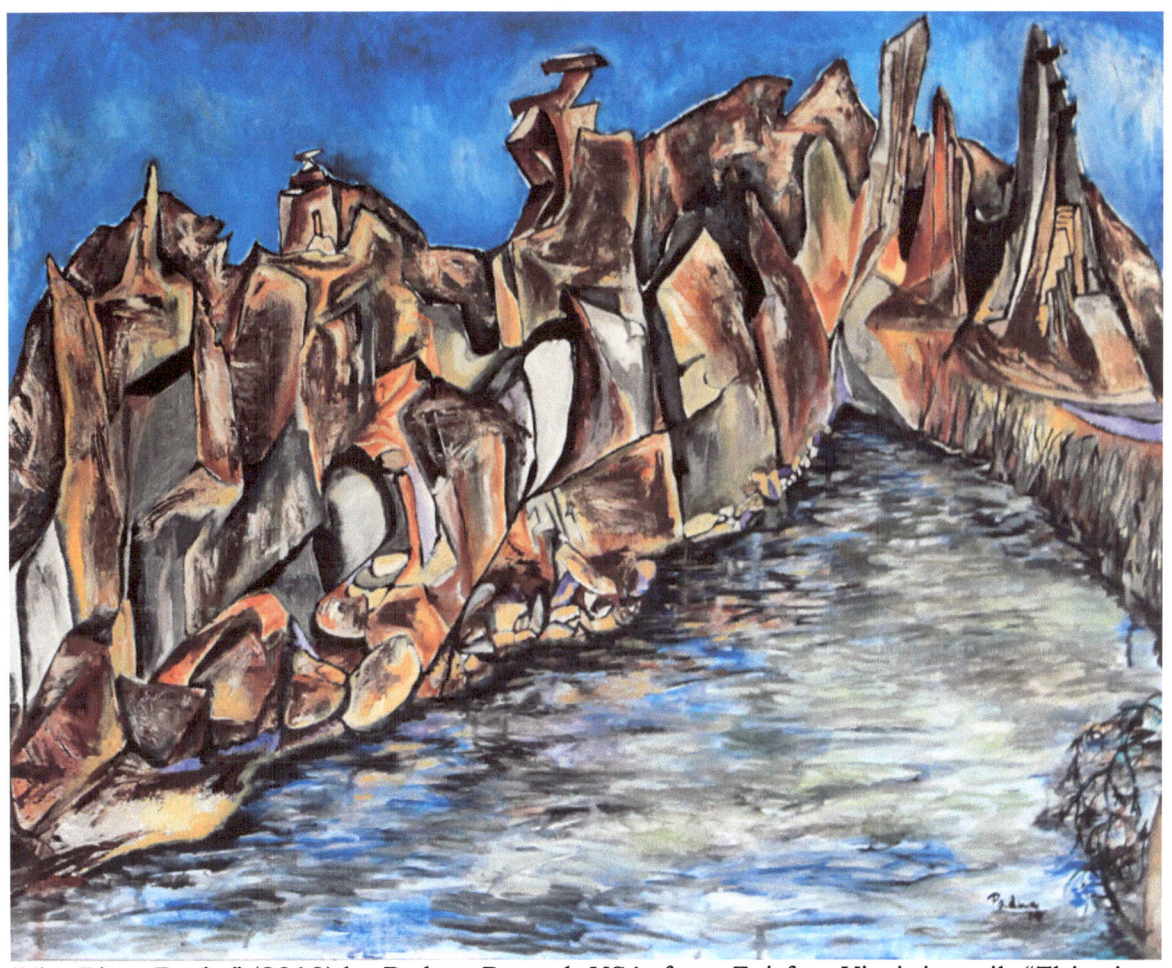
"The River Rocks" (2010) by Padma Prasad, USA, from Fairfax, Virginia – oil. "This river landscape is a collage from different pieces of landscapes; I am mostly a figurative painter and the rocks became my figures."

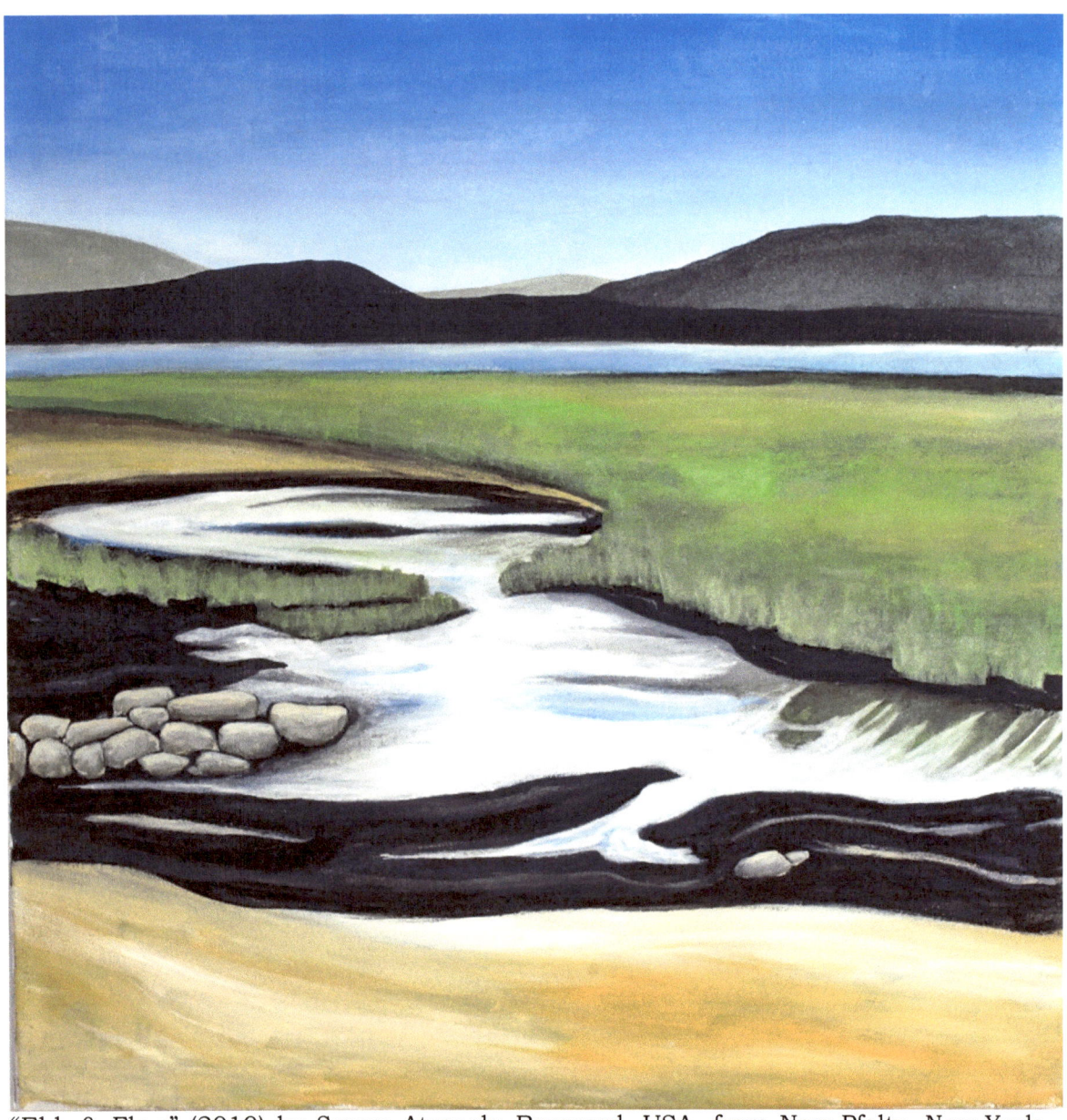
"Ebb & Flow" (2010) by Suzan Atesoglu Brassard, USA, from New Pfaltz, New York – acrylic on canvas. "When I see something that is profoundly beautiful or moving I take a mental picture. While the moment is fleeting, the memory is permanent. These indelible images become the basis for my work. On the canvas the landscape is simplified. The sky, water and earth are clean, pure and forever unadulterated."

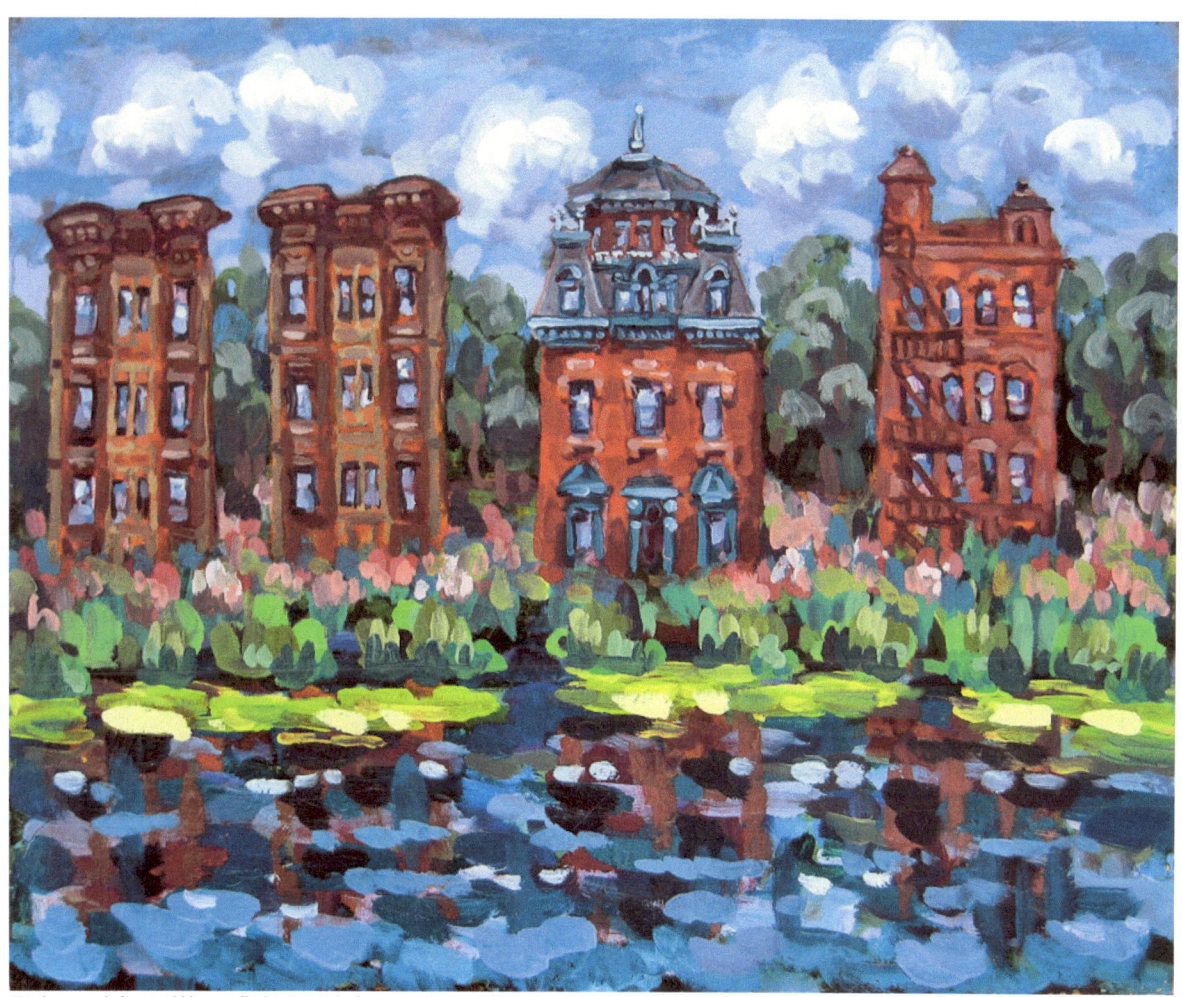

"Riverside Village" (2009) by John Lloyd, USA, from Brooklyn, New York – oil on board. "The painting is a fantasy based on a group of buildings in Brooklyn, 2 apartment buildings, a mansion and an old factory which I placed along the banks of a river in Brooklyn,"

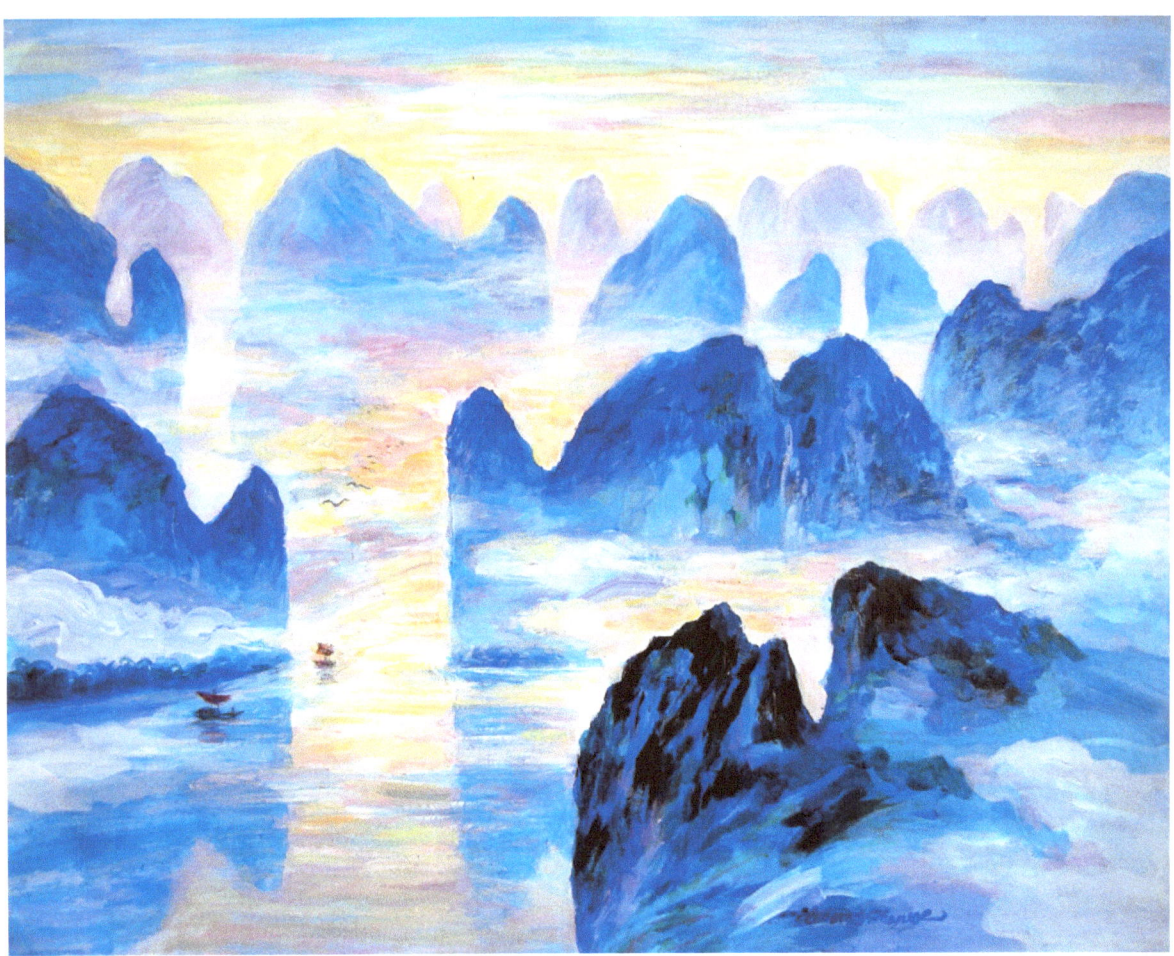

"The Lijiang River" (2005) by Ken Shanye Huang, Chinese-American residing in Silver Spring, Maryland. – acrylic on paper. "LiJiang is a beautiful river located in my hometown Guangxi, Southwest of China. The painting – 'The LiJiang River' is my tribute for its unique gracefulness and gentleness. Liken many of my other artwork in an essence that in which I have integrated the Chinese yin and yang philosophy with the western contemporary art concepts to express my deep love and respect for nature and life."

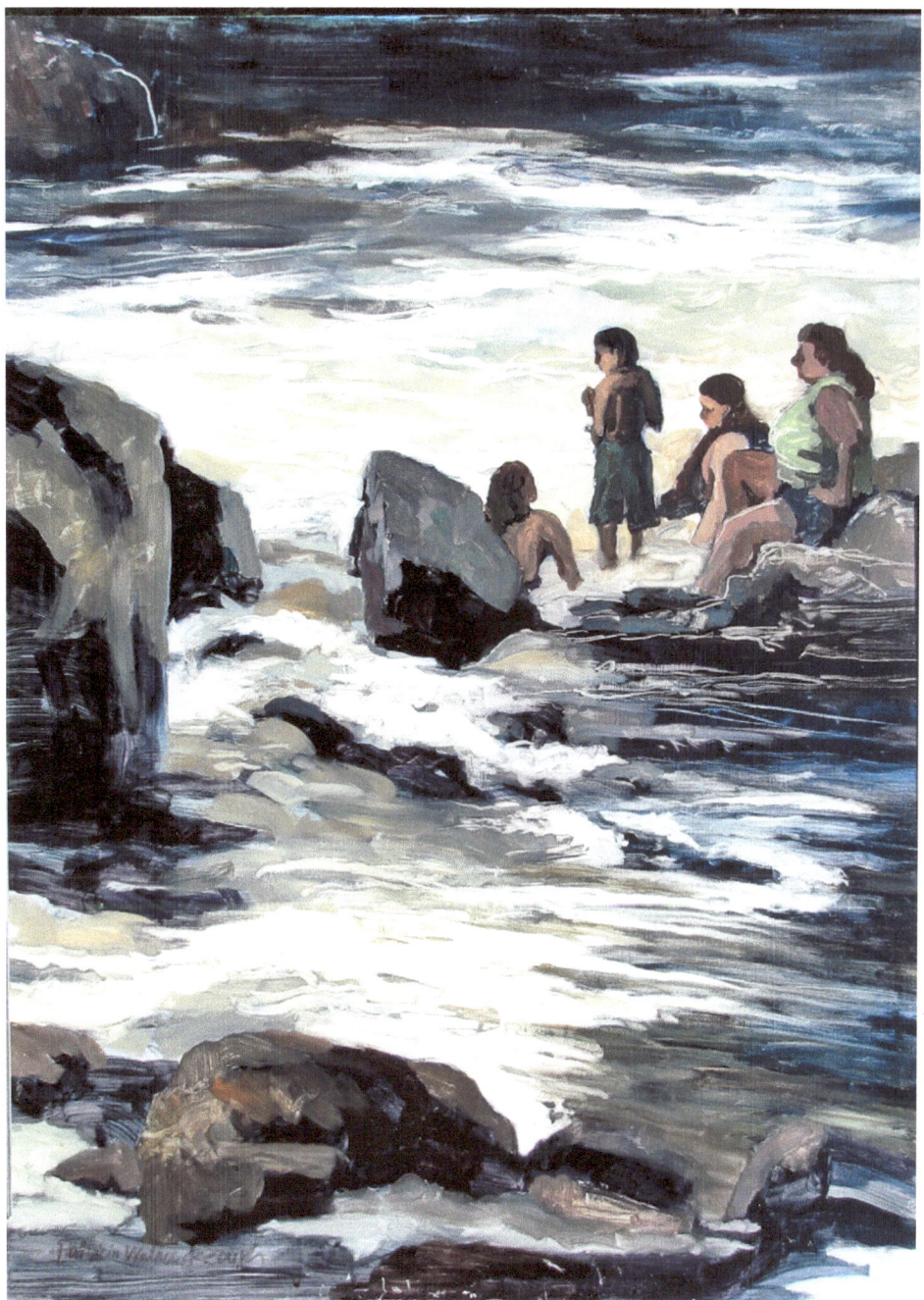

"Family on the Rocks" (2008) by Patricia Walach Keough, USA, from Carlisle, Pennsylvania – oil on board. "The setting for 'Family on the Rocks' is Buttermilk Falls on the Raquette River near Long Lake, NY. I took a photo of the family after having kayaked solo from the Forked Lake campground to the waterfall on a gray August day. The river was high and powerful ; the family played at the edge below the falls. I often paint at this spot where I have human subjects combined with moving water."

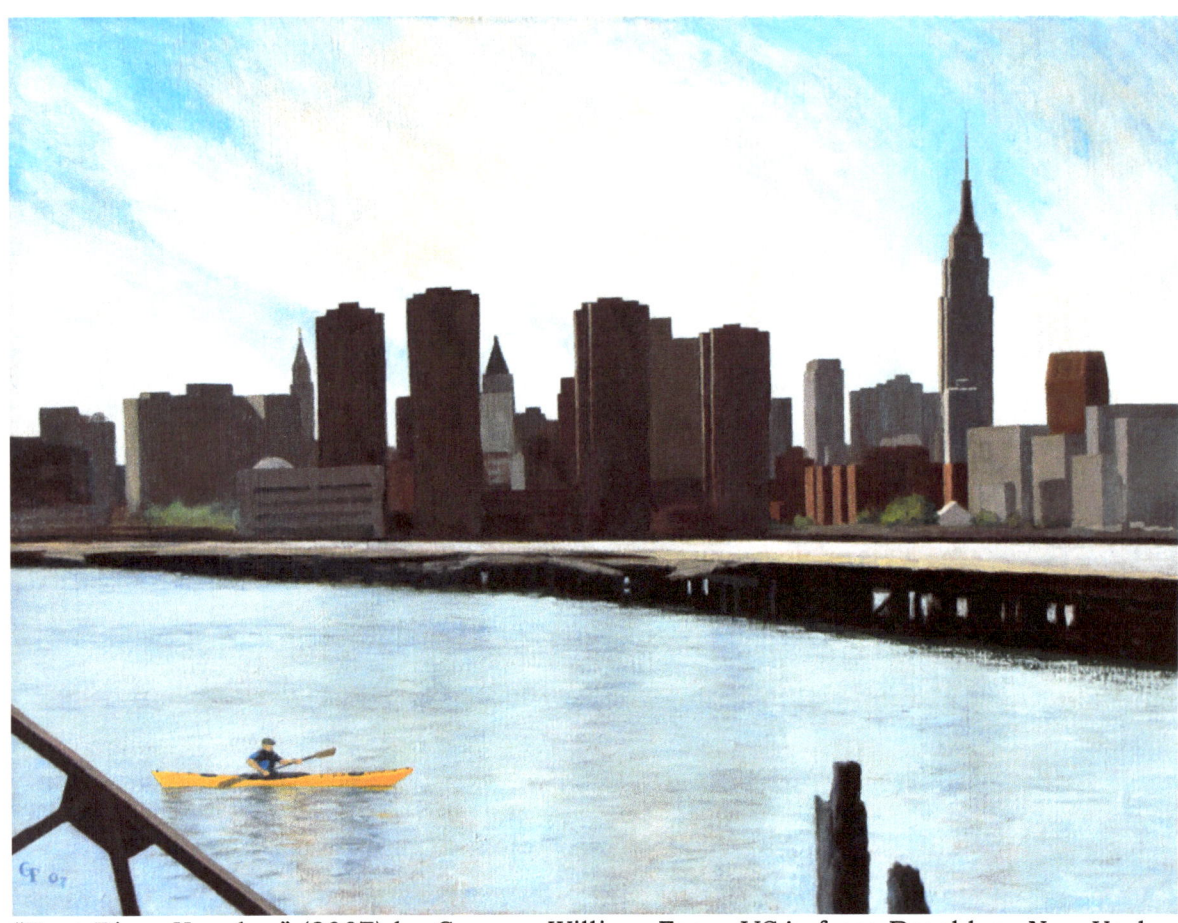

"East River Kayaker" (2007) by Gregory William Frux, USA, from Brooklyn, New York – oil on canvas. "The concerted efforts of the environmentalist community has lead to a gradual cleaning of New York harbor and a return to the waterfront as a place for recreation. My friend Monica Schroeder often takes her mango colored sea kayak out, braving the fierce currents of the East River. A summer kayak trip, across from the Manhattan island was the inspiration for this painting."

PHOTOGRAPHY

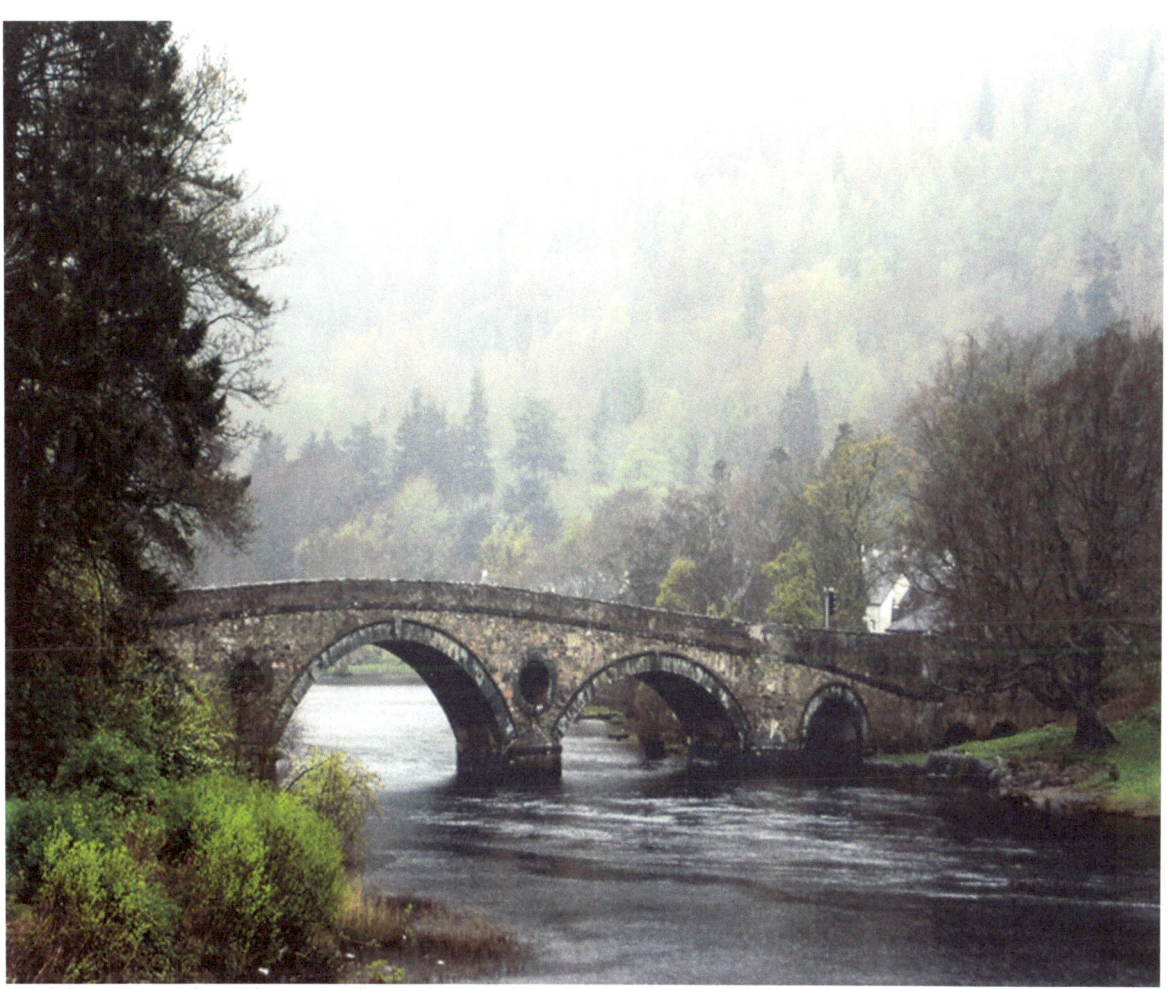

"Bridge Over the River Tay" (2008) by Kimberly Clark, USA, from San Antonio, Texas – photograph. "I had a dream about visiting Scotland that came true."

MIXED MEDIA

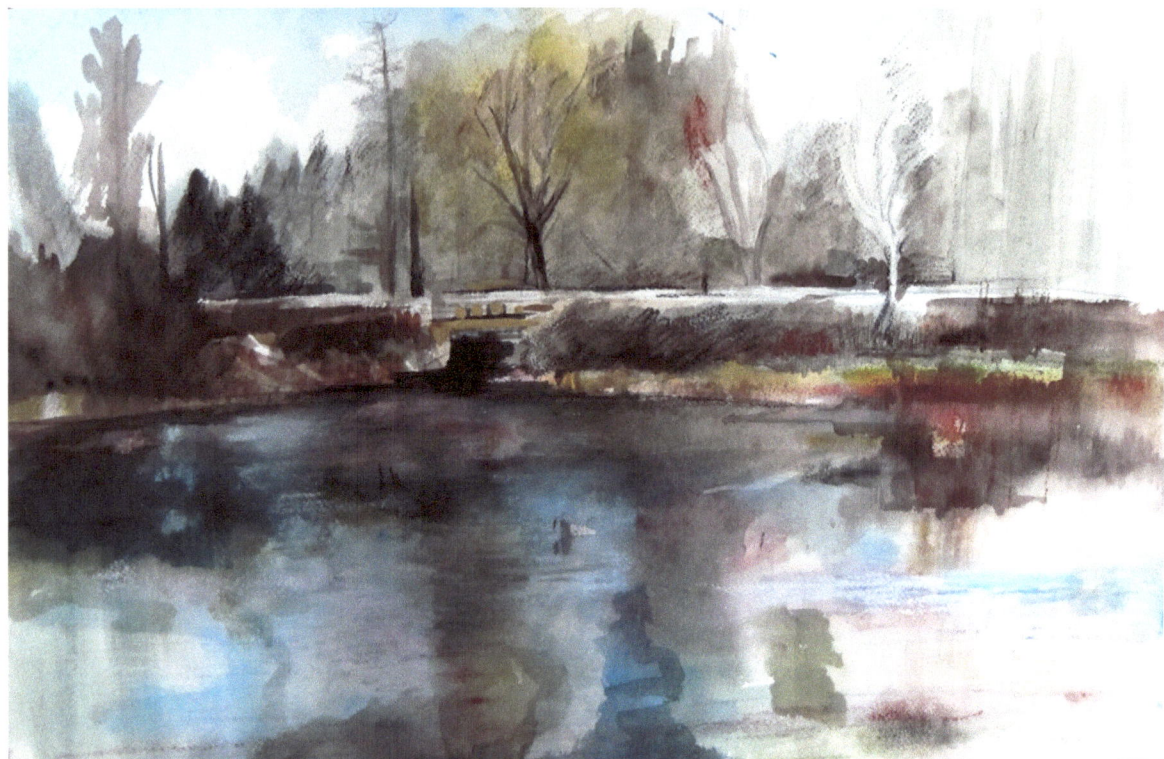

"Five Rivers in the Rain" (2009) by Rosalie Beck, USA, from Milwaukee, Wisconsin – watercolor, pastel, pencil, conte. "All of my paintings are done from observed reality. They are composites of the way things looked over a period of hours, days, sometimes weeks. In a sense, they are a record of a visual dialog between the painter and reality. Although they might be called "realist" my paintings always are based on an abstraction. Some quality- an arrangement of shapes, contrast of colors, or a quality of atmosphere will attract me enough to want to create a painting from it. Color in my work is naturalistically derived, but altered or intensified for emotional effect. For me, the layering of color stands for the metaphor of the rich and continuous feedback between artist and subject. Through this layering and enhancement I strive to create paintings, which are both sensual and intimate from places, which are commonplace and ordinary."

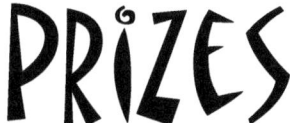

Grand Prize

The top entry of the competition received a $250 cash prize and was used as the cover image for this book.

This year's winner:

"The Lower Fork" (2009) by Ed Letven

Category Winners

The top entry in each category won $50 and was featured as the lead image in each chapter of this book:

Oil/Acrylic:

"9510 River Memory" (2009) by Joel Le Bow

Watercolor:

"Desplaines River" (2001) by Alli Farkas

Drawings/Sketches:

"By the River" (2010) by Nancy Ness

Mixed Media/Collage:

"Fishing Village" (2008) by Jing Chung

Traditional Photography:

"Dawn Breaks" (2008) by Sudipto Das (not in book)

Digital:

"Red Rocks" (2010) by Mark DeMent

Other:

"Not a Care in the World" (2008) by Lilianne Milgrom

Book / Exhibition Invitees

The following artists were selected by the jurors
to participate in the book and exhibition:

Digital
Barabara Richards
Deborah Orloff
Frances A. Miller
Jing Zhou
Kristine Campbell
Mark DeMent
Mark Kovalchuk

Drawings/Sketches
Greg Johannesen
Nancy Hess
Patricia Wynne
Rebecca Yates Shorb
Shannon Chong
Tatiana Myers
Veronica Winters
Whitney Knapp

Mixed Media
Carly Swenson
Harry Spitz
Janice Schoultz Mudd
Jing Chung
John Lyon Paul
Lian Zhen
Rosalie Beck

Other
Clemence Potier
Hem Jyotika
Joe Kluck
Lilianne Milgrom

Photography
Ellin Pollachek
Hugo Cruz
Judith Nylen
Kimberly Clark
Kurt K Weiss
Meryl Silver
Sarah Dedoelder
Sudipto Das

Watercolor
Alli Farkas
Greg Arens
Lauren Mulhern
Lian Zhen
Michael Gillespie
Sam Dixon
Sharon Way-Howard

Oil/Acrylic
Al Boze
Alex Mandel
Amihan Jumalon
Arlene Meyer
Barbara Fracchia
Claire Beadon Carnell
Connie Lane
Deborah Dorsey
Dena McMurdie
Dennis Shattuck
Don Michael, Jr.
Ed Letven

Ingrid Dohm
Jack Siegel
JoAnn Parsley
Joel Le Bow
John Hassler
John High
John Lloyd
John Treanor
Josephine Hodos
Julie Riker
Karen Silvestro
Ken Huang
Lian Zhen
Lynn Patron
Madeleine Avirov
Mark Frossard
Maya Gerr
Michael Gillespie
Padma Prasad
Patricia Walach Keough
Paul Hitchen
Ralph J Ryan
Randel Rogers
Renee Fineberg
Renee Leopardi
Robert Sunderman
Sam Dixon
Shannon Richardson
Suzan Brassard
Veronica Winters

www.ingramcontent.com/pod-product-compliance
Lightning Source LLC
Chambersburg PA
CBHW051153220526
45473CB00003B/756